Ken Brandvold

## *Praise for* The Prayer Experiment

Some books on prayer will drive you from the throne of God because they imply that it is a place reserved for the particularly spiritual or knowledgeable. However, every once in a while, someone will give the Body of Christ a practical and insightful book that draws Christians to God's throne with the joyful knowledge that they will be welcomed. If you are going to read anything on prayer this year, this is the one. It will change your life. Give it to people you love, too. You'll both be glad!

STEVE BROWN, PROFESSOR OF PREACHING AT REFORMED THEOLOGICAL SEMINARY
AND THE BIBLE TEACHER ON *KEY LIFE*

I've known Jay Dennis since our college days at Ouachita Baptist University, and I'm thrilled that he has allowed us all to see how God has used trials and troubles of his own life as a "Prayer Experiment," and introduced the "Jabez factor." Don't think this book is for "professional practitioners of religion," because its compelling style makes it a book all believers will love.

MIKE HUCKABEE, GOVERNOR OF ARKANSAS

I am not only impressed by *The Prayer Experiment*, I am excited by what this book could do within the Christian Community. This book needs to be worked into seminar material for churches that want to move forward in a way in which they've never done before. I would recommend that churches invite their membership to seminars on the content of this book. I am delighted and honored to be asked to recommend this book, and I heartily do so.

MILLIE DIENERT

This is not your typical book about prayer. It introduces you to a prayer that can change your life, then with gripping illustrations explains the remarkable prayer phrase by phrase. Enriching!

LUDER G. WHITLOCK, JR.
PRESIDENT, REFORMED THEOLOGICAL SEMINARY

Jay Dennis writes from a platform of personal integrity. Read this book and the Lord will "bless you indeed" as Jabez prayed.

DR. O. S. HAWKINS

Abraham Lincoln would have loved this book. Once during the dark days of the Civil War, Lincoln was asked about a sermon he had just heard. After favorably commenting on its beauty, eloquence and delivery, he observed that it failed – because we were not asked to do something great. Jay Dennis in *The Prayer Experiment* challenges us to pray big, believe big, dream big, and impact big. Thanks! I needed that.

DR. JAY STRACK

Jay Dennis is an impact player for Christ. When you read his new book, *The Prayer Experiment*, you will discover why . . . and how you, too, can know God's power in your life.

JACK GRAHAM

# THE **PRAYER EXPERIMENT**

DISCOVERING A PRAYER THAT COULD CHANGE YOUR WORLD

# **JAY DENNIS**
### WITH MARILYN JEFFCOAT

GRAND RAPIDS, MICHIGAN 49530

# ZONDERVAN™

*The Prayer Experiment*
Copyright © 2001 by Jay Dennis and Marilyn Jeffcoat

Requests for information should be addressed to:

Zondervan, *Grand Rapids, Michigan 49530*

---

**Library of Congress Cataloging-in-Publication Data**

Dennis, Jay.
    The prayer experiment: discovering a prayer that could change your world/
Jay Dennis with Marilyn Jeffcoat.
       p.   cm.
    Includes bibliographical references.
    ISBN: 0-310-23785-8 (hardcover)
    1. Prayer.   I. Jeffcoat, Marilyn.   II. Title.
BV210.2.D44 2001
248.3'2—dc21
                                   00-051301
                                        CIP

---

This edition is printed on acid-free paper.

*Interior design by Melissa Elenbaas*
*Chart and graph design by Beth Shagene*

Printed in the United States of America

---

01 02 03 04 05 06 07 08 /❖ DC/ 10 9 8 7 6 5

This book is affectionately dedicated to my best friend, the love of my life, and my partner in ministry, my wife, Angie. She is the greatest example I know of a real Christian. I could never repay her for the loving sacrifice she has made for me and our children.

# Contents

## Part Three: Impact . . . Your Chance
*Increase my influence and opportunities for you
and give me a sense of your continual presence and direction.*

## Part Four: Impact . . . Your Assurance
*Protect me and keep me from falling into Satan's traps.*

# Acknowledgments

**A** few acknowledgments are necessary for me to express my deepest appreciation:

To Marilyn Jeffcoat, my writing partner, without whom I could not have written this book. She is a gifted writer, a consummate encourager, a trusted friend, and truly someone after God's own heart.

To my precious children, Will and Emily, who encouraged, prayed for, and loved me, as well as understood Dad's many nights at the computer.

To the wonderful people of First Baptist Church at the Mall for their willingness to give their pastor the freedom to write this book. They are truly the greatest people on earth, because they have never learned to say "no" to God.

To my administrative assistant, Donna Costello, for her encouragement, prayers, insight, and humor, which helped to make this fun.

To my parents, Bill and Donna Dennis, for their unconditional love and support.

To Paul Engle, editor and friend, for his wise counsel, his encouraging spirit, his desire for excellence, and his passion to make an impact through the printed page.

To Bill Shiflett, whose wisdom and insight are beyond his years and who brings a much-needed joy to every situation.

To the staff team of First Baptist Church at the Mall, who picked up more than their share of the load while giving me time to write.

To Bruce Wilkinson whose emphasis on the prayer of Jabez has blessed multitudes, including me.

To the layman at our church who first challenged me to lead our people in a thirty-day prayer experiment.

# ▪ PART ONE ▪

## Impact . . . Your Choice

*Jabez was more honorable than his brothers.*

# Discovering a Prayer That Could Change Your World

Impact . . . gotta have it in order to make a difference in the world. I want it so badly in my Christian walk that I am willing to do whatever it takes to get it. This is the way I approach living my life, but sometimes God stretches me so far beyond the boundaries of my comfort zone that I often have to stop and reconsider what in the world I am doing. Since I became a Christian at age sixteen, I have been praying that God would increase my opportunities to have greater impact on my world. In fact, I have not just prayed for increased influence on *my* world, but I have been pushing the envelope in my faith expectations as I have begged God to increase my influence in *the* world.

*Personal Journal*

*Friday, September 18*

> *Trying to get away today was such a hassle! I knew it was going to be "one of those days" as soon as I walked out and discovered a flat tire on my car. As I changed the tire, I got grease or something all over my clothes, so back into the house I went to change into another set of "business casual." As I opened the front door to leave a second time, the dog bolted out the door. I had stopped again to chase this soon-to-be-an-orphan animal down the street, yelling, "Abbie! Abbie! Come here, girl!" Not a good start. . . .*

*When I finally got on the road, I had to stop by the office for just a minute to grab something I needed to carry with me—and this turned into an hour and a half of crisis management ordeal! Now I was really running late. Once on the way, I was not quite sure which turn to take—because the sign was down—so I headed down what I thought must be the right road—and, of course, it wasn't! That only cost me another fifteen to twenty minutes. More and more it seemed like I wasn't supposed to go on this retreat....*

*And now that I am here, I am beginning to wonder if it was worth it. It's so hard to get away from my responsibilities at the church. Plus, I hate leaving Angie and the kids again. And then to go somewhere for the weekend to be with people I don't even know, for a purpose that God has not yet made clear.*

*Oh, God, this has been a tough day ... not so much for what all has happened, but for what has not happened. I can't imagine why you've led me here. What difference can I make among all these community and business leaders? I know I have prayed that you will increase my impact, but how can that be possible here? I've gotta be honest with you, Lord. I feel like such an outsider here—like such a nothing little weenie among all these hot dogs.*

*God, you are definitely putting my living-on-the-faith-edge commitment to the test this weekend! You know I am willing to venture anything if I know you are in it. So, please, Lord, reveal your purpose in my being here....*

The story does not end here. God was writing a new chapter in my life.

## Be Careful What You Pray For

I have learned to take faith risks because I have a tremendous fear that somehow I'm going to "miss God" or miss out on what he wants to do in my life if I do not. I want to experience God unleashed in my life and to know that I have—without reservation—allowed him to work in and through me. When I come to the end of my earthly existence and a tombstone records the dates of my birth and death, I want the little dash in between those dates—which tells the true story of my life—to symbolize that God did something so big through me that it was obviously of him. I cannot be satisfied with a putting-in-my-years-for-a-gold-watch mentality. I am not content with a just-barely-getting-by spiritual existence. I want to impact my world for the God who has radically impacted my life. It's the least I can do, and it is the highest for which I can strive to attain.

As a serious Christian who passionately believes in God's promise to empower his people through his Holy Spirit to impact a lost world, I have had serious doubts about that being fulfilled practically in the lives of those who say, "I'm a Christian." Often I find myself questioning what significant impact I am having in my sphere of influence and what difference the church is making in society today. I am obviously not alone in that feeling. A recent Gallup Poll indicated that 70 percent of eighteen- to twenty-nine-year-olds believe religion is losing its influence in American life.[1] As I examine such surveys taken by both Christian and non-Christian pollsters, I am perplexed and increasingly troubled that we, as Christians, are making no measurable impact on lives and culture; yet, should this not be our passion?

When I discovered the prayer of Jabez, I found a prayer with which I could relate. When I tried praying it as a thirty-day prayer experiment, I found a prayer principle that changed my life, as well as the lives of thousands of others who dared to try it at my suggestion. While I make no claim that it is a sure-fire cure-all, I am convinced by years of repeated experimentation that this prayer experiment is a timely solution to a problem plaguing so many Christians: the lack of positive impact in the world. In detailing this experiment to you, I do not presume to be the Louis Pasteur of Christendom—only a fellow struggler who has desperately searched for a genuine answer to an important question, the question of meaningful impact in the world.

A word of caution to the wise: Be careful what you pray for, you might just get it—but not always the way you want it. If you choose to invest the time, energy, and faith necessary to perform this prayer experiment in your life, be prepared for some changes—dramatic changes—in your life. But these changes may not be anything you can presently envision. Time and again, I have seen this experiment turn individuals' lives upside-down and inside-out as they are reshaped for a new task. It has been amazing to watch God unleashed in experimenters' lives and ministries. God still does big things—even today. This prayer can change your world. Are you ready for it?

> ■
> Seventy percent of eighteen- to twenty-nine-year-olds believe religion is losing its influence in American life.
> —GALLUP POLL
> ■

## Just "Uh. . . Christianity"

On one episode of *The Simpsons*, son Bart asks his father, Homer, what his religious beliefs are. Homer replies, "You know, the one with all the well-meaning rules that don't work in real life. Uh. . . Christianity."[2] I believe the greatest threat to Christianity and the American church today is the threat of indifference or being ignored. It seems to be making little difference that there's "a church on every corner," eighty-five percent of our population call themselves "Christians,"[3] and sixty-one percent of Americans say that religion is very important in their lives.[4] Even though we are surrounded by an abundance of Christian books, tapes, CDs, radio programming, seminars, study resources, and Bible translations, positive Christian impact on culture and lives is not being felt as it should be. America has more unchurched people than the entire populations of all but eleven of the world's 194 nations! Most of them used to be churched but stopped attending.[5] Influencing other people's lives is not the priority for Christians that it used to be. A recent Barna Research Group survey found that since 1991 born-again Christians have become less interested in influencing other people (48% vs. 30%) and in making a difference in the world (58% vs. 39%).[6]

Warren Webster, veteran missionary to Pakistan, confessed before thousands of college students at InterVarsity's triennial Urbana Missions Conference this need for Christians to make a difference in people's lives. He said, "If I had my life to live over again, I would live it to change the lives of people, because you have not changed anything until you've changed the lives of people."[7] Born-again Christians must once again realize the importance of making a difference in the world for the cause of Christ. We must possess the desire to change the world, to influence the lives of people who have in many ways become inoculated against Christianity. True "impact Christianity" is what our nation and world desperately need. Anything less is a failure on our part, as believers in Christ, to carry out the Great Commission mandate (Matt. 28:19–20) of our Lord, Jesus Christ.

To go from a prevalence of "uh ... Christianity" to "impact Christianity" in our culture does not call for more people calling themselves Christians; rather, it calls for us who call ourselves Christians. . .

- to become who we profess to be in Christ Jesus
- to dynamically apply the truths of God's Word to our lives
- to be transformed Christians in plain view of a lost, but seeking world
- to be empowered by the Holy Spirit to make a significant difference in the world
- to live as transparent, authentic Christians who contagiously infect the world
- to make an obvious difference in the world that so desperately needs God's truth

If the Internet is a barometer of our contemporary mindset, then I find convincing evidence of the world's increasing curiosity and a deepening hunger for spiritual things. A recent report in the

*Wall Street Journal* examines religion's staggering presence on the World Wide Web and its exponential expansion.

> By some measures, religion is almost as big as sex online. Plug "God" into a Netscape search, and you'll get as many as 600,000 responses, remarkably close to the 775,000 sites listed for "sex." Yahoo! Inc. lists 17,000 sites devoted to religion and spirituality, compared with 12,000 about movies and 600 about home and garden.[8]

In *The Great American Paradox*, David Meyers cites even higher "God" online stats: "As of August, 1999, 'God' could be found on 5.6 million websites."[9]

Spiritual interest is not just reflected on the web, it permeates every aspect of our culture from movies to television programming, from books to magazine articles, from constructing Zen meditation gardens to dialing psychic networks. While today there is increased spiritual interest in Eastern mysticism, New Age thinking, and even witchcraft, we find there is a diminishing Christian influence in the world. With the world on a search for God, why is Christianity not making a bigger difference in people's lives? What should we as Christians and the church do to regain a genuine influence in people's lives? I believe that in order to influence our world, we must be willing to ask these kinds of hard questions and relentlessly to seek answers. That's where *The Prayer Experiment* is helpful.

## Whassup?!

A popular commercial features some guys conversing with each other using a term that's been around for a while in a distinct— and somewhat annoying—way. Phoning each other, they ask, "Wha-a-s-s-u-up?!" My trying to convey in writing how they sound is more than a little challenging. This one-word, male-bonding greeting comes out of their mouths sounds something like a laryngitis-stricken Darth Vader coughing up a fur ball as he

Ebonically greets Luke Skywalker. So, too, you may be asking, "Whassup with a thirty-day prayer experiment?"

Years ago while a student in seminary, I discovered the biblical recounting of what seemingly was an insignificant prayer by a "lesser known" guy in the Bible named Jabez. Making only one appearance in Scripture (1 Chron. 4:9–10), Jabez achieved distinction because he prayed. Here was a man who Scripture says was "more honorable than his brothers" (v. 9) and who impacted his world for God.

When I read the account of Jabez, something inside of me immediately resonated with this man. I knew I was like him in wanting to make a difference in my world. I thought that if what he did worked for him, perhaps it, too, could work for me. I knew that I wanted my prayers to make a difference—in my life and in the lives of others. As I read and reread Jabez's simple, but powerful, prayer, it became a profound reminder that God wants his people...

> to pray big
> to believe big
> to dream big
> to impact big.

I claimed his prayer as my own and began praying that prayer with the hope that God would "bless me indeed" (v. 10), as he had done Jabez.

Now, more than a decade later, this prayer continues to influence me everyday. As a result of this prayer, I have been amazed to watch mountains of impossibilities moved, countless "highly unlikelies" changed to glorious realities, and incredible miracles of God take place in my life and in the lives of so many other Christians.

In fact, without the prayer of Jabez's being such an important part of my life, I may have missed the opportunity to serve as pastor of my present church. You see, when I was approached by a search committee about my coming to First Baptist Church of

Lakeland, Florida, as their pastor, I struggled to know what to do. Being a minister who's willing to go wherever God leads me has never exempted me from wrestling with him when faced with such an important decision. I believe most ministers do. For me, doing God's will doesn't present nearly so big a problem as finding it. In my decision making about this church, I earnestly sought God's will in prayer and in godly counsel. For six months I daily prayed the prayer of Jabez, not knowing where my praying would take me. I believed my responsibility was to pray it in faith, and it was God's responsibility to answer it in whatever way he chose.

The counsel came. Several friends in the ministry advised me to forget about considering Lakeland. They felt it would be a poor career decision for me to go to what was then a smaller church in a smaller city and for less money. "Hold off," they told me. "Something bigger and better will come along if you just wait a bit longer." With all of the counsel I received, I did not sense God in what I was hearing. The answer was not apparent.

> What we experienced as the result of praying this prayer . . . could only be labeled a "God thing."

As I lay in bed wrestling with the yet-unmade decision that I was supposed to share with the search committee the next day, God got my attention. He reminded me of that which I had been praying daily for months. Addressing my indecision and uncertainty, God spoke to my heart and said, "Jay, I am answering your prayer. Don't blow it!" Finally, I had my answer. In faith and without hesitation, I said, "Yes!" to God—and to the committee.

Later God reminded me of a telephone call I had received earlier that week from a friend who had heard I was talking with this church about becoming their pastor. After talking with me for awhile about the decision I was about to make, my friend said, "Jay, may I pray with you over the phone?"

"Certainly," I said.

When he started praying, I could not believe my ears! This friend prayed, "Lord, I feel impressed today to pray the prayer of Jabez for my friend." Not knowing the significance of this prayer in my life, he proceeded to pray the words of this prayer to God on my behalf. *Wow!* I thought. *God* really *is in this!* And, in fact, God was.

After going to Lakeland as their pastor, I asked our entire church to commit to praying the prayer of Jabez for thirty days on two different occasions. What we experienced as the result of praying this prayer (in faith and in obedience to God) could only be labeled a "God thing." We experienced the blessings of God in such dramatic ways that we—as individuals and as a church—will never be the same.

Wait! Before you jump to the conclusion that I'm advocating some kind of name-it-and-claim-it, blab-it-and-grab-it approach to getting some mega-blessing from God, you must know that that is the farthest thing from what I am trying to promote. This is not about seeing the world (or being seen by the world) through rose-colored glasses. I am compelled to remind you that the greatest blessings are often born out of the greatest adversities. *The Prayer Experiment* may take you down a course of trials and tribulations before you realize the blessing of God upon you. You may have to decrease before your influence can increase.

Why, then, did I hold on to this prayer of Jabez? Because I felt a passion within me to experience something far beyond that with which I had become all too comfortable. In doing so, I was not seeking the strategies offered by seminars, the promised results of high profile conferences, the how-to's of implementing better programs, or the motivation to set higher goals. While these resources can greatly benefit us, there is always present a danger to circumvent the process and go for the quick fix or the "sure result." Be clear about this: *The Prayer Experiment* is not a goal; it is a process—a process of life-transformation.

> *The Prayer Experiment* is not a goal; it is a process—a process of life-transformation.

## Diagnosis: Prayer Anorexia . . . or Bulimia

The Massachusetts Medical Society reports that an estimated five million Americans—three percent of young women—are affected by anorexia nervosa and bulimia nervosa.[10] Approximately one thousand people die annually from these severe eating disorders.[11] Anorexia often begins with a relatively normal desire to lose a few pounds; however, because dieting only temporarily relieves underlying psychological problems, it soon becomes compulsive to the point of self-starvation. Even though eating is almost eliminated, the victim, obsessed with body image, frequently sees himself or herself as fat, even though the opposite is true.[12]

Like anorexia, bulimia can have dire physical consequences. While anorexics simply starve themselves, bulimics binge on food and then purge by self-induced vomiting. They also frequently use excessive exercise, diet pills, laxatives, and diuretics to reduce weight and temporarily relieve depression and other negative feelings.[13]

If you do not carefully watch your spiritual diet, your prayer life can be afflicted by common strains of these disorders. I believe that if Jesus were addressing the self-righteous Pharisees or his not-yet-with-it disciples today, he would speak in contemporary cultural terms—as was his teaching style—and expose their prayer anorexia. He would point out that these religious elites were starving themselves spiritually, because their prayers were nothing more than pious-sounding words and not getting them to the Source of any true spiritual nourishment. Even though they thought they were spiritually fat, the opposite was true.

I think that if the Garden of Gethsemane prayer vigil had occurred in this century, Jesus might have said to his sleeping disciple Peter, "Peter, your prayer anorexia is flaring up again." Jesus would have then explained that Peter had before him the broken Bread of Life, yet he was missing the benefits of feasting on him.

Jesus would also have a word for prayer bulimics, those who constantly study Scripture and consume lots of fattening information, and then regurgitate many sugar-coated words—which they label "prayer"—to keep them in spiritual shape. When they pray, out come words intended to impress people, but they do not connect with God. In their own eyes, they think they look like spiritual heavies, but instead they are malnourished light-weights.

Every Christian must guard against these two praying disorders. The Great Physician has given us the prescription for the sure cure. He gives the following treatment plan for prayer anorexia and prayer bulimia:

> And when you come before God, don't turn that into a theatrical production either. All these people making a regular show out of their prayers, hoping for stardom! Do you think God sits in a box seat?
>
> Here's what I want you to do: Find a quiet, secluded place so you won't be tempted to role-play before God. Just be there as simply and honestly as you can manage. The focus will shift from you to God, and you will begin to sense his grace.
>
> The world is full of so-called prayer warriors who are prayer-ignorant. They're full of formulas and programs and advice, peddling techniques for getting what you want from God. Don't fall for that nonsense. This is your Father you are dealing with, and he knows better than you what you need. With a God like this loving you, you can pray very simply.
>
> —MATTHEW 6:5–8 *THE MESSAGE*

Christians need to fill this prescription and take this prayer disorder preventative medicine several times a day. This is a prayer diet that really works.

## Hyde and Seek

The prayer of Jabez transformed the life of missionary John Hyde, who lived 1865–1912. The prayer moved his heart to pray with such great faith and fervor that he became known to others as "Praying Hyde." Through praying as Jabez, Hyde learned to pray the kind of prayers one prays when one truly expects God to answer. Dr. J. Wilbur Chapman wrote to a friend to tell the story of Praying Hyde's profound influence:

> I have learned some great lessons concerning prayer. At one of our missions in England the audiences were exceedingly small. But I received a note saying that an American missionary ... was going to pray God's blessing down upon our work. He was known as "Praying Hyde." Almost instantly the tide turned. The hall became packed, and at my first invitation fifty men accepted Christ as their Savior.
>
> As we were leaving I said, "Mr. Hyde, I want you to pray for me." He came to my room, turned the key in the door, and dropped on his knees, and waited five minutes without a single syllable coming from his lips. I could hear my own heart thumping and his beating. I felt the hot tears running down my face. I knew I was with God. Then, with upturned face, down which the tears were streaming, he said, "O, God!" Then for five minutes at least he was still again; and then, when he knew that he was talking with God ... there came up from the depth of his heart such petitions for men as I have never heard before.
>
> I rose from my knees to know what real prayer was. We believe that prayer is mighty, and we believe it as we never did before.... It was a season of prayer with John Hyde that made me realize what real prayer was. I owe to him more than I owe to any man for showing me what a prayer-life is.[14]

Through performing his own Jabez experiment, Hyde's life was changed, his influence increased, and the world dramatically impacted for Christ.

As you read this, you may be looking for something that can transform *your* life and *your* effectiveness, as was John Hyde's.

- You may be frustrated with your mediocre—or, perhaps, even your lack of genuine—Christian influence on others.
- You may feel like you've been put on "hold" and opportunities to impact your world for Christ seem to be passing you by.
- You may feel a lack of power and a sense of ineffectiveness in your personal prayer life.
- You may be concerned that your church is not changing lives or culture, but you are tired of glib answers and slick programs.

I know all too well these feelings and frustrations. I have struggled with each of these at some point in my life.

A believe-it-or-not, too-incredible-to-be-true Internet site reports that a hunter in Uganda was being sought by local authorities for illegally hunting gorillas. That's not all. His method of operation is quite distinctive. He first shoots the gorillas with a tranquilizer gun, then dresses them in clown suits. This story goes on to say six gorillas had been found wandering around dressed as clowns.[15] Whether or not there is any veracity in this account I have not been able to verify. I will say, however, that I have known some individuals dressed up as Christians who do not know the reality of who they profess to be. The world has been disappointed and shocked so often it has become numb with apathy when these clowns are exposed for who they really are.

Genuine transformation is needed in all of our lives for us to be who we say we are. The world desperately needs for us to be "the real deal." I know that *The Prayer Experiment* transformed my life—my way of thinking, my way of praying, my way of influencing other lives—and, likewise, I know that it can transform yours.

## Mr. Foreman, Do You Have a Verdict?

The trial is over. The courtroom is abuzz as the jury reenters. The foreman hands the verdict to the bailiff as order in the court is demanded. As the presiding judge reads the verdict, she asks, "Mr. Foreman, do you have a verdict?" To which the lead juror replies, "We do." Soon the rendered verdict is read aloud and the sentence is pronounced.

While I have not gone before the courts to try *The Prayer Experiment*—although a number of legal and judicial professionals have personally tried it—I have asked our congregation to put *The Prayer Experiment* on trial in their lives. The first time that our congregation committed to praying the prayer of Jabez for thirty days was during the first few months of my ministry in Lakeland. The results were immediate and unmistakably the work of God in our midst.

From concerted, faithful praying an atmosphere of revival emerged. Lives were touched and people changed. The church has never been the same since that time. It was thirty glorious days of heaven coming down! By the end of those days we had to move out of our sanctuary to our Christian Life Center in order to accommodate the growing numbers of worshipers.

> From concerted, faithful praying an atmosphere of revival emerged.

We sensed the Holy Spirit's presence in a fresh way. Praying this prayer created an atmosphere where God had the freedom to work. One of the most significant results of this prayer experiment was the change in the impact of our members on their world: where they lived, worked, went to school, played golf, and shopped. These Christians and our church had a new magnetism that attracted more and more people.

Two years later, the church committed a second time to putting *The Prayer Experiment* on trial again. We anticipated much the same results as before. Instead, we encountered a number of confusing surprises. Our church had already moved out of the gym and into the Lakeland Civic Center, which we had leased. We had plans to build a new worship center. All was going well with those building plans and the groundbreaking date was set. During the thirty-day prayer experiment, however, all those plans fell through. We found out that to build on our location would require an exorbitant amount of money being spent on closing one city street. God had closed the door. We were not sure what we would do.

To be honest, it seemed like *The Prayer Experiment* had turned into *The Murphy's Law Experiment*. If it could go wrong, it did. I felt like Job Jr. No one wanted to curse God, but I think they may have wanted to curse me for leading them into a second prayer experiment. Personally, I felt discouraged, because I couldn't see the blessings of God.

I was grateful when the thirty days were over. Had *The Prayer Experiment* failed this time? None of us quite knew, until two weeks later. It was then I received a phone call that would change everything. The principal owner of the old Lakeland Mall called one of our church leaders with the question, "Would you be interested in purchasing the old Lakeland Mall for your church?" He went on, "I have been thinking about this for a few weeks and I felt I had to approach you."

To put this call in perspective, the mall, which had been vacant for nine years—had 400,000 feet under one roof, 1800 parking spaces, two theaters, and a spa, and it was located on a beautiful lake. In addition, approximately 45,000 cars pass by that facility each day. Also, connected to the mall was a vacated Sam's Club warehouse facility. Wal-Mart Corporation was still paying thousands of dollars each month on the lease on that empty building. Here was the offer. If we could negotiate a buyout of the lease with Wal-Mart, the owner would take it off the asking price. God had already gone before us preparing the way. To make a long story short, Sam's Club paid us three million dollars to get out of the lease. After seeing God answer our prayers as he orchestrated all of these seemingly impossible events, the church voted overwhelmingly to buy the mall, sell our old church facilities, and move.

I could share with you miracle after miracle since that time of buying the mall. How did we relocate a church that has been in existence since 1895? Through prayer our people had become unified in purpose. There was no dissension, only enthusiastic support for what God was doing in our midst. Our members recognized this move as God's specific answer to our thirty-day prayer experiment. The prayer of Jabez had created a sense of expectancy and readiness to do whatever God would lead us to do. Heaven had come down and God had shown himself to us!

## I Dare You!

Over the years, I have had the privilege of introducing *The Prayer Experiment* to a number of churches and thousands of Christians. I know of no time this experiment has failed in its usefulness in getting Christians to think beyond what is and to believe God for what could be. I often get letters from individuals and pastors who are praying the prayer of Jabez—many on an on-going basis—and seeing God work through their prayers in mighty ways.

> Thank you so much for giving three days of your busy schedule to share with us. Only time, and maybe eternity will tell the full impact of the messages you shared with us. . . . The most exciting thing to me is the fact that so many of our folks are praying the prayer of Jabez every day with expectancy! Sunday night people began to give testimonies of how God is answering their prayers. Everyone gave God the glory. They talked for thirty minutes about how wonderful our God really is! Perhaps this is the beginning of revival.[16]

I believe it is an experiment worth trying. There is an urgency as never before to reach a world where we are losing influence. Some have said that we are only one generation away from paganism. The time is now for us to exert our influence on our world. We must offer something more than just talk about God flowered with our religious clichés. The world must see the Holy Spirit at work in our lives—transforming our lives—before it will listen to our message about Christ. *The Prayer Experiment* can facilitate that change.

*The Prayer Experiment* is more than repeating a prayer; instead, it offers focal points for your praying. Some have referred to this as "centering prayer," where genuinely getting into touch with God is central to praying. Calvin Miller explains, "Centering prayers are interested in relationship, not answers. Centering prayers want God alone—all of God— more of God—only God."[17] Praying the prayer of Jabez is a great vehicle—as a centering prayer—for drawing you more deeply into a relationship with God.

> ■
>
> I know of no time this experiment has failed in its usefulness in getting Christians to think beyond what is and to believe God for what could be.
>
> ■

If you are willing to risk performing an experiment that can change your life, your impact on the people around you, and your legacy of faith, then I encourage you to continue reading as I explain the experiment and its many implications to you. I dare you to join me in praying the prayer that could change everything, the prayer of Jabez:

> Lord, bless me indeed.
> Do something so big in my life that it is obviously from you.
> Increase my influence and opportunities for you,
> And give me a sense of your continual presence and direction.
> Protect me, and keep me from falling into Satan's traps. Amen.

Pause now. Pray the prayer of Jabez; however, before you do...

1. Name those in your world you would most like to see impacted for God through your life.

2.  As you pray this prayer, pray for those people you listed.
3.  After you have prayed this prayer, start expectant watch for—and seize—God-opportunities to touch those for whom you have prayed.

> Lord, bless me indeed. . .
> Do something so big in my life that it is obviously from you.
> Increase my influence and opportunities for you,
> And give me a sense of your continual presence and direction.
> Protect me, and keep me from falling into Satan's traps. Amen.

If you want God to start doing big things through you, you may want to continue the experiment.

# If You Think You're the Last Person God Would Use for Big Things...

*His mother named him Jabez.*

"**H**ighly unlikely." Would that be your response if asked if you believed God would do something big through you? Perhaps, you'd think about it for a moment and ask, "Just how big?" I guess I should qualify my question. Do you believe God would do something so big that it would make an obvious impact for Christ in your world? That's the question that usually evokes some sort of emotional response from Christians who don't really feel they are ever going to get the opportunity to make a big difference with their lives. At this point, the reasons vary, but the ultimate answer is almost always the same: "Not really." Believe me, I totally understand. That's exactly what I felt. My prayer had been, "God, please don't pass me by. Do something big in my life."

Why is this the way we think? Perhaps many of us have bought into the idea that nothing much will come of Average Joe. That's understandable, considering all the hype given the Hollywood beautiful, the Madison Avenue chic, the Wall Street powerful, and the World Series super-jocks. These larger-than-life icons—the Who's-Who, the Most-Likely-to-Succeed, and the Rich-and-the-

Famous—seem to be the ones destined to make it big in the world and to have a big impact on the world. Then, there's the rest of us—like Timmy's dad. He was guilty of bringing home office work just about every night. Finally six-year-old Timmy asked his dad why. His dad explained that he has so much work he couldn't finish it all during the day. Timmy reasoned, "Then, why don't they put you in a slower group?" In which group do you find yourself: mover and shaker or removed and shaken?

## Generic Is Priceless

"Do you prefer generic if we have it?" Well, I don't necessarily prefer generic, but my insurance provider certainly does. As the belts have tightened and the pencils have been sharpened, health insurance companies seek ways to make their bottom line the new standard of patient care. Generic drugs, drugs that no longer have their name protected by trademark and can be made and distributed by any drug manufacturer, are one means to cut the escalating costs of medicine. Generally generic is less expensive while its quality is the same. Rigorous FDA requirements ensure that the generic drug should treat an illness or condition with exactly the same effectiveness and as safely as the brand-name equivalent. Not only do health care providers prefer generic, so too does God. That certainly is encouraging news for all of us.

> The wise and almighty God of the universe seems to commonly opt for the generic, store-brand Christian who has a heart for him.

If you find yourself removed from the "in crowd' and shaken from the pack of "big dogs," then you may find it impossible to believe that God could use someone like you to do something significant for him. Let me assure you that while God certainly can use those on the elite list, he most often chooses to use those on the Least-Likely-to-Succeed, the "Who's He?"

or the "Who's She?" list. The wise and almighty God of the universe seems to opt commonly for the generic, store-brand Christian who has a heart for him and an earnest desire to be used by him to touch the world for Christ. He has been in the habit of using highly unlikelies to make a difference throughout history. The Bible contains story after story of highly unlikely individuals who were radically transformed—then used—by God.

- Joseph: the unlikely-to-survive young man who was thrown into a pit and then sold into slavery by his jealous brothers, only later to be transformed by God into the vice-pharaoh of Egypt and was used to save not only his family, but his Hebrew nation from extinction
- Moses: the unlikely boy-in-a-basket-thrown-in-a-river, who was transformed into the Hebrew leader and whose faith was rewarded with the parting of the Red Sea and God's entrusting him with the Ten Commandments
- Rahab: the unlikely prostitute who risked her life to hide Joshua's men in her home and was transformed by God into a woman of faith listed in the genealogy of Christ
- David: the young shepherd whose father reluctantly presented him during Samuel's king search and who later committed adultery and sought to cover up a murder while he was king; however, God transformed him into a man after his own heart
- Saul of Tarsus: the chief persecutor of Christians, who was transformed by God into the apostle Paul and shaped Christian thought to this very day

God constantly says, "Next!" He seems to delight in transforming highly unlikely individuals into transformed servants in order to impact the world. I know that is what he did for me. I am definitely one of those highly unlikely people. As a young ministerial student in college, I held one of my first revival meetings in a small, white frame, rural church. After preaching my heart out on "The Characteristics of a Committed Christian," I called for a time of personal commitment. I vividly recall an older, gruff-looking man in bib-overalls jumping over a pew in his haste to respond to the appeal to "get things right with God." He grabbed my hand, looked squarely into my eyes, and said words I'll never forget: "When I saw that you were preaching, I thought to myself, 'If God can use someone as homely as you, there's hope for me.'" I didn't know what to say. You know, I kind of wanted to kick him—in Jesus' name, of course—and then go off somewhere and lick my wounds.

His words hurt, because they were a painful reminder of feelings that had plagued me most of my life. I had always struggled with the feeling that some way, somehow, I didn't measure up. Enough never seemed to be enough. After that man made that statement to me, I must confess that every time I looked in the mirror, I would see a deficient me and would hear his indicting words like a tape recording being played over and over again. As I write these words, I am again reminded of the apostle Paul's words.

> Take a good look, friends, at who you were when you got called into this life. I don't see many of "the brightest and the best" among you, not many influential, not many from high-society families. Isn't it obvious that God deliberately chose men and women that the culture overlooks and exploits and abuses, chose these "nobodies" to expose the hollow pretensions of the "somebodies"?
>
> —1 CORINTHIANS 1:26–29 THE MESSAGE

Our heavenly Father often chooses to use his most highly unlikely children—like me and like you—to do significant things for him. As I have grown in my relationship to God and have found my security in him, I am thankful for those times when it has been obvious to others that it is not me, but rather God's Holy Spirit in me, who is at work. Through the process, God has shown me that it is only through prayer and drawing our true worth from his accomplished work that we can get beyond our feelings of inadequacy and rise above the painful things we feel. I am constantly amazed at our great God and his choice to use unlikely individuals.

## "Jabez Who?"

The common look given me when I begin to introduce individuals or groups to *The Prayer Experiment* is a puzzled "Jabez who?"-look. This is understandable. I was recently presenting *The Prayer Experiment* to a church and I got the "Who's that?" looks. That was no problem, however, for once I explained it, the prayer touched a lot of hearts and stirred great interest. In fact, one individual in the congregation was so excited about the prayer that she called our church asking where she might get a copy of "The Prayer of *Jezebel*"!

Even at my own church, there has been some confusion about exactly who this Jabez guy is. A lady who recently began attending our church wrote me a letter sharing her excitement about what was taking place at our church. She said that she was somewhat puzzled by a reference to an individual and his prayer. She wrote that she left church one day confused about the "prayer of *J. Best*." A Sunday or two later, she again heard about the prayer. So on her way home from church that day, she commented to her husband that this J. Best must be an important person in the church, because we kept referring to his prayer. Not until the scriptural reference was given did she figure out that it was not "J. Best"; rather, it was Jabez!

In case there is any misunderstanding or confusion, it's *Jabez*: J-a-b-e-z—not *Jezebel* or *J. Best*. Because of such experiences, let me also assume it is necessary for me to give a brief introduction to this individual. Jabez is found among all the "begats" in 1 Chronicles, in a section of an Old Testament book where it seems unlikely we would read something to apply to our present-day lives. Such an assumption, however, will cause us to miss a rich passage of Scripture and a brief portrait of an important biblical character.

Jabez's very name suggests that he was not a candidate to accomplish anything significant in the world's eyes, for his name means "pain" or "sorrow." We don't know why his parents named him *Jabez*, only that sorrow is evidently what he brought to his parents (1 Chron. 4:9) and carried with him throughout life. Just think about it: From his earliest memories Jabez could only remember a life defined by pain. Whatever his problem, it seems it would have prevented him from being a nominee for the most-likely-to-matter; yet amidst the hundreds of descendants of Israel listed in 1 Chronicles 1–11, Jabez stands out as one who did matter, one whose life made a big difference.

## God Factoring

It was the God factor in Jabez's life that made the difference and that turned this man of sorrow into a man of honor. Jabez relied on something beyond himself—something beyond his own limitations, or strength. He placed his hope in

> the healing power of prayer to free him from pain
>
> the elevating power of prayer to change his standing in the world
>
> the equipping power of prayer to accomplish that which he could not
>
> the promising power of prayer to bring God's blessing on his unlikely life.

I can easily put my own name in the place of Jabez's name. Many have asked, "Jay who?" when they have seen my name as a scheduled speaker. A number of times I have even been called "Joy Dennis." (If I didn't think they were referring to the fruit of the Spirit evident in my life, my male ego could be bruised by such confusion!) My identifying with Jabez is more than a lack of name recognition. From birth I, like Jabez, knew sorrow. I was born with club feet, and my earliest recollection is of the awful sound of the saw used to cut through the constantly replaced casts on my lower legs. Beyond this physical infirmity, I knew the pain of circumstances that early would label me as "highly unlikely" to amount to much, to do anything in life that would make an impact.

When I was eight years old, my father was inspecting a paper-cutting machine and noticed a jam inside of the machine. As he used his right hand to correct the problem, he slipped on a slick oil spot on the floor. When this happened, his hand was thrust into the machine and was severed. His life suddenly changed, as did mine. Painful is the memory of my dad's remorseful words: "I can't even throw a baseball or football to my son." My father endured thirteen surgeries and years of rehabilitation. With the loss of my father's income, our family had to learn to survive on $38.50 a week. My security in life was shaken. I felt alone and afraid. I remember being told that I now qualified for "free lunch" at school, which—because it embarrassingly wounded my pride—made me feel different from the other kids. (Because of feeling this way, I was unable to accept the help offered me.) Economically and socially, psychologically and spiritually, things had changed in my life.

I can only recall two really happy moments during those painful childhood years. One was when the doctor told us that my father could come home. I remember well when I heard the news. I was eating roast beef in the hospital cafeteria, and on hearing the news I was so excited I could no longer eat a thing! It was truly better than any Christmas I can recall. The second was when my then-hospitalized dad told my mom to buy me a toy with our meager resources. She bought me a little blue Tonka truck. As an eight-year-old, it became a symbol of hope against a stark background of sorrow and despair, including a devastating tornado that roared through our town and shattered many people's dreams. It was just one more thing that created deep inner fear and anxiety.

As I grew up, I learned to cope and survive by responding to all that was happening in my life with a strong determination to rise above it all. Yet, in my mind I could never quite measure up. I never saw the label "outstanding" as ever applying to me. My life being used by God to do something big for him was not only highly unlikely, but seemed to me like only a dream.

## Sermon on the Won't Amount

> ■
>
> Prayer can change "highly unlikelies" into "absolutely positivelies" who impact the world.
>
> ■

My perspective began to change when I was sixteen years old. As with Jabez, a prayer transformed my life: the "sinner's prayer" where I embraced my Savior's loving offer of salvation. My previous counterfeit religious experiences had left me empty, confused, and desperately in need of a God who was greater than my problems and my life circumstances. I was introduced to a God who has big plans for anyone who will dare say "yes" to him. When I reflect on those uncomfortable memories, they now serve as powerful reminders to me that without God, "no way"; with God, "yes, way!" Prayer not only changes hearts, prayer changes lives. Prayer can change "highly unlikelies" into "absolutely positivelies" who impact the world.

Such is well demonstrated through the praying of Maria Panteleyvna, the Russian woman who is better identified as Mikhail Gorbachev's mother. She prayed for many years that God would use her son to bring down communism. What seemed highly unlikely amazingly became reality before the world's eyes. The *Wall Street Journal* published an article entitled "The Russian Reformation"[1] that raised serious questions about the religious beliefs of Mikhail Gorbachev. Mark Helprin wrote that former President Reagan's press secretary, Larry Speaks, recorded in his memoirs that at the 1985 Geneva Summit Mr. Gorbachev confided in Reagan that he was a Christian. This claim was verified by intelligence, which indicated that Gorbachev was indeed a baptized Christian and that his mother went to church. To quote the article:

Maria Panteleyvna does not merely attend services. She is devout. Her son, baptized during Stalin's terror, worshipped at a time when doing so was an elemental commitment and an act of courage. In what may have been a prophetic metaphor, his paternal grandparents hid religious icons behind portraits of Lenin and Stalin. Today, when [former] President Gorbachev visits his mother each year on his birthday, she serves an Easter cake decorated with the initials for "Christ is Risen."[2]

The prayers and faithful devotion of a mother changed the life of this highly unlikely world leader.

Yes, prayer offered in the belief that God not only can—but will—turn the natural into the supernatural, the ordinary into the extraordinary, and the impossible into the possible. Prayer allows us family access to our heavenly Father as well as an earthly hope as a result. We can enjoy a higher kind of life, one empowered and directed from above. If offering a modern-day "Sermon on the Won't Amount," Jesus might say of such transformed Christians, "Blessed are those whom others consider highly unlikely, for they will impact their world."

> Blessed are those whom others consider highly unlikely, for they will impact their world.

## I Feel Your Pain

In his first bid for the presidency, Bill Clinton made popular the phrase "I feel your pain." The 1992 Clinton campaign organizers were confident they knew their constituents well. In having Clinton identify with the human common denominator of pain, they hoped to score big at the polls. (Obviously, it worked.) Pain—it transcends all social, economic, and political boundaries. We can relate. We all have experienced pain to varying degrees, and even, at times, we too have taken on the name Jabez.

Pain may have found its place in your life in such a way that you can easily identify with Jabez. Perhaps you've been told:

"You won't amount to anything."
"Why are you wasting your time?"
"You'll never make it."
"I don't love you any longer."
"You're useless."

Maybe you have been so overwhelmed by feelings of rejection, discouragement, and disappointment that you wonder, "Can God really transform my life and make a difference through me?"

A middle-aged woman suffered a severe heart attack. She was rushed to the hospital and soon found herself on the operating table. While undergoing emergency surgery the woman had a near-death experience. During the experience she saw God and asked if this was the end. God told her "no" and explained that she had another thirty to forty years to live.

After recovery, the woman decided to stay in the hospital and have a face lift, liposuction, a tummy tuck, and other "improvements." Before she left the hospital, she even had someone change her hair color to complete her transformation. She figured that she might as well make the best of the additional thirty or forty years she had to live.

When she had recovered from the last operation, the woman walked out of the hospital and was killed instantaneously by a speeding ambulance pulling up to the emergency room door. In heaven, the woman arrived in front of God and asked, "I thought you said I had another thirty or forty years. What happened?" To that God replied, "I guess I didn't recognize you!"[3]

Better than any plastic or reconstructive surgery is God's ability to transform life's sorrowful scars into rejuvenated faith. God is in life-makeover business. He often uses our weaknesses to make us strong and useful for Christ's sake.

## Star Search Auditions

Not long ago Ed McMahon cashed in on his fame as the "Heeeeeere's Johnny!" straight man to host his own long-running talent show, *Star Search*. Hopefuls and wanna-be's saw their careers launched, catapulted, or sometimes crashed on this popular television series. Stars were born through the ingenious efforts of this surprise-you-may-already-be-a-millionaire pitchman. Have you ever considered that God, too, is in the star-search business? He seeks Christians who are willing to "push the envelope" for him, who are willing to go beyond their comfort zones by saying "yes" to the opportunities for impact that he brings their way, who are willing to say "no" to paralyzing fear and doubt that will thwart their effectiveness.

It is important to remember that stars are placed with exactness by God. He puts us precisely where he wants us, in a place where we can make a difference and do what he wants us to do. Our world—our sphere of influence, our home, our job, our school, our after-hours-and-on-weekends life—is the stage on which we can shine our brightest for God. We should also consider that stars cause people to look up. That is precisely what we as Christians are called to do in our world. Never having a "look-at-me"—or even a "look-at-poor-ol'-suffering-me"—attitude, we are put on stage to perform our role in pointing people upward to God. For us to be God's kind of stars, we should examine God's Word for a biblical definition of *stars*: "Those who are wise will shine like the brightness of the heavens, and those who lead many to righteousness, like the stars for ever and ever" (Dan. 12:3).

When I think about stars shining for Christ, I think of Christians

- who completely allow God to infiltrate all areas of their lives
- who cheerfully accept and follow the terms of God's "contracts"
- who consistently tune in to God's voice through prayer and the Word

- who contagiously radiate joy in being released from the bondage of pain
- who consciously never say "no" to the God of possibilities-made-realities
- who are confidently assured that God can use them to impact the lives of others.

## "The Body" Versus Cassie

Minnesota Governor Jesse "The Body" Ventura wants you to believe that your having faith in God and trusting him to use you to do big things is "a sham and a crutch for weak-minded people."[4] Such reasoning is the true sham. God is real, and his desire to use you in a significant way is real. The question that begs asking must then be: "Is *your* faith in God and *your* desire to serve him real?"

For Cassie Bernall, it was as real as life itself. A typical seventeen-year-old junior at Columbine High School in Littleton, Colorado, Cassie was having a typical day on April 20, 1999, when she was called upon to have a profound impact on the world. With atypical courage, Cassie faced a martyr's death two years after she said "yes" to the possibilities of living a "sold-out" life for Jesus Christ. Listen to this poem she wrote a few months before her death—a poem later discovered by her brother:

> Now I have given up on everything else.
> I have found it to be the only way
> To really know Christ and to experience
> The mighty power that brought
> Him back to life again, and to find
> Out what it means to suffer and to
> Die with him.
>
> So, whatever it takes
> I will be one who lives in the fresh
> Newness of life of those who are
> Alive from the dead.[5]

Cassie declared, "I will be one who lives in the fresh newness of life." And so she was. The world was touched by this "average" teenager with anything other than average faith and devotion. God had transformed her from a teenager who a few years before was obsessed with death rock, vampires, and self-mutilation[6] into a bold Christian martyr. In the course of writing this book, Cassie's mother, Misty Bernall, poignantly shared in conversations how Cassie's short life had made an impact on others because of her choice to change and to live out her professed faith in God.

A fellow student Josh, who was near Cassie in the library that fateful day, recalls, "I could hear everything like it was right next to me. One of them asked her if she believed in God. She paused. . . and then she said yes. She must have been scared, but her voice didn't sound shaky. It was strong. Then they asked her why, though they didn't give her a chance to respond. They just blew her away." Another student recounts seeing Cassie with her hands clasped in prayer. Josh concurs that Cassie must have been visibly praying: "I don't understand why they'd pop that question on someone who wasn't."[7]

Concerning the impact Cassie made on others, a teen from her youth group explained, "Cassie raised the bar up for me and my Christianity."[8] You may be thinking, "I'll never be asked to take such a stand for my faith as Cassie did. I live an average life with average opportunities for possibly influencing the world for Christ." That's normal to think that way. What *The Prayer Experiment* is trying to do, however, is to get you to think outside the box. Who you are, where you are, what you do, or where you have been doesn't determine your impact for God. It doesn't matter if you are a stay-at-home mom or a CEO at a major corporation. It doesn't matter whether you are pastor or a student. God wants to use you in your sphere of influence to touch your world in a significant way. A popular Christian song asks, "Will you be the one?"

## "Well, You Can't Just Sit There"

We must move beyond complacency and a fear of failure.

We must not be afraid to act when it is our opportune time
to do so.
We must seize those golden opportunities for Christian
witness.
We must take a stand for Christ at all costs.
We can no longer just sit there making excuses,
hoping someone else will handle it.

Thirty-three-year-old truck driver Larry Walters did anything but just sit there. It had been Walter's dream for twenty years to construct and fly a clustered-balloon aircraft. To make his dream come true, Larry went to the local Army-Navy surplus store and purchased forty-five weather balloons and several large tanks of helium. Going to a friend's house in San Pedro, California, the night before his now infamous flight, Larry inflated the huge weather balloons with helium, rigged each balloon to his aluminum Sears-brand lawn chair, and tethered his aircraft—which he dubbed *Inspiration I*—to the ground. His plan was to float upward for a one-of-a-kind view of his surroundings and take some spectacular pictures. He judged he would get no higher than a hundred feet, but just in case he did, he planned to regulate his altitude by shooting out some of the balloons with his pellet gun.

On Friday, July 2, 1982, with a half-dozen friends holding the tethers, Larry donned a parachute, grabbed his pellet gun, a large bottle of soda, a portable CB radio, and a camera, and he then took a seat in his lawn chair. Instructing his friends to let him up slowly, Larry was soon in flight. Going just a bit higher—16,000 feet higher!—Larry was soon on his CB yelling for help. With no pilot or balloon training, Larry spent about two hours aloft. His flight took him into a flight landing approach of Los Angeles International Airport. At least two startled commercial pilots—one with TWA and one with Delta Airlines—spotted Larry, and one radioed the Federal Aviation Administration.

Shivering in the high altitude, Larry used his pellet gun to pop balloons in order to come back to earth. On the way down, his balloons got entangled in power lines, blacking out a Long Beach neighborhood for twenty minutes. The chair dangled from the power lines, five feet above the ground. Regaining his composure, Larry was soon able to get down safely.

Larry Walters caused quite a stir fulfilling his dream. All landings and takeoffs at LAX were diverted while Larry floated in his lawn chair at 16,000 feet. When they finally got him down, he was surrounded by TV crews, the police, fire and rescue squads, and plenty of curious onlookers. It was a major news event. When asked by reporters if he planned to do it again, Larry responded, "Since I was thirteen years old, I've dreamed of going up into the clear blue sky in a weather balloon. By the grace of God, I have fulfilled my dream—but I wouldn't do this again for anything." Another reporter asked, "What in the world made you do it the first time?" Larry Walters thought about it for a moment and said, "Well, you can't just sit there."⁹

> God is searching for those who have a heart that passionately desires to change the world for him.

In your Christian life, you can't just sit there when God is offering you the opportunity of a lifetime to impact your world for him positively. While what you do for Christ may not gain you notoriety or media attention, it *will* have its impact. Our friend Jabez did just that. He didn't just sit there feeling sorry for himself, he prayed!

In every town, every city, every church, every school, on every job, in every neighborhood, and on every golf course, God is searching for those who have a heart that passionately desires to change the world for him.

> For the eyes of the LORD move to and fro throughout the earth that He may strongly support those whose heart is completely His.
>
> —2 CHRONICLES 16:9 NASB

God is looking for those he can point to and say, "I want to use you." He isn't impressed with anything else or anything less.

## Got Prayer?

A huge advertising success has come from showing attractive, popular personalities, each with a white milk moustache holding a cold, thirst-stimulating glass of milk. The ad asks, "Got milk?" Picture the Christian who is making a big impact in his or her world, the kind of person who would be great to feature in an advertising campaign for Christianity, the kind of person whom God is using to touch lives in a significant way. Who would this person be? I believe it would be the common-variety, blue-light special Christian who has discovered the secret to being available to be used and to being used effectively for God. Of this person we would not have to ask, "Got prayer?" The evidence—not a white moustache, but a Spirit-empowered life—would make it obvious.

Be certain of this: The average Christian does not have to have an average impact. While prayerlessness on the part of Christians leaves them feeling impotent in their effectiveness and discouraged about their usefulness, prayerfulness brings Christians feelings of confidence and assurance in what God can do in their lives. A connection with God in prayer yields a force the world cannot comprehend.

> Be certain of this: The average Christian does not have to have an average impact.

Jesus, of course, understood the role of prayer in a Christian's life. He often relied on prayer when the world's draining of his (human) strength demanded his getting his battery recharged. He regularly engaged in prayer as a necessary source of guidance from—and communion with—his heavenly Father. He also emphatically communicated to his disciples that prayer was the invaluable key to their making an impact on the world. On some level they must have understood this. They never asked him how to walk on water or how to heal the sick. But they did ask Christ, "Lord, teach us to pray" (Luke 11:1).

Likewise, prayer should be the source of your strength and guidance. Your influence in the world will be determined by your prayers. It has been said that much secret prayer means much public power.[10] Do you want to make a real difference in the world? You can only do so through prayer, as it is what makes a difference in lives and in life events. The author of the insightful book *The Kneeling Christian* writes: "Let us not forget that the greatest thing we can do for God or for man is to pray. For we can accomplish more by our prayers than by all of our work. . . . When we pray God works."[11] I want you to know that I have seen what I alone can do, and I am ready—more than ever—to see what God can do!

## Raise Your Hand If You Know the Answer

When I preach or teach on *The Prayer Experiment*, I usually give the group an opportunity to commit to praying the prayer of Jabez for thirty days. Depending on group dynamics and the Holy Spirit's leading, I will ask the individuals who are willing to commit to praying this prayer daily either to stand or to raise their hands. Every time I have done this, the majority of those present have indicated their willingness and desire to participate in this prayer experiment for the prescribed number of days. I believe people are eager to commit to this because they know they need to pray, and most have wanted to establish effective prayer habits. While Christians know they should pray—and pray consistently— they struggle to make the time in their schedules to do so.

I was sickened to read that the average pastor prays only three minutes a day.[12] Not that I don't appreciate the time pressures pastors feel, but I find it amazing that we as pastors can settle for so little, so little of God's power displayed in our lives, in our ministries, and in our churches. Can you imagine the impact praying pastors would have in their worlds? How defeating it is for pastors—like other Christians—to work so hard, yet pray so little.

Snoopy, the cherished *Peanuts* cartoon pet, sat droopy-eyed at the entrance of his dog house, lamenting, "Yesterday I was a dog. Today I'm a dog. Tomorrow I'll probably still be a dog. SIGH. There's so little hope for advancement!" Perhaps you feel like Snoopy: hopeless, with little expectation of God's doing something significant in and through your "flea-bitten" life. An old saying suggests, "If you keep doing what you're doing, you'll keep getting what you've got."[13] Is there a cycle of ineffectiveness or discouragement you need to break? If your desire is "Lord, don't pass me by. Please use me. Let me be the one," be encouraged. God delights in empowering and using his children—especially those who call on him.

> I tell you the truth, anyone who has faith in me will do what I have been doing. He will do even greater things than these, because I am going to the Father. And I will do whatever you ask in my name, so that the Son may bring glory to the Father. You may ask me for anything in my name, and I will do it.
>
> —JOHN 14:12–14

If you think you are the last person God would use for the big things, think about the unlikeliness of Jabez. Discover, as he did, the power of prayer. Let me challenge you to undertake this thirty-day *The Prayer Experiment*, praying daily the prayer of Jabez. This experiment is one of the easiest things to do, yet the results can be so profound. Your thinking will change. Your desire to be used by God to touch other lives will become a daily passion. You will find yourself becoming like an eager schoolchild with your hand raised, pleading, "Call on me, God! Let me be the one!"

Pause now. Pray the prayer of Jabez; however, before you do...

1. Think of those big things you would like for God to do through you.
2. What is preventing you from achieving those things? As you pray this prayer, ask God to help you live by faith and overcome these hurdles.

3.  Commit to God's doing the big things through you—
    even today.

> Lord, bless me indeed. . .
> Do something so big in my life that it is obviously
> from you.
> Increase my influence and opportunities for you,
> And give me a sense of your continual presence
> and direction.
> Protect me, and keep me from falling into Satan's
> traps. Amen.

If you are tired of status quo Christianity and desire to move beyond it, you may want to continue the experiment.

# 3

# Motivated to Go Beyond
# Status Quo

*Jabez was more honorable than his brothers.*

Is there anything average about you? See how your daily requirements compare to the following facts[1] about the average person:

The World Health Organization surveyed 120,000 students in twenty-six European countries, the United States, and Canada and found that the average American young person smokes less, watches fewer hours daily of television, eats less healthily, exercises less frequently, and acts less congenially than young peers in other countries.[2] *American Demographics* reports that today's average teen prefers Julia Stile, Mandy Moore, vans, yellow, popular, Taco Bell commercials, Seth Green, PlayStation, The Rock, bowling bags, floral motif, and rhinestones over Jennifer Aniston, Puff Daddy, Reebok, Black,

| Nutrition Facts | |
|---|---|
| **Serving Size** | **% for Average Person** |
| Claims to never cheat on expense account | 82% |
| Women: Loves to cook | 78% |
| Men: Loves to cook | 56% |
| Sings with the car radio | 78% |
| Confesses to lying regularly | 70% |
| Always wears jewelry | 70% |
| Drinks orange juice daily | 70% |
| Eat the cake before the icing | 69% |
| Sets watch ahead by at least five minutes | 68% |
| Reuses gift wrap | 57% |
| Exceeds the speed limit | 55% |
| Regifts unwanted presents | 54% |
| Sneaks into movie theatres | 50% |
| Eats Oreos whole | 50% |
| Twirls stringy pasta | 50% |
| Drinks coffee black | 50% |
| Sleeps with two pillows | 49% |
| Uses mouthwash twice a day | 45% |

angel, Geico commercials, Adam Sandler, Sega, Steve Austin, Messenger bags, and butterflies.[3]

## Average Joe Christian

Average may be okay when referring to a person's sleeping, gifting, eating, driving, or exercising habits, but when we associate it with living the Christian life, average is far from the standard set throughout the pages of the New Testament. *The phrase "average Christian" is an oxymoron.* Average has been defined as the best of the sorriest and the sorriest of the best. Christians who are just average are not going to impact the world. In fact, they are going to be ignored by the world because nothing within them sets them apart.

A media-reinforced caricature of Christians portrays us as narrow-minded, intolerant, uptight, boring, unintelligent, and wacko. In the eyes of the world...

> Christians who are just average are not going to impact the world. In fact, they are going to be ignored by the world because nothing within them sets them apart.

### Average Joe Christian:
- carries a huge black Bible
- wears a leisure suit, wing-tip shoes, stiffly starched white shirt
- reeks of Old Spice cologne and Ben-nongay
- parts his slicked-down hair on the right side—of course
- drives a Yugo with a "Honk if you love Jesus!" bumper sticker
- punctuates every sentence with "Praise the Lord"
- believes that education is of the devil
- goes to church every time the doors are open
- doesn't smile, dance, drink, smoke, or cuss
- should be labeled "born against."

Sure! Such caricatures are ridiculous, but still there's a kernel of truth behind this exaggerated depiction. As offensive as the above caricature is, a truer portrait of the status quo Christian is equally—if not more—disturbing: The average Christian looks and acts like those who don't profess to have a relationship with Christ. The danger in this scenario is not that Buffy or Biff Believer is going to be persecuted, but worse—they are going to be ignored because they blend in so well.

**A status quo Christian:**
- believes the Bible is God's Word and owns at least one,
  but doesn't daily read it or allow it to affect life
- believes he or she should go to church and is even a baptized member,
  but isn't seriously committed to its mission and ministries
- believes in the power of prayer,
  but only ardently prays when a 911 situation arises
- believes in heaven as one's eternal reward,
  but never tells anyone else how to get there
- believes in being moral,
  but believes tolerance is to be practiced toward others who are not
- believes Christians should make a difference in the world,
  but is hidden in plain sight at work, at school, and out in the world
- believes he or she is being transformed into the image of Christ,
  but has become the enemy of vibrant Christianity.

Jeve Moorman has said that status quo is Latin for the mess we're in. It is accepting the way things are and, most likely, the way things will stay. If I were to give a name to those who live in a status quo mentality, I would call them *in-betweenites*. They remain content to be stuck somewhere between excellent and awful. Status quo or average Christianity just doesn't cut it.

If we are facing major surgery, we don't want an average doctor.
If we are being sued, we don't want an average attorney.
If we are being audited, we don't want an average CPA.
If we are flying in a storm, we don't want an average pilot.
If we are recruiting, we don't want an average team player.
If we are going to impact our world...

God does not want us to be just an average Christian.

These are the words of the Amen, the faithful and true witness, the ruler of God's creation. I know your deeds, that you are neither cold nor hot. I wish you were either one or the other! So, because you are lukewarm—neither hot nor cold—I am about to spit you out of my mouth.

—REVELATION 3:14B–16

## Wasted Years in Mediocreville

In *An Enemy Called Average*, John Mason describes mediocrity as "a region bounded on the north by compromise, on the south by indecision, on the east by past thinking, and on the west by a lack of vision."[4] It doesn't take a rocket scientist to figure out that society is in a mess—morally, ethically, emotionally, and spiritually. The reason? The change agents—Christians—have become stuck in what Jimmy Buffett might call Mediocreville. Too many have become addicted to average, satisfied with status quo, and complacent with mediocrity. Because Christians are virtually indistinguishable from those who profess no relationship with Christ, their impact is not being felt beyond the walls of their homes, churches, and youth groups.

Teenaged Brian was skinny as a bean pole and pimply as a strawberry. His awkward social skills meant nobody really wanted to have anything to do with him. He was truly a loner. Although it almost appeared as if it were by choice, it really wasn't. He came to a church youth group, back in the early 1980s in South Florida, which included the usual teenage cliques and groups. But nobody wanted to include Brian. The whole youth group visited an amusement park one Saturday. When the youth pastor decided to pair them up, nobody wanted to pair up with Brian, and so he wandered by himself all day long through that amusement park feeling unloved, ignored, and untouched. Three or four months after the amusement park incident, he just sort of silently slipped away. Nobody at the church really even noticed.

The youth pastor moved on to take a job at a seminary. Years later one of the former students in the youth group, now a grown man, called the youth pastor. As they were talking he said, "Pastor, do you remember Brian in the youth group?"

The pastor said, "Brian? Ah, no. Can't think of any Brians."

"You remember, Brian Warner."

"Brian Warner?" More than a decade had passed and he didn't remember any Brian.

"You remember that skinny fellow with the pimply face who was such a loner and nobody wanted to have anything to do with him?"

"Oh, yeah, that kid. Yes, I remember him. I wonder whatever happened to him."

"Well, he changed his name."

"Oh, what does he call himself now?"

"Well, he took the first name of a woman who committed suicide, Marilyn, and he took the last name of a man who was a masked murderer, Manson. He has formed a band. Today he's a big hit among the shock rock crowd—Marilyn Manson."[5]

Brian now calls himself "Antichrist Superstar." He has millions of fans, but two in particular stand out: the two young gunmen at Columbine High School in Colorado.

If just one person had reached out to him on that one-day trip,
if just one person had been friendly,
if just one person had said, "Come with me,"
if just one person had loved him,
if just one person had shared Jesus with him,
    things may have been far different today.

We do not need to be content with mediocre Christianity, but we can change the world. However, we must not let the devil beat us to the opportunity. We never know when we may have the chance to make a difference in the life of a Brian Warner.

## Myths in Advertisement #1 : You'll Get Over It

As students at Ouachita Baptist University, a friend and I were invited to conduct a weekend revival in a staid, old church. My friend was asked to lead the singing and I was asked to preach. When we arrived, we were greeted by the pastor who warned us, "Don't expect much to happen this weekend." This less-than-affirming leader explained he had been there for several years, and nothing much had happened during that time. I guess as he sized us up, two unlikely-to-make-a-difference college students in his eyes, his feelings about nothing much occurring that weekend were confirmed in his mind. I had a sneaking suspicion that this fellow really didn't want God to do much through us.

Though a little discouraged by our reception, my friend and I—left alone in the church—began fervently and urgently praying that God would move in that place. Well, God did! People got saved, and the preacher got upset. I don't think he was upset that people got saved, but that something happened. His self proclaimed prophecy was failing right before his eyes.

> If just one person had shared Jesus with him, things may have been far different today.

After the final service, he took my friend and me out to eat, and I noticed he kept staring at me. Finally, after what seemed like forever, he pointed his finger at me, and gave me this advice: "You'll get over it."

"Pardon me?" I said.

"You'll get over it! All you guys think you are going to be the next Billy Graham and are going to win the world, but you'll get over it."

That's been almost twenty years ago, and—praise God—I'm still not over it! I am more excited and enthused every day about the possibilities of what I might be allowed to see God do. I don't ever want to get over it!

Christians serve as God's P.R. team to the world—advertisements for Christianity. In Scripture we are called "letters of recommendation" from Christ (2 Cor. 3:2–3). Every believer—knowingly or unknowingly—launches his or her own advertising campaign, which will either positively impact or negatively impair the cause of Christ. The people of the world are not looking up to find God; they are looking around at those who profess to know him. They are studying Christians to determine if there is reality behind the "Christian ad campaign" that can change their lives.

When our profession of faith and practice are inconsistent, the world accuses us of false advertising. Society is not impressed with our God-talk or moved by our Holy Joe bumper stickers and cute little clichés. When they view scandals and moral indiscretions among those in the ministry, Christianity becomes just one more religious myth among the many—definitely an advertising campaign gone wrong.

- When Gerber started selling baby food in Africa, they used the same packaging with the beautiful baby on the label as appeared in the United States. Later they discovered that in Africa—since many people cannot read—companies routinely put pictures on the label of what's inside the jar!
- A Miami-based T-shirt vendor printed shirts for the Spanish market that promoted the Pope's visit. Instead of "I saw the Pope" (el Papa), the shirts read "I saw the potato" (la papa).
- Pepsi's "Come Alive with the Pepsi Generation" translated into Chinese reads, "Pepsi brings your ancestors back from the grave."
- Clairol introduced the "Mist Stick" curling iron into Germany only to find out that "mist" is slang for "manure."

- When Parker Pen marketed a ballpoint pen in Mexico, its ads were supposed to have read, "It won't leak in your pocket and embarrass you." Instead, thinking that the word "embarazar" (to impregnate) meant "to embarrass," the company's misguided ad read: "It won't leak in your pocket and make you pregnant."[6]

When we say, "Jesus can change your life,"
   yet our lives are
     no different...
when we say, "Christianity can bring you hope,"
   yet our lives are
     filled with despair...
when we say, "Christ can bring you peace,"
   yet our lives are
     wracked with turmoil...
when we say, "God is the answer,"
   yet our lives are
     consumed with doubt and fear...
when we say, "Christianity can help you to overcome,"
   yet our lives are
     in bondage to strongholds...
when we say, "Prayer works,"
   yet our lives are
     void of prayer's power...
when we say, "The Bible is God's Word,"
   yet our lives are
     not transformed by its content...
...we could be accused of false advertisement.

## Original Recipe

For years, Colonel Harland Sanders carried the secret formula for his Kentucky Fried Chicken in his head as he transported the spice mixture in his car. The Colonel developed the formula in the

1930s when he operated a roadside restaurant and motel in Corbin, Kentucky. His blend of eleven herbs and spices attracted a loyal following of customers at the Sanders Court and Café. "I mixed the spices in those days like mixing cement," the Colonel recalled, "on a specially cleaned concrete floor on my back porch. I used a scoop to make a tunnel in the flour and then carefully mixed in the herbs and spices."

> While Christians are called to be authentic, they are not called to be anonymous.

Today, the recipe is locked away in a safe in Louisville, Kentucky, and only a handful of trusted individuals know that multimillion-dollar formula. The security precautions protecting the recipe would make even James Bond proud.[7] Many have tried to copy the Original Recipe®, but it's still not the real thing. There's just nothing like that finger-licking good chicken from the Colonel's place.

One day after a morning church service a preacher stood at the door, shaking hands with those leaving. He grabbed a man's hand, pulled him aside, and challenged, "You need to join the Army of the Lord!"

The man replied, "I'm already in the Army of the Lord, Pastor."

The pastor questioned, "How come I don't see you except at Christmas and Easter?"

He whispered back, "I'm in the Secret Service."

Unlike the Colonel's highly guarded recipe, the original recipe for Christianity is to be shared with everyone. While Christians are called to be authentic, they are not called to be anonymous. Too long this delicious recipe for living the dynamic life in Christ has been locked away in lives of those in the ranks of the "Secret Service."

Paul shared with the believers in the Greek city of Thessalonica the recipe for producing a profound, contagious lifestyle. One ingredient is an authentic encounter with God through Jesus Christ, known as salvation. Here's how the apostle describes this essential ingredient: "You turned from idols to serve the living and true God" (1 Thess. 1:9). Whereas religion is concerned with doing something to attempt to gain God's approval, Christianity is centered on establishing a personal relationship with God.

Recognize other distinctive ingredients of original-recipe Christianity shared by Paul: "Be joyful always; pray continually; give thanks in all circumstances, for this is God's will for you in Christ Jesus" (1 Thess. 5:16–18). How important it is to understand how to blend these ingredients in your life. Do not confuse the ingredient joy with happiness. Happiness depends on circumstances, but joy is derived from an unchanging relationship with Christ. It's an inside job, having nothing to do with what happens around you, but having everything to do with what happened to you the moment Jesus entered your life. It's not a shallow giddiness that laughs at everything that happens, but an inner calmness that trusts in God no matter what.

> Joy is a confidence that operates irrespective of our moods.
> Joy is the certainty that all is well, however we feel.
> Joy is not a matter of simple will or all the world would have it.
> Joy is the by-product of spending time with the Lord.[8]
>
> In thy presence is fullness of joy.
>
> —Psalm 16:11 NASB

In the later years of his life Martin Luther appeared to be gloomy. One day his wife, dressed in black, came into his study, provoking Martin to ask, "Who's dead?"

She immediately responded, "God is."

To which Martin asked, "My soul, why should you talk like that?"

"Because of your gloom," replied his perceptive wife.[9]

If we make a commitment to add the ingredient of ongoing prayer to our life, it doesn't mean we should lock ourselves away, get on our knees, and close our eyes twenty-four hours a day.

Correctly measured, this ingredient calls for our living in an atmosphere of prayer that will bring genuineness to our daily walk with God. Concerted, as well as abiding, prayer brings the obvious and attractive presence of God on our lives and gives us the power to change things.

Giving thanks in all circumstances seems like a hard ingredient to acquire in the midst of the typical fast-paced blur of postmodern life surrounded by sirens, crises, and scandals. But we must realize that this does not mean to feel grateful or glad about everything that happens. Catch this distinction: Paul is not suggesting that believers give thanks *for* all things—rather, *in* all things. In doing so, we are acknowledging God's control—not our control or Satan's control—over life's circumstances. We give honest thanks because God remains in charge, not only of the direction of the entire universe, but also of the details of our lives.

## Lifestyles of the Elite and Complete

Robin Leach, host of the program *Lifestyles of the Rich and Famous*, enjoyed taking his television audience to exotic places where only the upper echelon of society normally visits. The covet-fest, made popular in the 1980s, would visit unusual travel destinations, lavish surroundings, and world-class sites to entertain the audience with fantasies of what "the other half" lives like. When we watch such shows, most of us feel the green monster envy provoke the sense that we will probably never experience this kind of lifestyle. We pass it off thinking, "Well, it must be nice. Some got it and some don't." I have observed that this kind of response is not limited to our perspective of the rich and famous who live without Christ in their life. Sadly, it also creeps into our thinking about fellow Christians.

Dwight L. Moody encountered this mindset when he brought a "pew full" of boys and girls off the streets into a church that he anticipated joining. The presence of Moody's guests so disturbed the aristocratic, affluent church that when he presented himself for membership, the church board suggested Moody take a month to pray about his desire to join.

A month later the church board asked Moody, "Did you follow our suggestions?"

Moody affirmed he had.

"And what did the Lord say?"

"He told me not to feel bad about it, because he has been trying to get into this church himself for the last twenty-five years!"[10]

These members obviously suffered from an "I'm better than you" spiritual complex.

If I were going to host a show about spiritual elitism, the haves vs. the have-nots, I would call it *Lifestyles of the Elite and Complete*. This religious superiority complex manifests itself in the thinking. . .

"I'm flying first class spiritually and you're flying coach."
"I have these gifts of the Spirit, you do not."
"I use this version of the Bible, you do not."
"I belong to this denomination, you do not."
"My church is better than your church."
"We sing praise choruses, you do not."
"You ordain women, we do not."
"God told me to tell you . . ."

People have actually visited our church and told me to my face, "I'm here to set you straight." In most of these situations, I soon learn that they have come to "straighten me out" only after they have gone to every other church and couldn't get a foothold. And it's not just me as the pastor they want to "help." Within a week of one man's joining our church, he stood in the office declaring that he was the answer to help fix our music. Sometimes these "saints" just want us to know how much better everyone is doing it than we are.

*The Prayer Experiment* is not about spiritual elitism, but about the potential for any believer to make a difference for God. Understand me well: Any faithful, praying Christian can make a noticeable difference in his or her world. I suspect a lot of believers simply harbor the defeated feeling of "Why even bother? I could never attain spiritual 'greatness.'" To them I respond that the last time I checked, the Bible is full of ordinary people whom God used to make a big difference in the world. The Bible also shows how God passed over many religious elites in order to use the common person, who had been overlooked by society.

Jabez was an ordinary, run-of-the-mill person with many of the same insecurities and obstacles in his life that we face. Yet he dared to live above—and pray above—average. He adopted a vision for his life that left no room for conceding to the status quo. Jabez experienced a holy dissatisfaction with where he was in life, not wanting to live contentedly in a place called "The Comfort Zone." So he broke out of his pain-limiting existence by one simple act: prayer.

Jabez prayed diligently and persistently that God would do something so big in his life that it was obviously from him. He prayed that he might acquire more real estate that would serve as an indicator of God's giving him greater influence and opportunities. When God answered his requests, Jabez didn't act superior about this blessing. Rather, he used it to lead others in a God-directed path. No wonder Scripture says of him that he was "more honorable than his brothers." Jabez maintained the testimony of being a person of godly character.

## Making the Honor Roll

Parental pride is obvious whenever you see one of those "My child made the Honor Roll at. . ." bumper stickers. Moms and dads delight in reading school notices listing their child on the honor roll. Their child is being rewarded for working diligently and rising above average. Even insurance companies consider this achievement significant and reward these students with lower premiums—which has been a great motivation for my teenaged son since he pays his own insurance!

Hebrews 11 records the Bible's longest honor roll with the names of individuals who broke with mediocrity and impacted the world.

The act of faith is what distinguished our ancestors, set them above the crowd.

—HEBREWS 11:2 *THE MESSAGE*

---

### God's Honor Roll

**Abel** . . . . . . rose above average
by giving God his best, instead of his leftovers.

**Enoch** . . . . rose above average
by living a "Yes, God, yes! Anything for you" life.

**Noah** . . . . . rose above average
by building a boat at God's command even though there was no water.

**Abraham** . . rose above average
by going without knowing and trusting God to provide.

**Sarah** . . . . . rose above average
by believing God would do the impossible.

**Isaac** . . . . . . rose above average
by determining what was right rather than doing what he wanted.

**Jacob** . . . . . rose above average
by passing the faith of his fathers along to his family.

**Joseph** . . . . rose above average
by living victoriously even in the face of death.

**Moses** . . . . rose above average
by choosing commitment over convenience.

**Rahab** . . . . . rose above average
by risking personal harm to protect the people of God.

---

The outrageously funny comedy *Cool Runnings* was inspired by the true story of Jamaica's first Olympic bobsled team. With the help of an ex-champion (John Candy) as their coach, four unlikely Jamaican athletes left their sunny tropical island home to enter the chilly Winter Olympics to compete in a sport about which they knew nothing—bobsled racing. As these four inexperienced bobsledders are training for the competition, the words "You gotta rise above it" is being sung in the background. Finding the courage in each other to give it their all, they met the challenge and soon became heroes—taking the world along for the ride.

Here's exactly what Jabez did. Without a doubt, he made God's honor roll in his courage to think big, pray big, and live big. He knew there had to be more to life than what he had experienced. He found the answer on his knees. He connected with an extraordinary God, plugged into his supernatural power, and rose above...

his circumstances,<br>
his limitations,<br>
his own abilities,<br>
his critics,<br>
the rest.

## Billionaire Garbage Man

Voted by *Forbes* magazine as one of "Corporate America's Most Powerful People," H. Wayne Huizenga presides over a multibillion-dollar business empire that includes everything from professional sports teams to the nation's largest car retailer. It all started from a single garbage truck. Following his father's advice that you can't make money working for someone else, young Wayne set out to make his mark in the business world. At age twenty-five he started the Southern Sanitation Service with one used dump truck and a few accounts. Six years later he owned twenty trucks and was servicing customers in a huge area. Along with his uncle, Huizenga then embarked on a buying spree and acquired ninety trash haulers in the next nine months. This new company, Waste Management, ultimately became the largest garbage removal company in the country with a revenue of over one billion dollars.

At age forty-six Huizenga retired—but not for long. During a three-year period he acquired more than a hundred businesses, ranging from bottled water and lawn-care services to hotels and office buildings. While these businesses produced a $100 million annual revenue, Huizenga had not struck the deal that would make him a household name.

Three years after his retirement, Huizenga and two partners purchased the controlling interest in a little chain of video stores called Blockbuster, which included eight stores and eleven franchises. Huizenga's grand-scale approach to acquisitions turned Blockbuster into the largest video-rental chain in the world—all within one year.

Making money so quickly that he could not spend it all on Blockbuster, Huizenga went on another buying spree—this time purchasing all or part ownership of the Miami Dolphins, Joe Robbie Stadium, the Florida Marlins, the Florida Panthers, the Super Club Retail Entertainment record chain, Republic Pictures, Sound Warehouse, and Music Plus. Becoming one of the wealthiest men in America, Huizenga felt the need to move on and sold Blockbuster to Viacom for $8.4 billion and began seeking out new industries to conquer.

After acquiring another trash-hauling business, Republic Industries, Huizenga then trained his sight on a new target, the retail automotive industry, and began building a nationwide chain of new- and used-car outlets. Within six months, he bought 65 auto dealerships with 109 outlets selling 31 brands, opened 11 used-car AutoNation superstores, and purchased three rental-car agencies, including Alamo and National. By 1999, AutoNation Inc. owned 412 new-car dealerships and 29 used-car stores and operated nearly 4,000 rental car locations worldwide, making it the world's largest auto retailer and the United States' second-largest provider of vehicle-rental services.

Even though Huizenga is one of the world's richest men, money is not the driving force behind his ventures. What drives him is the one-on-one competition between himself and a rival.[11] When I hear stories of such entrepreneurial spirit, I am inspired to dream even bigger for the cause of Christ. If we Christians were as passionate about our strategies for reaching the world as we are about making money or a name for ourselves, what a difference that could make on society. If we craved the Savior's touch as much as the Midas touch, what an amazing difference we could realize in our lives and the lives of others.

> ■
>
> **It is a wretched waste to be gratified with mediocrity when the excellent lies before us.**
>
> —ISAAC D'ISRAELI, 1834
>
> ■

I have to fight being disheartened when I read statistics that indicate at least 44 percent of the world's 1.6 billion Christians should be identified as "nominal." According to a British research organization, this huge block of professing believers rarely attend church because they value spirituality over organized religion or because they feel uncomfortable in church as a result of their own lifestyle or cultural differences.[12] No wonder the world is not impressed with the difference Christians make! Who in their right mind would be attracted to or motivated by the walking dead? Oh, that God would resurrect in each of us an obsession for rising above mediocrity and striving for excellence in carrying out his kingdom work on earth.

## Caped Crusader

> *Faster than a speeding bullet, more powerful than a locomotive, able to leap tall buildings in a single bound, it's. . .*
>
> —FR. *SUPERMAN*

Occasionally, when facing an opportunity disguised as a challenge, and I, as a senior pastor, have been called upon to...

> weigh the options,
> discern God's will,
> formulate a plan,
> make a decision,
> while keeping everyone happy,
> ministering to our members' needs,
> reaching out to the community,
> and furthering the cause of Christ.

I have jokingly been called "Superpastor." To which I have responded tongue-in-cheek, "The dry cleaner still has my cape and I can't possibly do a thing without it." What a ridiculous thought! I don't own a single cape or wear a shirt with a huge "S" on it, and I definitely stay away from tights! However, like other Christians, I do find myself in situations where I need superhuman strength to perform the seemingly endless and overwhelming feats before me.

Thank God that we don't really have to fly from challenge to challenge with only a cape and a superhero costume. None of us is called to be the Cape Crusader or SuperChristian, only a yielded individual transformed through Christ into a ready-to-soar-to-new-heights, super-empowered child of God.

Sanfra professed Christianity, but would have little, if anything, to do with coming to church. Whenever I finally spotted her sitting in our worship service, I thought, "Wow, I'm glad she's here ... but I'm so surprised." For years, many had tried to get Sanfra to come to church with little success—that is, until she started attending around the time we began praying the prayer of Jabez for the second thirty-day experiment. Sanfra kept coming back.

Within that electric, prayer-saturated atmosphere, Sanfra made a genuine commitment to Christ and was baptized. Since that time, she has become a vocal witness for Christ through her life and through her successful business. She never skips our worship services now, for fear that she might miss God's doing something big.

Her vibrant faith has become contagious—above average and far beyond status quo. She has become an impact Christian, able to access the superhuman power of God on high.

Transforming prayer made all the difference in Sanfra's life. It, too, can help you, not to leap tall buildings, but to soar above those who settle for an average Christian life. Sanfra discovered— as many average Christians could as well—the secret to soaring is unaverage prayer.

Pause now. Pray the prayer of Jabez; however, before you do...

1. Realize that as you pray this prayer, you are asking God to transform your life from being average to extraordinary, granting God permission to accomplish that in whatever way he chooses.

2. Think of any "Brian Warner's" God has placed in your world. Pray for them and commit to active faith involvement in their lives.

3. Ask God to point out any "Average Joe or Jill Christian" or status quo areas in your life. Seek his help in rising above mediocrity.

> Lord, bless me indeed...
> Do something so big in my life that it is obviously from you.
> Increase my influence and opportunities for you,
> And give me a sense of your continual presence and direction.
> Protect me, and keep me from falling into Satan's traps. Amen.

If you are ready to impact your world by making yourself available to God in spite of drawbacks, you may want to continue the experiment.

# ▪ PART TWO ▪

## Impact . . . Your Availability

*Lord, bless me indeed. . .*
*do something so big in my life that it is obviously from you.*

# ■ 4 ■

# When Praying Doesn't Remove Your Problems

*Lord, bless me indeed.*

**A** woman in Mobile, Alabama, took her little boy to the grocery store. She picked him up, set him in the seat in the grocery cart, and started up the first aisle. As she was piling groceries in the cart, her child spotted stacks of chocolate chip cookies on a shelf. Immediately the boy cried out, "Mama, Mama. Can I have some chocolate chip cookies?"

"No, you can't," she said brusquely. "I told you not to start begging for things."

The woman started up the next aisle and the kid wailed, "Can I have just a couple of chocolate chip cookies?"

"No! Now sit down!"

Halfway up the next aisle the kid pleaded desperately, "Mama, can I have just one chocolate chip cookie?"

"I said sit down!"

She continued to pile more and more groceries in the cart until there was hardly any room left for her boy.

When she finished her shopping, she pushed the cart to the end of the checkout line. As the woman looked at the child, she noticed he was glaring back at her with a bright gleam in his eye. She sensed something was coming. She just knew it. Then this little boy, about three years old, in little pajamas, rose slowly out of his cart seat, turned his big brown eyes toward heaven, and cried out, "In the naaaame of *Jeeeesuss!* Give me some chocolate chip cookies!"

Everyone in the grocery store started cheering and clapping their hands. The exasperated mom shook her head, walked up the aisle, and got the child some chocolate chip cookies.[1] Crying out to the Lord certainly worked for this young man, but it doesn't always bring this sort of result. Sometimes we can pray with all fervency; yet, the problem remains.

## "I Prayed and It Got Worse!"

Knowing how passionately I believe in the power of prayer, people often share with me their prayer experiences. Recently, as I was taking a diverse group of men through *The Prayer Experiment*, one of the guys spoke up about an incident when praying didn't produce the results he expected. He had just paid a visit to the Kentucky Derby and placed a bet on a long-shot horse. Then, remembering our discussions on the power of prayer, he asked God to help his horse win. Anticipating what God was going to do, the man said he listened excitedly, only to hear that the favorite horse had won and his horse had come in fourth. My friend was dead serious when he announced to our group, "Prayer doesn't always work!"

While we can understand why God may have chosen not to give my friend what he had asked, we all must confess that we have had—at one time or another—that same feeling: Prayer doesn't always work.

> We pray and problems persist...
> We pray and failures still happen...
> We pray and a loved one still dies ...
> We pray and nothing seems to happen ...
> We pray and things only get worse ...

Standing over the freshly-dug, tiny grave, peering at the little casket holding their precious, lifeless twin girl, these parents, who love God, with tears streaming down their cheeks, asked, "But pastor, we don't understand. We prayed for her."

We stood in the hospital morgue as a wife identified the body of her godly husband, who had said "goodbye" that morning and a few hours later was killed in an automobile accident. While no one said it aloud, the whole scene screamed, "How could this happen? This man prayed all the time."

The young couple held hands as they sat across from my desk and expressed the frustration and confusion they were experiencing: "Pastor, we have been through in vitro fertilization—all the expense, the emotional draining, and the embarrassment—four times now, and we still can't have a baby. Why? We would be loving parents. We have prayed our hearts out to God."

Arriving at his home shortly after he called, I tried to console the husband whose wife had just packed her bags. His words to me reflected his desperate need to know God was still hearing and answering prayer: "Pastor, I can't believe it. My wife has left me and my daughter for the night club scene. She claims that she has found the man of her dreams. Oh, God! I pray and pray for her, and she only gets deeper and deeper into sin."

Surrounded by his wife, family, and friends, a veteran man of God who had touched thousands of people for Christ lay dying in the hospital. While this prayer warrior had prayed God would heal him, healing did not come, and the doctor spoke the somber words: "He's not going to make it. You must let me know if you want me to disconnect the life-support system."

I live out these gripping scenes with the people in my congregation on a much-too-frequent basis. But my church isn't unique. I dare say that every Christian will face similar trying circumstances at some point in his or her life or in the lives of family and friends. Even the apostle Paul prayed and it got worse for him! He prayed that God would remove the problem he was facing, and God did not.

> To keep me from becoming conceited because of these sur-
> passingly great revelations, there was given me a thorn in my
> flesh, a messenger of Satan, to torment me. Three times I
> pleaded with the Lord to take it away from me. But he said
> to me, "My grace is sufficient for you, for my power is made
> perfect in weakness."
>
> —2 CORINTHIANS 12:7–9A

We must remember:

Prayer is not an instant cure-all.
Prayer is not a quick-fix exercise.
Prayer is not guaranteed get-whatcha-asked.

## Waving the White Flag

In September, 1862, at the battle of Munfordville, Kentucky,
Colonel John T. Wilder found himself surrounded and outnum-
bered six to one by General Braxton Bragg's Confederate forces.
An Indiana lawyer, Wilder lacked the combat experience and confidence to decide between fighting or surrendering. What he
needed was professional advice—even if it came from the enemy.
Waving a white flag, Wilder entered the Confederate's camp and
approached Major General Simon Bolivar Buckner, respected for
his integrity.

General Buckner demurred when Wilder asked him what to
do. Instead, he referred the Union commander to General Bragg,
who invited Wilder to count the number of cannons trained on his
forces. Wilder stopped counting at forty-six. "I believe I will surrender," he said. Wilder promptly turned over 4,267 prisoners to
General Bragg, along with ten guns, five thousand rifles, and other
supplies. General Buckner said later, "I would not have deceived
that man under those circumstances for anything."[2]

I am not sure how long waving a white flag has been the sign
of surrender in warfare, but I know that I have often had to wave
it in the heat of battle in own my life. Unlike the Civil War

account, my waving the white flag is not yielding to the enemy or even asking for his counsel. Rather, it is my signaling God that I no longer have it within me to continue the struggle without his divine intervention.

Prayer is an act of surrender that:

- takes the horrible, the painful, the impossible, and yields it to God
- turns control over to God, who works in and through all things
- tears down resistance to God's commands
- trusts God to overcome the enemy
- touches the embattled soul with healing, peace, and rest
- tells the world there's Someone Else who has the answers
- transforms a defeated prisoner into a triumphant child of God!

"I give up. Tell me why it happened. Why would God allow this?" The questions came like rapid fire when the news of Phyllis's death circulated. A fantastic wife and a mother of three girls, Phyllis was a great person, a wonderful Christian, a true servant. While traveling on Interstate 4 between Lakeland and Kissimmee, she was killed instantly in an automobile accident.

At her funeral it became obvious that her tragic death was some sort of divine appointment that God was already using to touch lives. To those packed in our old sanctuary, I purposefully and clearly shared the victorious Good News of a Savior's timeless love. Phyllis's friend Sharon was there. Like many others, she was heartbroken, confused, and numb. While she did not typically attend church on Sunday, at the funeral she was exposed to a compassionate God, who really cares even though we cannot explain why horrible things like this happen. As she heard the truth of how God can work in our lives—even through tragedy—the Lord began speaking to her heart. Out of this tragedy, Sharon began a life-transforming journey of faith.

Today Sharon attends church and a Bible study regularly. She is growing in her faith and learning to trust God more completely. God is using her to make a difference in others' lives. Yes, Phyllis is gone. But out of her untimely death have come some incredible blessings. People came to know Christ as their Lord and Savior through that funeral service. It may not surprise you to learn what we found after her funeral—she had taped to the mirror of her bathroom a prayer she prayed everyday: the prayer of Jabez. Did the experiment work for her? Ask Sharon and ask those who will now be in heaven because Phyllis dared to pray, "Increase my influence and opportunities for you."

> God is not some heavenly genie that shows up to grant three wishes to whoever prays.

Through such circumstances I am again reminded—in a profound way—that our prayers are never wasted. While these unexplainable life events are incredibly painful and confusing, our faithful Lord, who is in charge of all things, continually works for our good (Rom. 8:28).

After a hurricane hit Miami, a woman wrote the following letter to the *Miami Herald*, expressing her frustration at how she felt God had "jilted" her:

> I've never believed in God or in prayer. I thought it was all superstition. But, since the storm was coming, I gave it a try. I asked God to protect my house—but it got damaged anyway. So just wondered, what do you say about those who say they believe in God and prayer?

Soon afterward the newspaper printed the editor's response:

> Madam, I don't know much about prayer either, but I think perhaps God was busy taking care of his regular customers.[3]

I would add to the editor's response by saying God is not some heavenly genie that shows up to grant three wishes to whoever prays. Prayer is a dynamic instrument by which true believers tell their heavenly Father, "Whatever, whenever, however—I wave the white flag!" The Father does what he does best: remains in complete control.

## S-s-s-smokin' Masks, Levi's, and T-Files

Jim Carey stars as Stanley Ipkiss, a bumbling bank clerk who goes from zero to hero when he puts on a curious wooden mask in the movie *The Mask*. Stanley is transformed from shy guy into a s-s-s—smokin' party animal. Consequently, he gets into more trouble that he can handle. This loser-turned-"oooooooh . . . somebody stop me" superhuman taps a power not his own when he is disguised in the mask.

God's greatest blessings, too, are often masked. These blessings-in-disguise often appear looking like unwelcomed intruders and unanswered prayers. Because of our lack of understanding or faith or patience or strength, we give up too soon, get frustrated, and begin to doubt God's goodness—or, at least, his willingness to do something about what we are facing.

Back in 1850, during the California Gold Rush, a young man from Bavaria came to San Francisco, bringing with him some rolls of canvas. He was twenty years old at the time, and he planned to sell the canvas to the gold miners to use for tents. Then the profits from his sales would finance his own digging for gold. As he headed toward the Sierra Nevada Mountains, he met one of the gold miners with whom he shared his plans. The miner said, "It won't work. It's a waste of your time. Nobody will buy your canvas for tents. That's not what we need."

While he listened to the gold miner's discouraging words, the young man silently prayed for God to show him what to do. He quickly got his answer when the miner went on to say, "You should have brought pants. That's what we need—durable pants! Pants don't wear worth a hoot up there in the diggings. Can't get a pair strong enough." Right then, the young man from Bavaria decided to turn the rolls of canvas into pants—blue pants—that would survive the rigors of the gold-mining camps.

Levi Strauss had a harness maker reinforce the pockets with copper studs, and the pants sold like hotcakes! He called the new pants "Levi's." Nine hundred million pairs of these pants—whose style has remained basically unchanged for more than 130 years— have been sold throughout the world.[4] Probably each us owns at least one pair of these "canvas tents," an idea initially masked as defeat.

> Unless there is a total cooperation with God, we will often miss the blessing within the challenge.

No one is exactly sure what the "thorn" problem was in the apostle Paul's life, although many have offered their speculations. I believe the reason it is not identified in his writings is so that Paul's readers can readily relate to what he was saying. "Thorns" in our lives serve a real purpose. Like Paul's thorn, they keep us humble, remind us that we cannot make it without God, and keep us hopeful that God is not finished with us yet. Sometimes thorns may even be the answer to our prayers; yet we, like Paul, beg God to take the problem way. The thorns in our lives may be masked so that they do not immediately resemble—in any way—blessings from above. Unless there is a total cooperation with God, we will often miss the blessing within the challenge, because we are only able to see the thorn.

Most of us have some familiarity with these "T-Files" (Thorn-Files) episodes:

*T-Files Episode #1*: "This pain is unbearable."
*T-Files Episode #2*: "This situation is impossible."
*T-Files Episode #3*: "This temptation just won't go away."
*T-Files Episode #4*: "This memory continues to haunt me."
*T-Files Episode #5*: "This problem will never be solved."
*T-Files Episode #6*: "This person destroyed my marriage."

*T-Files Episode #7*:  "This burden is too great."
*T-Files Episode #8*:  "This job was all I had."

We each can replay our own "T-Files" episode and give testimony of how it demanded we depend on God. One other thing: We can be pretty certain there will be new episodes of the "T-Files" produced in our lifetime.

## On-the-Job Training

Finally, I was able to slip away for a nice, relaxing date night with my wife. Our dinner reservation allowed us just enough time to eat and to catch a movie before we needed to return home to resume parental responsibilities. Nights like this are too good to be taken for granted—or squandered. Shortly after the hostess led us to our table, we were seated and began looking at our menus.

Presently not one, but two servers appeared at our table. The server-trainer said—if my memory serves me correctly—"I'm Frick and this is Frack. Frack is in training and doesn't know anything. He will keep his mouth shut and watch." Well, we must have been server-in-training's first-ever patrons. I have never seen such a botched attempt at shadow serving ... to the point of being painfully humorous. If it could be spilled, dropped, juggled, or mishandled it was. (Angie constantly gave me the I-dare-you-to-laugh look, so I knew better!)

From his ineptness, I assumed this young man had never eaten out, much less ever waited tables before. Frick and Frack eventually got the job done, I had my sanctification tried and tested, and—because the dynamic duo had eaten up so much time on the clock with their on-the-job training—our plans for a movie were but a memory never realized.

I well understand on-the-job training is essential for excellence. Doctors must survive stringent internships before they are ready to practice solo. Teachers must practice-teach before they are ready for the classroom. Plumbers must learn the trade as apprentices. Even pastors must practice preaching and complete an internship before graduating from seminary. Christians face not a brief period of on-the-job training (O.J.T.), but a lifetime of training and equipping. It readies us for effectively reaching and teaching a changing, godless world.

> Our O.J.T. is not always pleasant, and is often. . .
> extremely demanding,
> physically taxing,
> emotionally draining,
> spiritually exhausting,
> socially challenging.
> And sometimes it just plain hurts!

At times we are tempted to say, "You know, God, I wouldn't have done it that way." Sometimes we actually think—although we don't say it—we know better than God how to handle our lives.

> We say, "Oh, no! Here comes another problem."
> God says, "Pay attention. Here comes a platform for a blessing."
> We say, "Not another obstacle."
> God says, "What an opportunity I am giving you!"

> It is all part of our O.J.T. to do the work our Lord has called us to do.

Paul, too, received O.J.T. It was more than the extraordinary revelation he received prior to his first day on the job as ex-persecutor-turned-apostle. Because he was such an extraordinary individual, God needed to equip him with the training necessary to enable him to relate effectively to the common person. The thorn in the flesh was all part of the training. While it may have looked like a constant irritation from Satan, God allowed the whole thorn thing in order to make his newly called disciple the useful messenger who would change the world.

Remember, God never allows something to pass through his hands and into our lives unless there is a reason, a divine purpose.

For Paul, the reason for God's allowing this thorny problem in his life was so he would not get puffed up with pride. Every time I read the biblical passage where Paul explains God's purpose for this (2 Cor. 12:7–10), I think about the old saying, "He who gets too big for his britches will be exposed in the end." Paul's thorn was a gift from God to cover his weakness. But because Paul did not think the thorn was a good thing to keep in his life, three times he asked God to perform thorn surgery and remove it. Three times God said, "No way. You need this more than you think." God had something better in mind. Paul couldn't see it, but God did.

> God never allows something to pass through his hands and into our lives unless there is a reason, a divine purpose.

So it is in our lives. Often we cannot see why God fails to remove—or at least improve—a serious problem. That's where the trust factor comes in: Even though it appears as though God is inactive in answering our prayers, he is constantly present with us and doing what is most beneficial in our lives and for his glory.

Jabez prayed, and it is true God answered his prayers in an obvious way. But when you search the two verses about his life, you will notice Jabez still battled the "thorn" that had plagued him all his life. He, too, had had O.J.T. for the life of expanded influence with which God blessed him. Prayer did make a difference, but the difference wasn't in removing his pain. Rather, it was in blessing him through it.

## The Screwtape E-Mails

"You've got mail" could be the opening line in a contemporary version of C. S. Lewis' *The Screwtape Letters*. As you may recall, Screwtape (a.k.a., senior devil) sends his nephew, Wormwood (an immature junior devil), letters of advice containing strategies to win over "Patient's" young Christian heart. Screwtape advises Wormwood to attack through the undramatic and routine temptations that everyone faces throughout daily life:

> Never having been a human ... you don't realize how enslaved they are to the pressure of the ordinary.... Thanks to processes which we set at work in them centuries ago, they find it all but impossible to believe while the familiar is before their eyes. Keep pressing home on him the ordinariness of things.... Teach him to call it "real life."[5]

Screwtape advises Wormwood to attack Patient's mental and emotional states. Also to be attacked is Patient's relationship with the "Enemy" (God). By making Patient have doubts about his relationship to God, he would be unable to survive the battle.

A contemporary version of this story, *The Screwtape E-mails*, would have Screwtape e-mailing his nephew, Wormwood, with advice on how to consume a believer's time and energy with "real life" matters:

*––Original Message––*

*From: Screwtape [mailto:screwtape@hell.com]*
*Sent: Sunday, April 1, 2001 12:01 AM*
*To: Wormwood*
*Cc: Satan*
*Subject: Patient's "Health"*

*Wormwood:*

> *Thanks for IM-ing me yesterday with an update on your progress with destroying Patient's "health." While I am pleased you are making progress, do not be deceived. The Enemy has many effective countermoves to each and every successful move you make. It is imperative you stay on Patient constantly today. Don't relax for a minute! Double the distractions. Start with car trouble, then problems at work. Interrupt anything that might be running smoothly with an annoying crisis. Send in irritable co-workers. Don't allow Patient a chance for lunch or even a coffee break. As*

*Patient is wearing down, have the school call to say that Patient's child has sprained or broken an ankle in P.E., and someone should come immediately to take the child for medical treatment. While en route to the school, Patient should be pulled over for speeding. Make sure he cannot find the car registration. Then . . . remember the migraine? It's always a good time for one to kick in. I'll make sure to check in on your progress mid- or late-afternoon. If things go as planned, we both will be LOL. ;-)*

    *Affectionately,*
    *Uncle Screwtape*

Paul says that his thorn was delivered as a messenger of Satan—perhaps initiated by a Screwtape e-mail! The name *Satan* means "adversary." This adversary uses real-life adversity, pain, and crisis to try to defeat the believer. However, make no mistake: Public Enemy Number One is under God's control. He and his lackeys can only do what God allows them the freedom to do. The book of Job teaches us that Satan must seek permission from God before he can do what he does. In many ways, even Satan himself is just a messenger boy used by God to get our attention.

We don't know why Jabez's parents named him what they did. Maybe they were bitter at his birth because of the financial burden he brought to them or because of a physical handicap. No matter the reason, his "real life" problem became the point from which God would perform a miracle. So, when the diabolical messenger boy delivers our "thorn," we must decide which course we will take.

God wants to use our thorn to bring out the best in us.
    Satan wants to use our thorn to bring out the worst in us.
God wants to build us up.
    Satan wants to tear us down.
God means it for our good.
    Satan means it for evil.
God designs these setbacks for our protection and blessing.
    Satan designs these setbacks for our defeat and destruction.

It's our call!

## Enough Is Enough!

| | |
|---|---|
| "Watch your driving! " | Enough is enough! |
| "Stop your whining!" | Enough is enough! |
| "Another bill?" | Enough is enough! |
| "I can't handle any more!" | Enough is enough! |
| "You did what?" | Enough is enough! |

We all want to cry out those words when we think we just can't take one more thing. Yes, God promises not to put more on us than we can handle—in his strength—but sometimes we wonder if God has gotten our load limit mixed up with someone else's.

We just experienced a year that will go down in the Dennis family history as the year from non-heaven. Nothing went right. My wife, Angie, faced surgery. I developed a chronic throat problem. The septic tank backed up in the house. The roof fell in—literally! And those were just some of the problems that cost us many thousands of dollars in never-ending personal and house repair bills.

Add to that the bodywork that had to be done on Angie's car after an accident. It was unbelievable—even my little dog quit liking me. I asked God what I had ever done to him. Enough was enough! But, I want to tell you that year's trials became the platform for God to do some awesome things in our lives. Enough was enough! However, I'm not talking about exhaustive frustration. I am speaking of God's grace being enough—more than enough—to get us through the "more than enough" problems we were facing.

As that good-news-challenged year was coming to an end and Christmas was approaching, my wife and I looked at our financial resources and realized we simply did not have the money to do much for our family and loved ones. As we had done throughout these tough times, we shared our hurts and our concerns with God. We presented to him what seemed like an impossible situation and asked him to meet our needs as he had done so faithfully in the past.

A few days prior to Christmas, we received a letter at our home from a woman who had been attending our church and with whom we had just made a friendship. In it she wrote, "I heard about the sacrifice you made for the building program, please accept this as a gift from God." It was a check for our family for $4,000.00! God had done it again—and right on time. The Dennis family learned again that God never fails. His enough was enough to get us through—even when it seemed impossible.

God didn't answer Paul's prayer the way he wanted. He wanted the problem removed; instead, God gave him something better: grace. Grace is God's giving you what you need—exactly when you need it—to help you face whatever comes your way, even though you've not earned it and don't deserve it. God told Paul that his grace was sufficient, enough to allow Paul to handle his problem. God allows just enough problems in our lives every-day to conform us to the likeness of Jesus Christ, but he also gives enough grace to deal with them.

At a Billy Graham crusade, the late Corrie ten Boom shared the story of how, as a child, she went to her father and said, "Papa, I don't think I have the faith to handle real trouble. I don't know what I'd do if you should die. I don't think I have the faith that some people have to face trouble."

Corrie's father looked at her tenderly and said, "Corrie, dear, when your father says he will send you to the store tomorrow, does he give the money to you today? No, he gives it to you when you are ready to go to the store. And if you are going on a train trip and need money for a ticket, does your father give you the money when you decide you may take the trip? No, he gives it to you when you are at the depot, all ready to buy your ticket. Corrie, God treats us the same way. He doesn't give you faith until you have a need. When you do, he will certainly give it to you."[6]

By not removing Paul's problem, God provided a wonderful platform to display his awesome power. In the end, that would be better than removing the problem. When we pray, we need to remember the words of our Lord to Paul when he said, "My grace is sufficient for you, for my power is made perfect in weakness" (2 Cor. 12:9).

> Power . . . available to us from God
> > Provision . . . whatever we need provided by God
> > > Plenty . . . "enough" to meet our "enoughs"
> > > > Pointed . . . and targeted right at our need
> > > > > Present . . . God always responding on time
> > > > > > Personal . . . to handle our unique situation.

Enough grace is enough to meet your challenges head-on. Remember, the grace of God is best seen against the backdrop of our own inadequacies.

## High-Five Anyway

The high-five is an animated expression of winning where one person with palms extended connects with another person doing the same. Derek Smith of the 1980 NCAA champion University of Louisville basketball team claims to be its originator. He was quoted in *The New York Times*, *The Sporting News*, and other publications as saying that he and his teammates Wiley Brown and Daryle Cleveland wanted something "a little odd" to set them apart in victorious celebration. The high-five was created and fine-tuned during preseason practice and introduced on national TV in 1979.[7]

The high-five, which has become the congratulatory standard on fields and arenas across the globe, means:

"Yes!"

"We won!"

"We conquered!"

"Victory!"

We see the high-five when a football player makes an awesome play. We see the high-five when a golfer sinks the difficult put. We see the high-five when a student graduates. We see the high-five when good news has come to someone. However, we don't expect to see the high-five from Paul as he deals with this aggravating thorn in the flesh. Yet, he does! He praises God—he high-fives God—anyway. He has come to the end of himself, exactly where God wants him to be, and then turns the next play over to God.

> "My grace is enough; it's all you need. My strength comes into its own in your weakness." Once I heard that, I was glad to let it happen. I quit focusing on the handicap and began appreciating the gift. It was a case of Christ's strength moving in my weakness. Now I take limitations in stride, and with good cheer, these limitations that cut me down to size—abuse, accidents, opposition, bad breaks. I just let Christ take over! And so the weaker I get, the stronger I become.
>
> —2 CORINTHIANS 12:9–10 *THE MESSAGE*

When I read Paul's words, I can visualize his saying:

"Let that thorn keep sticking me  . . . high-five anyway!"
"Another night in 'Prison Hotel'  . . . high-five anyway!"
"Another low blow  . . . . . . . . . . . . . high-five anyway!"
"Constant criticism  . . . . . . . . . . . . high-five anyway!"
"Physical beatings  . . . . . . . . . . . . . high-five anyway!"
"Character attacks  . . . . . . . . . . . . . high-five anyway!"
"A dead end  . . . . . . . . . . . . . . . . . high-five anyway!"
"Alone  . . . . . . . . . . . . . . . . . . . . . high-five anyway!"

In the early part of last century, the boll weevil devastated southern cotton crops, hitting particularly hard in southern Alabama. The disaster was a wake-up call for the need to diversify. The farmers of that area started raising peanuts, soybeans, corn, sorghum, fresh vegetables, and other crops. The economy improved so much that the residents of Enterprise, Alabama, actually built a monument to the boll weevil in the center of town.[8]

We don't have to wait until our trials are over to acknowledge God. While we may not be able to erect a monument to point to what God has done and is doing, we are able to offer him a high-five in our hearts and in our praise. In doing so, we lift our eyes...

- from the battle to the victory
- from the problem to the answer
- from despair to joy
- from what we can see to what we cannot
- from our weakness to his strength
- from our way to his way.

As you undertake *The Prayer Experiment*, get ready for a struggle. While it may appear that this prayer has backfired on you, remember Jabez, remember Paul. And no matter what, get your hand ready and high-five God anyway!

Pause now. Pray the prayer of Jabez; however, before you do...

1. Think about a time that you prayed and it got worse. What was God trying to teach you through that? Commit to consistently praying—no matter what happens.
2. Ask God to give you whatever on-the-job training you need today in order to better serve him.
3. Present to God the most significant trial you are currently facing and ask him to transform it into a blessing.

---

Lord, bless me indeed...
Do something so big in my life that it is obviously from you.
Increase my influence and opportunities for you,
And give me a sense of your continual presence and direction.
Protect me, and keep me from falling into Satan's traps. Amen.

---

If present problems have dampened your dreams, but you are willing to undertake a risk for God, you may want to continue the experiment.

# Risk Dreaming
# God-Sized Dreams

*Do something so big in my life.*

Dreams can be so compelling and yet so bizarre. Surely they must have some purpose. Sigmund Freud asserted that the function of dreams was to preserve sleep. But that one-hundred-year-old theory has been challenged by those who study sleep habits and now know that dreams happen regularly—at least five or six times per night in an active stage of sleep called REM sleep. Contemporary dream theorist William Domhoff has now appeared on the scene asserting, "The best evidence for now is that dreams have no physiological or psychological function." Other theorists disagree, suggesting possible purposes of dreaming: coping with psychological stress, preserving psychological and physical health, spurring us toward spiritual enlightenment, integrating new information and skills with stored memories—and the list continues.

Popular dream hustlers will tell you that if you buy their books or attend their workshops, you, too, can have and understand dreams as amazing and memorable as theirs. Dream groups, dream work sessions, dream time exploration groups, and dream journey circles are gaining in popularity across our country. These groups explore dreams through many dream study techniques, including Gestalt, dream theater, living dream images, sand play, shamanic dreaming, healing sessions, visualization, dream interpretation, dream mask-making, and the like.

Often those whom I counsel will mention their dreams, wanting to discuss the spiritual dimensions. Others share dreams that reflect fears or stress elements in their lives. Occasionally others will spout off some nonsense or fantasy they may have on their mind—as in "I had this dream about . . ."—because it allows them to reveal something personal about themselves and not divulge whether their claim to "just dreaming it" is true or not.

I tend not to remember my sleeping dreams. Sure, like most, I have had dreams of being unprepared for an exam or speaking engagement, of driving an out-of-control car, of falling, of nightmarish frights. In my life, however, it's the lucid dreams that I dream when I am awake that I recall and that are meaningful to me.

## Daydream Believer

Living near Disney World carries distinct advantages, especially during the spring when EPCOT hosts its annual Flower Power concerts. This year was no disappointment as the pop stars of my younger years once again appeared at the American Pavilion. Ah! Hearing the voice of Davy Jones singing "Oh, what can it mean to a daydream believer" immediately transports me back to another time, a time I dreamed of what could be in my life.

While I may not resonate with dream discovery or dream analysis, I have always been a big dreamer, especially when I am wide awake. As a young boy I dreamed of being a doctor and helping people in my small hometown. That dream faded as I began to understand God's purpose for my life, especially at age seventeen when I sensed God's call to a life of ministry. As a young man I dreamed of having a beautiful and godly wife along with wonderful children. I have been incredibly blessed to see this become a dream come true. As a young seminary student I dreamed of preaching to thousands. God has given me this desire of my heart. Now my dream is to impact my world with the message of Jesus

Christ—whether it's with one person, a small group, a large congregation, anywhere, or everywhere. The more God allows me to see this dream become a reality, the more I daydream about the possibilities. In fact, I dream about it all the time.

I guess you could say that I am a daydream believer, especially when the dreams focus on what God might do in my life. T. E. Lawrence declared, "All men dream but not equally. Those who dream by night in the dusty recesses of their minds awake to the day to find it was all vanity. But the dreamers of the day are dangerous men, for the many act out their dreams with open eyes, to make it possible."[1] Edgar Allan Poe also understood daydream believers when he remarked, "Those who dream by day are cognizant of many things that escape those who dream only by night."[2]

> All men dream but not equally.
> —T. E. LAWRENCE

I dream best with my eyes wide open. As I have consistently prayed the prayer of Jabez over the years, I have become more aware of God's answering big dreams. It's not just being on my knees in prayer, but it's living in an atmosphere of the awareness of God that allows me to see God at work all around me. While I most often physically shut my eyes when I pray, the eyes of my heart are wide open when I am expecting God to answer my dreams—scanning the scene and expectantly searching for that experience or event when my God-dream meets an earth-reality.

Jimmy was playing after dinner while his mom and dad, absorbed with household jobs, lost track of the time. Some of the light from a full moon seeped through the windows of their home. When his mom finally glanced at the clock and realized it was past Jimmy's bedtime, she called out, "Jimmy, it's time to go to bed! Go up now. I'll come and settle you later." Unlike his usual stalling routine, Jimmy went straight upstairs to his room.

An hour or so later his mother came up to check if all was well, and to her astonishment found that her son was staring quietly out of his window at the moonlit scenery. "What are you doing, Jimmy?" she asked.

"I'm looking at the moon, Mommy," Jimmy matter-of-factly replied.

"Well, it's time to go to bed now," his mom lovingly said.

As the reluctant little boy settled down, he said, "Mommy, you know one day I'm going to walk on the moon."

Who could have known that the boy in whom the dream was planted that night would survive a near fatal motorbike crash that broke almost every bone in his body and would bring to fruition this dream thirty-two years later when James Irwin stepped on the moon's surface, just one of the twelve representatives of the human race to have done so?[3]

Dreams—especially dreams born of God—can change lives, give purpose and meaning to life, as well as allow the dreamer to impact the world in unpredictable and amazing ways.

## A Monster Living Under My Bed

Santana has racked up all sorts of music awards for his release titled *Supernatural*. This much-acclaimed CD features a track entitled "Put Your Lights On," which speaks of an angel standing guard over a frightened individual who fears a monster living under his bed. He warns others, "Leave your lights on. You better leave your lights on." As a child I wanted to have the lights left on after I went to bed so that if something was going to get me, either the lights would scare it off or I could see what was about to get me. I never wanted to look under my bed for fear that my suspicions of a monster or something worse (like a mouse!) would do me in.

How often are we as dreamers frightened and need to have the light left on because we fear monsters living under our beds? The childhood monsters under the bed have run off, and new, grown-up monsters have taken residence under our beds. These creatures of the dark have insidious forms and tormenting approaches. Their names are fear, guilt, insecurity, worry, anger, turmoil, and bitterness. Sometimes even less obvious "monsters"—concerned family members, well-intentioned friends, or people with whom we work—can crawl under our beds, too.

Not just monsters under our beds get us, but the imaginary monsters in our own minds can gobble up our sweet dreams. Self-imposed dream-stifling is nothing new.

Charles H. Duell, U.S. Patent Office director, 1899, said:
"Everything that can be invented has been invented."

H. M. Warner, Warner Bros. Pictures, c. 1927, said:
"Who wants to hear actors talk?"

Grover Cleveland, 1905, said:
"Sensible and responsible women do not want to vote."

Robert Milikan, Nobel prize winner in physics, 1923, said:
"There is no likelihood man can ever tap the power of the atom."

The Michigan banker who advised Henry Ford's lawyer not to invest in the new motor car company said:
"The horse is here to stay, but the automobile is only a novelty."

Gary Cooper said,
"*Gone with the Wind* is going to be the biggest flop in Hollywood's history. I'm just glad it'll be Clark Gable who's falling flat on his face and not me."[4]

Often feelings of uncertainty, inadequacy, and insecurity hold us back from dreaming big dreams. These attitudes are reflected in a conversation Charlie Brown had with his good friend Linus. "You see, Linus," Charlie said, "it goes all the way back to the beginning. The moment I was born and set foot on the stage of life, they took one look at me and said, 'Not right for the part.'"

That must have been the way Jabez felt as he was growing up. All of his life Jabez lived with broken dreams and fallen rainbows.

With a name the equivalent of "Major Disappointment," he no doubt felt inadequate and insecure and had every reason to fail dreaming big things for his life. His prayer, however, indicates that he broke out of the role in life that everyone assumed he would play. He dreamed beyond his circumstances and dared to believe that God could—and would—use him to make a difference in his world. I'm sure he had plenty of dream busters who were in his life, those who would point out:

> why it couldn't be done
> why it wouldn't work
> why it cost too much
> why it didn't work on paper
> why the timing wasn't right.

Can't you just hear those people saying to Jabez, "Who do you think you are to dream such big dreams?" Despite all the flak he must have taken, Jabez stubbornly pursued his dream, and this gotta-have-it attitude he expressed in his dare-to-dream-big prayer.

Jabez saw prayer not as a Sears "Wish Book" catalog of dreams too big to come true, but as God's word full of come-true promises. In *An Enemy Called Average*, John Mason counsels: "Always involve yourself with something that's bigger than you are, because that's where God is."[5]

Bigger dreams, however, are not easily attained. I have found that the harder I have to pray and the more I have to trust faithfully in God's ability to pull it off, the better God seems to like it. Often we try to pursue our dreams on our own and even tell others, "Look what God is doing." But we are setting ourselves up for failure. God-sized situations require God-involved activities. If God is in charge, realizing dreams come true will not require our manipulating individuals, orchestrating situations, or forcing the issue. Perhaps you've heard the Fox News Network oft-repeated slogan, "We report, you decide." When it comes to dreaming big dreams for God, "We obey, he provides."

## Boogying to the Faith Walk

Growing up under Baptist influence put a definite crimp—or should I say "limp"—in my dance life. I confess I have never really learned how to get down and boogie. I suppose I have feared that the ghosts of Baptist past would come to haunt me. Plus, I knew I would get out on a dance floor and look like a fool. Okay, I will admit there were times when I was growing up that in the privacy of my room behind closed doors with a towel stuffed underneath the door, I kind of got in the groove, bebopped vigorously, and did a little shake, rattle, and roll.

But as an adult, I will have you know that I have finally learned to "get down" to a new step. No, you don't need to call the deacons of my church to report any wild behavior on my part. I am definitely not a John Travolta wanna-be. I don't know Swing from Salsa. I have not traded in my coifed hair, polished shoes, and Sunday-go-to-church attire for grunge apparel, body piercings, or tattoos that might help me gain entrance to the hottest rave club. Yet, it's likely you can find me practicing the faith walk at just about any hour of the day or night. I love to practice it everywhere—and with anyone who will dance with me! The faith walk is definitely not to be mistaken for Michael Jackson's passé Moonwalk, where one robotically dance-slides backwards. If you correctly do the faith walk, you are propelled forward in your faith as your eyes are fixed on God.

> So we fix our eyes not on what is seen, but on what is unseen. For what is seen is temporary, but what is unseen is eternal.... We live by faith, not by sight.
>
> —2 Corinthians 4:18; 5:7

Every Christian faces an ongoing struggle between faith and sight:

> Faith looks to God as the Source;
> sight trusts in possessions, power, and people.
> Faith focuses on "Who";
> sight is limited to "how."

Faith measures the size of God;
   sight is controlled by the size of problems.
Faith seeks God first;
   sight takes matters into its own hands.
Faith waits on God;
   sight rushes ahead with self-solutions.
Faith is based on what God said;
   sight is based on how we feel.
Faith's seeing-eye-guide is the Bible;
   sight's guide is only what is visible.
Faith looks beyond the circumstances to the possibilities;
   sight looks at how bad things are at the moment.
Faith believes God even when it seems nothing is happening;
   sight is controlled by the senses and feelings.
Faith doesn't require that it works out on paper;
   sight demands facts and figures first.
Faith leaves it in God's hands;
   sight picks it back up, and worries and frets about it.

The winner of the heavy-weight Faith versus Sight match is determined by you, as a Christian. While God will coach you and even referee the match, you stand in the center of the ring. You won't hear the words from the ringside announcer shouting, "In this corner, there stands Faith," and the heavenly grandstands going crazy with applause. Nor will you hear, "In the other corner, there stands Sight," and the devil and his groupies wildly doing the wave. Who will win the match? The best dancer.

## Big Dreams in Small Packages

Movie-star-turned-celebrity-pitchman William Shatner enthusiastically proclaims priceline.com as a new type of e-commerce: "This is big. This is really big!" The former Captain Kirk appeals to the consumer's desire to barter for the best deal to be found. Consumers utilizing this website enter the prices they're willing to pay for products or services, and then priceline.com contacts participating sellers to determine whether they can fulfill the customer's offer. More than 2 million people have used priceline.com to purchase airline tickets, hotel rooms, groceries, and new cars and trucks, as well as to secure long distance services, home financing, and rental cars. Shatner is right. As their profits have continued to soar, this means of fulfilling people's dreams has become big—really big.

Jabez prayed in faith, daring to believe in God rather than getting muddled in his circumstances or problems. Had he measured the size of his problems, he would have never gotten beyond where he was; instead, he measured the size of his God. Every issue was dwarfed when compared to the awesome almighty nature of God. It took a great faith for Jabez to pray as he did. He fully expected an answer from God; however, I'm sure he was surprised—like we, too, are often surprised—at how much more God chose to do beyond his expectations. God began to work in big ways in Jabez's life as a result of his faithfully praying: "Lord, do something so big in my life that it is obviously from you." I can just imagine Jabez's saying, "This is big. This is really big!"

> Had Jabez measured the size of his problems, he would have never gotten beyond where he was; instead, he measured the size of his God.

God is full of serendipitous surprises for people of faith, but in the context of some qualifying God-conditions. The word "honorable" in 1 Chronicles 4:9 gives us a helpful hint. Jabez had honored something. His word? His commitment? Another clue is given in his request for blessing by God. How could he do so? The whole blessing aspect of this prayer points to a vow made by Jabez to God. While I will discuss this particular vow formula in more depth in the last chapter, let me say now that scholars believe Jabez made a vow, or a solemn promise, to God within the context of this prayer. Implied in this prayer is his vowing to do God's will faithfully, to follow God's Word obediently, and to live earnestly a no-turning-back life for God.

More than a decade ago, Tom Hanks starred in the movie *Big*, in which he portrayed a young boy, Josh Baskin, who finds himself in a man's body the morning after he made a wish, at a magic wish machine, to be big. The biblical character Jabez was also transformed by praying for God to do something big. How big? "Big" is a relative term, not measured according to the size of what God is going to do, but by the impact of what he does.

Many of God's big blessings appear to be "small stuff" in the world's eyes. The tongue is a small thing, yet capable of giving big blessings. With it you can tell someone how to be saved, you can encourage someone who has lost his dream, and you can confess sin to God. The Bible is a small thing, yet it has the power to change our lives and our perspectives so we can dare to dream again. Your knees are small, yet from them you can touch heaven. In the language of the Old Testament, the Hebrew word for "to bless" means to kneel. A connection exists between prayer and blessings. Words are small, yet from them can come big blessings. Saying the word "yes" to God's will brings untold blessings, and saying the word "no" to that which is not in his will keeps you from messing up your life.

The Bible shares many stories about God's wrapping big blessings in small packages.

- The small stone David used to kill the giant Goliath produced the big blessing of a king and a nation in the making.
- The small rod Moses used to part the Red Sea produced the greatest miracle of the Old Testament.
- The small town of Bethlehem produced the Savior of humankind, Jesus Christ.

As a high school student I had the privilege of working in a nursing home, where my responsibilities included painting, mopping, cleaning, mopping, mowing grass, mopping, stocking groceries, and—did I say?—mopping. This proved to be not only an eye-opening experience, but a joyful one, too. I fell in love with the residents—well ... except for this one woman who took my full bucket of white paint and poured it out like a freely flowing river going down the hall. This culprit then got in the middle of the paint and started going round and round in her wheel chair laughing and hollering, "Help! Somebody, come here and help me!"

That less than pleasant but now hilarious memory is quickly offset by another occasion when one nearly blind resident stopped and asked, "Jay, is that you?"

"Yes, ma'am," I replied.

Although she was poor, this precious lady knew I was graduating from high school and wanted to do something for me. Grabbing my hand and placing a crisp five-dollar bill in it, she said, "I just wanted you to have this." That five dollars seemed like a million dollars to me because of the affirmation and encouragement it conveyed. I had always been more than a hired worker to her, I was a young man with big dreams. She believed in my daring-to-change-the-world attitude and my dreams to use the Gospel message to accomplish it.

## Sleepwalking Christians

Sleepwalking, also known as parasomnia, is a disorder affecting 18 percent of the population. It occurs when a person is in a mixed state of being both asleep and awake. You are awake enough to carry out certain functions, but still asleep and not aware of, or able to remember, these actions.[6] I have known quite a few Christians who seem to be suffering from a spiritual sleepwalking. They seem to be carrying out certain perfunctory functions of the Christian life, but not awake to the big things God wants to do through them. They don't seem to be aware of what God wants to do in their lives.

> The time has come for you to wake up from your slumber, because our salvation is nearer now than when we first believed.
>
> —ROMANS 13:11

As I look back on our congregation praying the prayer of Jabez for the first time in September of 1996, I am reminded of the movie *Awakenings*. Robin Williams and Robert De Niro portray a reclusive researcher turned clinical psychiatrist and a post-encephalitis patient who has been in a sleep state for thirty years. Williams' character, Malcolm Sayer, sets out to solve the medical mystery of why Leonard Lowe, the De Niro character, and the other patients in this psych ward have been catatonic for so long. After giving increasingly higher doses of an experimental drug, L-dopa, Lowe—followed by the other patients—miraculously wakes up. Something of a sleeping beauty, he is an endearing, childlike individual who nudges Sayer out of his own emotional dormancy and into his own awakening.[7]

> ■
>
> **The spiritual health crisis many face today is a sleeping sickness of the soul.**
>
> ■

Praying the prayer of Jabez at high dosages for thirty days caused something to happen among people in our congregation to bring them out of their spiritual catatonic state, to reawaken their faith, to put an expectancy in their praying, and to give them a renewed sense of God's presence. I saw men who had been Christians for years begin acting like new believers. I saw women praying with a new zeal. These were great people who loved God, yet now the words of this prayer became the prescription they needed for a God-anointed passion in their lives. My office was flooded with calls and letters of testimonies of what God was doing in people's lives. Many made the decision to make the prayer of Jabez a lifetime experiment.

One such call came from a friend of mine who had been praying the prayer of Jabez six times a day for two weeks. He had just received news of a potentially serious heart problem the day he underwent a stress test. Howe—a confident, self-assured, assertive, successful businessman—explained to the physician that he just did not have time in his busy schedule to deal with this problem. Finally his family intervened and was able to convince him to slow down long enough to have the recommended heart catheterization.

The day he went into the hospital to undergo this procedure, he was introduced to another physician who had been brought in on stand-by to perform a balloon angioplasty if test results warranted it. After the "heart cath" was performed, Howe was told: "We are sorry. We've made a mistake. You have the heart of a twenty-year-old." Howe knew they had made no mistake, and he was phoning to tell me so. He knew God had answered his prayers for protection and blessing. He awakened to the obvious fact that God had chosen to heal him, because he had a plan for his life.

The spiritual health crisis many face today is a sleeping sickness of the soul. Many individuals have Christ's resurrection power within, but that untapped resource is dormant in their lives, having little effect on daily living. The Christ-in-me potential never gets fully tapped. A person prays, yet without zeal. He reads the Bible, yet it doesn't transform his life. She goes to church, but it doesn't affect her decisions Monday through Saturday. He claims Christianity, but you would never suspect it by the way he looks and acts. She would never intentionally hurt the cause of Christ, yet her sameness to the world causes people to wonder if being a Christian makes any difference in her life.

## Roller Coasters, Skydiving, and Jesus

*Time* magazine reported in a recent issue that Americans have entered a new millennium embarking on a national orgy of thrill-seeking and risk-taking. "By every statistical measurement available, Americans are participating in and injuring themselves through adventure sports at an unprecedented rate."[8] Psychologist Frank Farley of Temple University points out that risk-takers are thrill-seekers—whether it's mental, physical, or criminal. Would you be one of those identified as a risk-taker? Here's an exercise to show just how daring you are:

☐ Have you ever sung in public with a karaoke machine?

☐ Have you ever ridden on a "rocket fast," inverted, multi-looped roller coaster?

☐ Have you ever moved to a new city without knowing anyone or having a place to live?

☐ Have you ever eaten something you could not identify?

☐ Have you ever gone mountain climbing, snowboarding, or skydiving?

☐ Have you ever played "truth or dare" and answered "dare"?

☐ Have you ever colored your hair an entirely different color?

☐ Have you ever slept out of doors without a tent in the rain?

☐ Have you ever ridden on a motorcycle with someone else?

☐ Have you ever gone to another country without speaking the language?

The greater the number of questions you answered affirmatively, perhaps the more likely you are a risk-taker. Risk-takers are often characterized by being "open to experience," curious, creative, and comfortable in trying their luck in uncertain or dangerous activity. Does this sound like you? Maybe you take your risks in other ways. Is your attitude one of "if at first you don't succeed, so much for skydiving"?

Jabez, in a sense, was taking a risk by praying such a prayer. He had probably experienced disappointment after disappointment in his life. I'm sure he had tried to break out of his mould many times and was probably met with "better luck next time." Jabez could have easily slid into a "what's the use" mindset about trying to advance in this life, but he did not. He dared to pray specifically for God to do something "so big" in his life.

The kind of risk Jabez took was a calculated one called *faith*. Faith is not a blind belief, but a belief based on the faithfulness of God to act in the lives of those who trust in him.

> The fundamental fact of existence is that this trust in God, this faith, is the firm foundation under everything that makes life worth living. It's our handle on what we can't see.

The act of faith is what distinguished our ancestors, set them above the crowd.

—HEBREWS 11:1–2 *THE MESSAGE*

The Christian life should not be characterized by playing it safe, but by launching out into life's seas with the purpose of making an impact for God. Ships in the harbor are safe from the storms, but they are not safe from dry rot. God never intended for us to play it safe or do the convenient thing. Only as we take some risks for God will we experience God-things. Sir Francis Drake wrote of this calculated risk-taking:

> Disturb us, Lord, when we are too well pleased with ourselves, when our dreams have come true because we have dreamed too little, when we arrive safely because we have sailed too close to the shore.
>
> Disturb us, Lord, when with the abundance of things we possess, we have lost our thirst for the waters of life; having fallen in love with life, we have ceased to dream of eternity; and in our efforts to build a new earth, we have allowed our vision of the new Heaven to dim.
>
> Disturb us, Lord, to dare more boldly, to venture on wider seas where storms will show your mastery; where losing sight of land, we shall find the stars. We ask you to push back the horizons of our hopes; and to push into the future in strength, courage, hope, and love.[9]

We must venture beyond the safe terra firma under our feet into the vast unknown seas to pursue big dreams for God. We also must realize that when we do take risks for him, we may be met with a variety of reactions:

"You're crazy!"—the response of those who cannot believe we'd consider doing such a risky thing.

"You're what?"—the response of many unbelieving people who simply cannot understand why we would embark upon such a course.

"You're not!"—the response of well-intentioned people who may attempt to talk you out of it and tell you why it won't work, why you should wait and see, and why the timing is not right.

Don't misunderstand me, God uses people to help give us direction and to help us avoid some foolish things. That's why it is vital to have people of faith and character as those in whom you confide. We, however, cannot be held back by the un-God-informed reactions to our risk-taking for God.

In seminary I encountered many middle-aged men and women who left high-paying, executive-level jobs, pulled up roots with their family, came to seminary, and then lived like paupers while they worked on their degrees. Why would they do such a thing? They dared to take such a risk for God because they believed that in doing so, they could make a difference in the world. I have seen successful doctors leave their practices and go to a remote mission site to use their medical skills in ministry. Why would they do such a thing? They dared to take such a risk for God because they believed that in doing so, they could make a difference in the world.

> Christian, risk is putting your life and reputation on the line for God.

Christian, risk is putting your life and reputation on the line for God. As you attempt great things for God, get ready for the doubt storms. Make preparations, seek God's shelter, and ride them out with prayer's provision. Samuel Johnson said, "Nothing will ever be attempted if all possible objections must be first overcome." Every significant thing that has been done for God has had the common thread of risk.

The greatest risk of all time was Jesus' death on the cross. He risked our following him, our trusting in his being the true Messiah, and our accepting him as the only true Way to salvation. We can appreciate what he accomplished through this eternally significant risky behavior.

D. L. Moody scribbled in the margin of his Bible, adjacent to the experience of Jesus' feeding of the five thousand, "If God be your partner, make no small plans." God invites us to risk-living in order to impact others in the supernatural God zone, rather than cautiously operating in the safe zones of the natural world.

## Dreamers and Doers

After his older brother was shot down and killed in World War II, Dick Clark listened to the radio to ease his painful loneliness. He began dreaming of someday becoming an announcer on his own show. *American Bandstand* became the product of this man's dream.

Two brothers-in-law had a simple dream of making seventy-five dollars a week. They started their own business that advertised a single product served thirty-one different ways. Baskin-Robbins ice cream was a dream come true for its founders—as well as ice-cream lovers everywhere.

Ray Kroc sold paper cups to restaurants in the 1920s. Confident he could make more money in the restaurant business, he bought out two brothers, kept their name on the business, focused on building a fast-food restaurant chain, and built McDonald's into a billion-dollar industry.[10]

Each year Disney presents the Disney Dream and Doer Award to students who are selected by their Central Florida schools for extraordinary accomplishments and for exhibiting qualities that would identify them as dreamers and doers in their worlds. The award, presented in an impressive awards ceremony at Disney World, bears this quote by Walt Disney:

> Somehow I can't believe there are any heights that can't be scaled by a man who knows the secret of making dreams come true. This special criteria, it seems to me, can be summarized in Four C's. They are curiosity, confidence, courage, and constancy. . . and the greatest of these is confidence. When you believe a thing, believe it all the way, implicitly and unquestionably!

Written not on a plaque, but on the pages of God's Word, the writer of Hebrews summed up the highest quality of a spiritual dreamer and doer: "What is faith? It is the confident assurance that something we want is going to happen. It is the certainty that what we hope for is waiting for us, even though we cannot see it up ahead" (Heb. 11:1 *Living Bible*). That confident assurance comes through praying.

When individuals seek my counsel about future choices in their lives, I often ask them the question, "If you could do anything in your life—fulfill any dream—what would it be?" Let me ask you the same thing. Sit back, kick your shoes off, put down this book, and answer that question. Are you dreaming big enough? Pause now. Think about it. It's important for you to start dreaming—and dreaming big—especially about your impact in the world. God is a God of wild and outrageous dreams. "God can do anything, you know—far more than you could ever imagine or guess or request in your wildest dreams!" (Eph. 3:20a *The Message*).

How can you become a dreamer *and* a doer? Alfred Lord Tennyson reminds us, "More things are wrought by prayer than this world dreams of." As you commit to praying the prayer of Jabez, you will be saying with Dorothy, "Toto, we're not in Kansas anymore." You may remember her story: her encounter with the Munchkins and then her adventuresome travels down the Yellow Brick Road to the Emerald City to see the wonderful Wizard of Oz.

But unlike Dorothy, once you have begun faithfully praying this prayer, you will not want to click the heels of your ruby-red slippers three times and say, "Take me home to Aunt Em!" in order to wake up from your dream and return to Kansas. For as you prayer this prayer, you will go places in your spiritual journey far grander than Dorothy ever journeyed, encountering God-opportunities all along the way. It's not somewhere over the rainbow; rather, it's Someone who hung the rainbow to whom you pray this prayer and share your grandest dream.

Pause now. Pray the prayer of Jabez; however, before you do:

1. Discuss with God your dreams for significant impact. Ask him to make you aware and to protect you from dream-busters in your life.
2. Ask God's help in dealing with those things that may be crippling your doing the faith walk.
3. Consider any risks inherent in your praying this prayer and then consider the size of God. Seek his strength and power as you pray anyway.

> Lord, bless me indeed. . .
> Do something so big in my life that it is obviously from you.
> Increase my influence and opportunities for you,
> And give me a sense of your continual presence and direction.
> Protect me, and keep me from falling into Satan's traps. Amen.

If you are ready to move from dreaming to doing, you may want to continue the experiment.

# ▪ 6 ▪

# God Really Can Do It Through You

*Do something so big that it is
obviously from you.*

**A**n eight-year-old girl was trying to teach her younger brother how to ride a bicycle. After several fruitless attempts, the little brother finally steadied himself. As he wobbled from side to side, he excitedly shouted, "I'm moving! I'm moving!" His older sister, in a cold voice that evoked disdain and a much keener wisdom, replied, "Yeah, you're moving all right, but you are not going anywhere!"[1]

God wants us to be verbs, not just nouns. We are who we are called to be in Jesus Christ, who calls us to be on the move—and going places—for him, doing what he has called us to do.

Christianity is more than a person . . .
> a follower of Christ, a child of God.

Christianity is more than a place . . .
> a church, the Holy Land, heaven.

Christianity is more than a thing . . .
> a religion, the one true Way.

Christianity is more than a concept . . .
> theology, beliefs, laws.

Christianity is not just something we are . . .

> but something we do.

It is active.

It is a verb.

Christianity is the obedient and vibrant response of those who have been made alive in Jesus Christ and are being renewed and transformed daily in the image of the One:

> they love!
> they worship!
> they serve!
> they proclaim!

## "You've Crossed into . . . The Impossible Zone"

For five seasons and 156 episodes, from 1959 to 1964, the above words of Rod Sterling and the "do-do-do-do-do-do-do-do" theme music opened the imaginative and successful show that immediately placed millions of viewers on the edge of their sofas and easy chairs:

> You unlock this door with the key of imagination. Beyond it is another dimension. A dimension of sound. A dimension of sight. A dimension of mind. You're moving into a land of both shadow and substance, of things and ideas. You've crossed into . . . *The Twilight Zone.*
>
> —*THE TWILIGHT ZONE* INTRO

The success of *The Twilight Zone* can perhaps be traced to its simple premise: Ordinary people are thrust into extraordinary circumstances.

As ordinary Christians we sometimes find ourselves thrust into extraordinarily difficult circumstances. We all cross into—do-do-do-do-do-do-do-do—*The Impossible Zone.* This zone is the area of life where we find ourselves trapped in an endless maze of frustrating situations that go on and on and on, causing us to throw up our hands and concede. It's a place where God's presence is often not obvious. *The Impossible Zone* plays mind tricks on us, convincing us there is no way out of this labyrinth of impossibilities.

A lot of Christians get stuck in *The Impossible Zone* because someone has told them there's absolutely nothing they can do but learn to live with it. Destined for a life of hopeless resignation, they settle into a little house or condo on It-Can't-Be-Done Street, which runs parallel with Learn-to-Live-with-It Boulevard.

Jesus crossed into *The Impossible Zone* when he was confronted with Mr. Philip Disciple wanting to know how in the world they were supposed to feed this hungry, expecting-to-eat-right-away crowd, who had gathered to hear him speak. This impossible episode, as recorded in John 6, involved a huge gathering of thousands and the obvious fact that there was no way all these people could be fed.

Jesus challenged Philip, "Where shall we buy bread for these people to eat?" The Bread of Life himself was giving Philip the faith test ... and Philip was about to flunk it. From our two-thousand-year-later perspective, the answer should have been obvious. Duh. It was like Colonel Sanders asking, "Is there any place to get a good chicken dinner around here?" Or Ronald McDonald asking, "Do you folks know where I can get a burger?" Yet Philip could not think of any place open that could accommodate such a large group—especially without reservations. He also missed the opportunity to say, "Jesus, I don't know about places to get something to eat, but I know you. And I know you have the power to perform a miracle right now. Jesus, with you there is no such thing as an impossible situation."

As our church remodels the old Lakeland Mall, we have made a pay-as-we-go commitment. The go stops when the paying ceases. Early on we were faced with the huge challenge of completing our Adult Sunday School facilities within a few weeks because we were moving out of our old facilities. It would cost us a half million dollars to do this work, but we were financially strapped. We found ourselves in a seemingly impossible situation. From where I was standing, it looked like the Red Sea on one side and Pharaoh's army on the other.

Over the months, the people had been incredibly faithful in giving, in pledging, and in sacrificing. Now I had to go back to them again and say, "We need for God to provide more resources. Things are looking right for a miracle." Because I had confidence in what God could do, I shared the need with the church and asked them to go into Jabez-mode praying again. Within three weeks, God did it again! We saw $500,000 come in, the job was completed, and the move was made. Even though our people had already given their lunches, God was pleased to accept their remaining snack meals and multiply their resources to their delight and for his glory.

> ◼
> **From where I was standing, it looked like the Red Sea on one side and Pharaoh's army on the other.**
> ◼

Today, the areas of our mall that were once in disrepair, dark, and ugly are now beautiful, useful, and vibrant places, where God's Word, the spiritual Bread, is being shared to transform lives. The idea of a "Food Court" takes on new meaning for us as it beautifully describes what God did—and is doing—among us at our mall.

Jabez was well acquainted with *The Impossible Zone*, yet he had figured the way out. Using a strategy of prayer combined with faith and action, Jabez found what would get him out of that place where he had lived for so long and bring him into a place of impact for God. He dared to believe that the way things were was not the way things needed to remain. He prayed to the One of whom it is said, "For nothing is impossible with God" (Luke 1:37). Whatever his pain or sorrow, he refused to concede that his lot in life was to stay where he was, living a mere existence, and not the abundant life. With God at work all around him, why should he settle for a giving-in-to-it mentality? He prayed and things happened.

## Adrift on Rubber Ducky III

Steven Callahan was sailing his small sloop, the *Napoleon Solo*, from the Canary Islands bound for the Caribbean when the boat sank during a heavy gale. He escaped in a small inflatable raft, the *Rubber Ducky III*, and embarked on a remarkable 1,800-mile journey that lasted for seventy-six days. Each day of his ordeal was a continual fight for survival. The solar stills intended to produce fresh water malfunctioned. Sharks attacked the small five-and-a-half-foot raft. Ship after ship—nine in all—passed by without seeing the sailor in distress. Every day was a delicate balancing act:[2]

> I must work harder and longer each day to weave a world in which I can live. Survival is the play and I want the leading role. The script sounds simple enough: hang on, ration food and water, fish, and tend the still. But each little nuance of my role takes on profound significance.... It is a constant struggle to keep control, self-discipline, to maintain a course of action that will best ensure survival, because I can't be sure what the course is.[3]

After forty days at sea, Callahan noted ironically that he had reached the maximum amount of time that his raft was guaranteed by the manufacturer. Nevertheless, he had cause for celebration for he estimated that he had, in that amount of time, drifted more than halfway toward the Caribbean. He had also managed to seal the leaking distillation stills.

His situation was momentarily stabilized, but disaster struck again on day forty-three. A speared swordfish ran the sharp tip of his spear into the lower tube of the raft, creating a gaping hole four inches long. Huge air bubbles rushed through the hole until the tube was completely deflated. The *Rubber Ducky*, now kept afloat only by her top tube, floated a mere three inches above the water.

For eight days Callahan tried to patch the leak. It had to be repaired if he was to survive. Depressed but determined, Callahan came up with a tourniquet device to keep air in the lower tube. The repair worked, and his spirits were lifted:[4] "My body hungers, thirsts, and is in constant pain. But I feel great! I have finally succeeded!"[5]

The raft continued to slowly drift westward. Each day presented new problems. The restricted diet and exposure continued to take its toll on Callahan, but Callahan's creativity enabled him to adjust to his surroundings:[6]

> By now the habitat in which I live, Duckyville, has become a neighborly suburb. The fish and I are so familiar I can chat with them individually. . . . I recognize a dorado's nudge, a trigger's peck, or a shark's scrape the way you recognize different neighbors' knocks on the back door.[7]

On day seventy-five, Callahan sighted the light from a lighthouse! The following day astounded fishermen sighted *Rubber Ducky III* and rescued him. Callahan—the only person in history to have survived more than a month at sea in an inflatable raft—was soon safe ashore on the island of Marie Galante, near Guadeloupe, in the eastern part of the Caribbean Sea.[8]

When faced with insurmountable challenges and obstacles, Callahan counted and considered his resources on board.

> What equipment have I got? Space blanket, flare gun, useless lighter, plastic bag. . . . What else have I got? First aid kit, bandages, scissors, twine, and line. And the stuff I have already used—spoon, fork. . . .[9]

Philip, the disciple, failed to count on the Jesus factor when faced with all those unexpected dinner guests and nothing to serve. He showed a definite deficit in math skills:

> He was subtracting by taking God out of the picture.
> He was multiplying the worry and fear.
> He and the other disciples were divided over what to do.
> He failed to add the Jesus factor.

Philip pulled out his calculator to punch the numbers and it didn't add up. He started figuring without regard for the presence of Jesus. "Eight month wages would not buy enough bread for each one to have a bite or enough soda for each to have a burp! It won't work. It can't be done" (John 6:7, author's paraphrase). It was getting late, and the longer he worked on this math problem, the hungrier the people got.

## Toxic People

In her popular book *Toxic People*, Lillian Glass explains, "A toxic person is anyone who has poisoned your life, who is not supportive, who is not happy to see you grow, to see you succeed, who does not wish you well. In essence, he or she sabotages your efforts to lead a happy and productive life."[10] I agree with Dr. Glass that toxic individuals are poisonous in our lives. Some operate without malicious intent; others deliberately seek to dump on our lives. I would love to tell you that no toxic people inhabit our churches, but if I did my nose would grow.

> Toxic people can poison our lives and our ministries if we fail to remain on guard.

Unfortunately many toxic churchgoers whom I have encountered claim to be defenders of the faith and the keepers of tradition. I've heard them say, "I was here when you came, and I will be here when you leave." Whenever they have said this— and, over the years, some have—I have gotten the distinct impression they believed they were called to help me with the latter. On one occasion a man, who was furious with me because I would not divulge a confidence, came up to me after church to blurt out, "You are a sorry pastor!" I wanted to say (but resisted), "Sir, tell me how you *really* feel." Toxic people can poison our lives and our ministries if we fail to remain on guard.

One-time president and head coach of the Boston Celtics, Rick Pitino, is a master at rebuilding basketball programs at the college and NBA levels. As a motivational speaker and author, he teaches how the route to business "overachievement" begins with a winning attitude. Although he does not use the term "toxic people," he describes them to a toxic "t" in his ten-step plan called *Success Is a Choice*:

> We all know the person that comes to work everyday and is always griping about something. The conference room is either too hot or too drafty. The coffee's cold. My boss doesn't listen to me. Nothing is ever right. You know the type. You are always going to be surrounded by negative people. They're in your workplace. They're in your family. They're among your circle of friends. There is no way we can get rid of them. They're the ones who tell you that you can't do this, can't do that, the ones who tell you that your dreams are just childhood fantasies that you'll never be able to accomplish. They may not mean to be harmful. They may be well intentioned and might not even know they're doing it. But their negativity is a poison to everyone around them, polluting the atmosphere, coloring everything. They are the Fellowship of the Miserable, and they are the killers of the dream. . . .
>
> They look for reasons why things won't work. They look for things to blame. They are the first to complain when things aren't going right.[11]

- Toxic people leave a trail of toxic waste wherever they go.
- They are difficult and discouraging rather than positive and uplifting.
- They pour cold water on God-ideas rather than enthusiastically supporting them.
- They love to blame rather than take personal responsibility.
- They delineate all the problems rather than attempt to offer viable solutions.
- They make others want to quit or spit rather than explore and soar.

- They stifle creativity and proactivity rather than enjoy what God might do.

Following in-home visits for a capital stewardship campaign in a former church where I pastored, enthusiastic members returned to the church to meet and to share the impact of their visits. As this electric meeting began winding down, a man in the back—looking as if he were waiting for everyone to get all this excitement out of their systems—walked up to the front. He made a sweeping gesture as he proclaimed, "It ain't all good!" Then, predictably, this toxic individual proceeded to share with us every detail of the negative visit he had just experienced and to lecture us on our need to be slow in "getting all worked up" about what we thought God was doing. I just knew he had the gift of discouragement and simply wanted to exercise it that night.

I'm sure Jabez had toxic people around him. We cannot know for sure, but given his name, his parents sound like they could have easily been a toxic influence in his life. Growing up, he undoubtedly faced ridicule by those who felt superior to him. Certainly there would have been those who meant well, but felt compelled to remind him how unlikely it would be for him to make a significant mark on the world. Can't you imagine their discouraging—and probably less than discreet—comments?

"Poor thing . . ."
"Bless his heart . . ."
"His poor parents . . ."
"What are his chances?"

In spite of their toxicity, Jabez's attitude was far from polluted. I can hear him thinking:

If God is God—and he is,
if God is all-powerful—and he is,
if God is everywhere at once—and he is,
if God knows all things—and he does,
then why not?

Jabez refused to have his life's dream for impact contaminated by tainted thinking, impure motives, and foul advice. He instead made the choice to seek and trust God. We, like Jabez, are confronted with a choice. Will we dare to believe God and take his word for it, or will we believe Toxic Tommy, Negative Nina, Critical Carl, or Pessimistic Paula? We face a choice of either giving God the boot or telling these folks to go join "Negaholics Anonymous."

## Skipping Sunday Lunch

Bubba was terribly overweight, so his doctor put him on a diet. "I want you to eat regularly for two days, then skip a day, and repeat this procedure for two weeks. The next time I see you, you'll have lost at least five pounds."

When Bubba returned, he shocked the doctor by losing nearly twenty pounds. "Why, that's amazing!" the astonished doctor exclaimed. "Did you follow my instructions?" Bubba nodded. "I'll tell you, though . . . I thought I was going to drop dead that third day," he said. "From hunger, you mean?" the doctor asked. "No, from skipping!"

Imagine skipping Sunday lunch after having been in church for hours. Imagine being asked to skip Sunday lunch if you were a kid. Imagine your parents taking you through the drive-thru and buying your lunch on the way to church, and then having one of the ushers come up and ask you to give up your Happy Meal so that others might eat. Perhaps the real miracle of the feeding of the multitude was the little boy's decision to give up his lunch. He didn't fight, kick, scream, or throw a temper tantrum. He willingly gave up his lunch to Jesus. His actions expressed the attitude, "Jesus, it's not much, but you can have it all."

Truett Cathey, Chick-fil-A founder and CEO, started with one restaurant called the Dwarf Grill in an Atlanta suburb in 1946, opened the first Chick-fil-A chain restaurant in 1967, and now operates one of the largest privately held chain restaurants in the nation. He has adopted as the "CFA Corporate Purpose" the following:

> As members of the Chick-fil-A family, we are committed to making the spirit of our corporate purpose evident to everyone we encounter: *"To glorify God by being a faithful steward of all that is entrusted to us. To have a positive influence on all who come in contact with Chick-fil-A."*[12]

Cathey, a committed Christian who recognizes God's ownership of all he has acquired, has never allowed any of the Chick-fil-A restaurants to be open on Sunday. In spite of this unheard-of-in-today's-market stance, Cathey's company has surpassed other restaurants that are open seven days a week. In giving up his Sunday lunch, Cathey has allowed Jesus to multiply what he has and to bless his company with over one billion dollars in sales.

Jabez took what he had and gave it all to God—as if he were putting his whole life in the offering plate. Even though he faced limitations, he was confident his God could take little and make much out of it. God could and would use Jabez, because he was surrendered to him. Likewise, in our lives, it's not what we possess, but what Jesus possesses of us that matters. Many, however, fail to surrender their lives because they have a bad case of the "if onlys":

> "If only I had the right personality ..."
> "If only I had more money ..."
> "If only I were in a better environment ..."
> "If only I had the right breaks in life ..."
> "If only people understood me ..."

Still others suffer from the "what ifs."

> "What if it doesn't work?"
> "What if people laugh at me?"
> "What if I fail?"

"What if God doesn't come through?"
"What if I lose my health?"
"What if I can't afford it?"
"What if no one else helps?"
"What if I look like a fool?"

Jabez surrendered his "if onlys" and his "what ifs" to God. The little boy gave his lunch to Jesus. That's how miracles begin.

## Surprise!

When my daughter, Emily, was two years old, she was quite the budding artist. One day as my wife and I were visiting with someone who had dropped by our home, we suddenly noticed Emily had left the room and was quiet—a combination that always made us suspicious. I immediately went on search for "Em" and found her in our bedroom. She had discovered her mother's red fingernail polish, opened it, removed the tiny brush in the polish, and began painting our new bedroom suite.

By the time I caught her, she had painted her heart out. Apparently she thought red streaks would bring out the beauty of our oak furniture! When she saw me, she had this look of "Surprise, Dad!" Well, I can certainly say her dad was surprised. More than a decade has passed, and we still have that bedroom suite. To this day, each time I look at her handiwork, I relive the surprise again.

"Surprise," however, is one word that can never be applied to our heavenly Father. Our all-knowing, sovereign God is never caught off guard by surprise. We will never hear God saying things like:

"How could this have happened?"
"Wish I had known that."
"You're kidding!"
"He did what?"
"I had no idea!"
"Oops!"

*New York Times* bestseller *Don't Sweat The Small Stuff . . . And It's All Small Stuff* reveals ways to calm down in the midst of incredibly hurried, stress-filled life. "Without question, many of us have mastered the neurotic art of spending much of our lives worrying about a variety of things all at once." Author Richard Carlson offers a number of strategies, such as: "Think of your problems as potential teachers."[13]

When Jesus asked Philip for a solution to the food shortage, he was trying to teach Philip through this problem (John 6:5). When the only solution was a miracle, Scripture says of Jesus, "He already had in mind what he was going to do" (John 6:6). When it comes to Jesus, it all truly is small stuff. While we get surprised and rattled by things that happen to us, he does not. He has a plan for whatever happens in our lives. He knows the answer before the problem arises.

The Mutz family has proved to be an incredible blessing to our church. They are also quite a sight to behold as all thirteen of them—Dad, Mom, and eleven children—walk into church, fill up an entire row, and worship God as a family. I find it heart-warming to visit in their home and experience a loving, caring, sharing community where God is at the center. This dear family is a picture-perfect example of selflessness in action as each member not only assumes his or her own role, but also feels a sense of responsibility for the others—helping a younger sibling out with homework, drying tearful eyes, or just putting the arms back on Barbie. What a joy and privilege to be allowed to participate in their family devotions, a daily practice in their home.

When they received the news that number eleven was on the way, everyone was excited. Would the new family member be a boy or a girl? Surprise was looming, however. When little Emma was born, something was not quite right. She had Down's syndrome with associated heart and stomach problems. As the family gathered together in a meeting, the parents, Bill and Pam, allowed all the children to share their feelings, positive and negative. In that meeting God did an awesome thing. They agreed Emma was truly a gift from God—health challenges and all. And she certainly is! The Mutz family took what could have been a devastating surprise and gave it back to their Lord, who ably and purposefully works through life's surprises.

The Sunday we dedicated Emma to the Lord, I could not hold back the tears. God's presence was noticeable with this family and this precious child. God had allowed her miraculously to survive dangerous heart surgery and has blessed her with a sweetness that can only be described as heavenly. Emma is like sunlight that brightens everyone's day. God has already used this child full of surprises to touch and warm hearts for him.

> Things will come up.
> Crises will happen.
> Trouble is certain.
> Problems are a fact of life.
> Issues will arise.
> Dilemmas will confront us.
> Challenges are always ahead.

My red-fingernail-polished bed and dresser serve as reminders that while I am often surprised by things that happen in my life and ministry, God is not. When these surprises come my way, God knows exactly what needs to be done and how to do it. My part is to cooperate through surrendering my lunch to him.

## "Ya-ba-da-ba-do!"

> "To do is to be."—Socrates
> "To be is to do."—Plato
> "Do-be-do-be-do."—Frank Sinatra
> "Ya-ba-da-ba-do!"—Fred Flintstone

By nature I am a proactive person who likes doing, especially when I feel like I am in tune with God's will. Doing gives a sense of forward momentum in my life, propelling me beyond what I have awaiting me each day and beyond even my expectations.

However, doing without a God-purpose has—at times—been my undoing.

As I mature in my walk with the Lord, I have grown in my intense desire to be more completely his. Out of a love response to him, I seek ways more genuinely to express my devotion to him— to *do* something to show my love for him, to be the person who reflects a more than casual relationship with him. One of the more uncomfortable things I do is examine the content of my days and ask the Father to show me those things that I need to give back to him. As I hold my life's "lunch bag" and look inside for things the Holy Spirit might prompt me to surrender, I find that time immediately jumps out at me. Because it is such a limited, precious commodity in my life, I think—as I cling to the clock inside my bag— "How could I possibly give God any more of my time?" Maybe you've felt that way, too.

God wants our clocks, our watches, our daytimers, our Palm Pilots, our calendars, our no-white-space schedules. The flashing 12:00 on my VCR is a reminder that I need to reset my time . . . in my life. Time is our most valuable resource. It is life itself. When we give God our time, we are giving him our life. How is our time more completely released to him?

- By spending time with him in prayer and the study of his Word
- By serving him through doing eternally significant work
- By reaching out to and caring for people in his name
- By listening to and encouraging those in need
- By living the committed life.

A gift certificate well represents another thing in my lunch bag I have been prompted to surrender. I feel compelled to give Jesus back the gift certificate he gave me along with the gift of my salvation. Every Christian is a "gifted" child of God. His Holy Spirit has gifted each one of us to do the work of the Father. God wants those gifts back! We are not to keep them, but to keep on giving these ever-increasing resources in our lives back to him. He also wants our talents—whether they be singing, playing an instrument, constructing buildings, painting, cooking, listening. When we give our talents to Jesus, he multiplies their effectiveness.

I'm a fan of the multi-platinum, country/bluegrass performer Charlie Daniels. This gifted and talented performer has won a Grammy and three Country Music Association trophies, yet we may see him singing, playing, and sharing his testimony in Christian settings, such as a Billy Graham Crusade. Charlie doesn't just talk about God, he communicates his deep faith and commitment to Jesus through his music, which he recognizes as a talent on loan from God.

> His Holy Spirit has gifted each one of us to do the work of the Father. God wants those gifts back!

When Charlie's wife Hazel faced a serious illness and surgery, he commented, "When your back is to the wall, God's word has over 7,000 promises to stand on. . . . Throughout my life, I've learned to do three things well: love my wife and family, sing and play the fool out of a fiddle, and experience the fullness of God by standing on his promises."[14] God is able to use this man who has given his lunch—in the form of a fiddle-shaped lunch box—back to Jesus.

Lest you think you are unimportant or that your gift is not as glamorous as some performer, consider this. When President Reagan was shot in 1981, the nation's government continued to function as though the attempted assassination had never taken place. During that same year the garbage collectors of Philadelphia went on strike for three weeks and brought the city to its knees. Although most would say the presidency is far more important than sanitation services, the trash collectors proved to be indispensable. Likewise, in the church some people may appear to have insignificant gifts, but the absence of their service can prove to be debilitating to the body of Christ.[15]

## Heart on the Auction Block

My lunch box contained one other object: my most prized earthly possession, a Martin guitar. I know, it was a tight fit, but I got it in there. Let me explain. I had dreamed of owning a guitar like this for a long time. It came with a lot of sacrifice. I put it on layaway and paid a little here and a little there until finally it was all mine.

During our capital stewardship campaign, I preached a series of messages entitled "All Rise." The purpose of this series was to motivate members to rise to the occasion and make the necessary sacrifice, the millions of dollars needed, to transform that old mall into our new church. As we approached the commitment "ingathering" day, I was troubled over what I was going to give. Repairs on our house had wiped us out, and we had no money to give. However, I knew that I, as the leader, had to set the example for the people. If I asked our members to give sacrificially, then I needed to lead the way.

Finally God spoke to my heart and gave me the solution: "Jay, what is the most important material possession you own?"

"Lord, you know it's my Martin guitar."

"That will do. Give it to me."

I wish I could tell you that I was excited about what I felt God was leading me to do, but I wasn't—and neither was my wife, who knew how much I loved that guitar. God assured me that if I would obey him in this, he would do something so big in our church that it would be obviously from him.

Three weeks before our big day of giving, I preached "A Life That Gives." At the end of the message I asked that the television cameras be turned off as I did not want anyone to get the wrong impression of what I was about to say and do. I then proceeded to tell the people about my struggle with knowing what I could possibly give and to explain what God was leading me to do. I brought out my guitar and gave it as my offering to God. By that point, tears were flowing like a river within the church. A spirit of sacrifice was spilled out on that service. People began to come to me saying:

- "I'm giving up my baseball card collection."
- "I'm giving up my Beanie Babies."
- "I'm giving up my jewelry."
- "I'm giving up my car."
- "I'm giving up my boat."
- "I'm giving up my land."

What an amazing sight as individuals, couples, and families searched their hearts to see what they needed to give back to God. Revival broke loose, and God moved mightily in our midst! This proved to be the turning point in our campaign as God began freeing up our people. When we had that ingathering day, we raised over one million dollars in cash with additional millions pledged.

We held an auction to sell all the donated items, and it turned out to be a huge success, with donations amounting to tens of thousands of dollars. Several of our people bid against each other for my guitar—with the top bid being $2,700.00. I admit I had mixed feelings about seeing it sold, but I was glad God had led me and helped me to do this. God was so good in teaching me and the other members about how to turn loose our possessions so that he could bless and multiply our gifts.

The following Sunday one of our Sunday school directors asked me to drop by and visit his class. Everyone was so excited about what God was doing among us, and I was certain I was going to hear inspirational testimonies from those enthused adults. As I walked into the classroom, things did not go at all as I had expected. Immediately my eyes caught sight of my guitar. I felt like I had seen an old friend. I wasn't sure what was going on until they explained that they had chipped in and purchased it for me. As they presented it to me, I was completely taken off guard. My hands were shaking and I was fighting back the tears as I took it out of its case and began to sing and play. I could not believe what God had done. I was amazed and humbled with his faithfulness. Joy flooded my soul while I lifted songs of praise to God.

As I walk through our awesome still-to-be-completed mall, the halls, the rooms, the roofs, the carpets, the air conditioning, the fire security system, the paint, the wire, the lighting all serve as reminders of how Jesus takes and uses our limited possessions—our lunches—to touch lives, reach lost souls with the Gospel, restore broken lives, shape hearts and minds, and free individuals from all kinds of struggles. When we wonder what our money can do, we need to remember our lunches can be used to do the same thing a little boy's lunch did—impact lives in a big, big way.

Undertaking *The Prayer Experiment* will create an atmosphere where God can use you, no matter who you are, and what you have, no matter how meager. He can take even a low-budget meal and transform it into a gourmet, seven-course spread. If you are truly hungry to see God work, pray the prayer of Jabez and watch him do it again. It starts with a lunch and a prayer.

Pause now. Pray the prayer of Jabez; however, before you do:

1. Think of the verbs that should describe the way you are living your Christian life, but are presently ones on which you need to work. Commit to doing so today.
2. What *Impossible Zones* are you now facing? Ask God to supernaturally transform these situations.
3. Think of the toxic influences in your life. Seek God's help in handling them. Consider as well whether you are a toxic influence on anyone else. With God's help, change the way you are influencing that person.

> Lord, bless me indeed. . .
> Do something so big in my life that it is obviously from you.
> Increase my influence and opportunities for you,
> And give me a sense of your continual presence and direction.
> Protect me, and keep me from falling into Satan's traps. Amen.

If you are ready to make a God-impression on the world, you may want to continue the experiment.

# ▪ THREE ▪

# Impact . . . Your Chance

*Increase my influence and opportunities
for you and give me a sense of your continual
presence and direction.*

# Making a God-Impression

*Increase my influence . . . for you*

**S**ome Christians make better scents than others. Not that they have masked body odor by splashing on some Obsession or cK One. Instead, they carry a scent that is more divine than any of these over-the-counter products. Some individuals just seem to exude an aroma that makes other people think of God and be drawn closer to Christ.

It has been said that prayer is the perfume of everything an individual does for God.[1] Likewise, authentic praying Christians may be compared to a fragrance, perfume, or scent. We may be rightly labeled the "God-scent" to a world who doesn't have a nose for the things of God.

## Follow Your Nose

Ah, the sense of smell can be so captivating! Most of us are attracted to something that smells good and are repelled by something that does not. As humans, we can discriminate between 4,000 and 10,000 different odor molecules.[2] Our sense of smell communicates many of the pleasures of life:

> steaks cooking on a grill
> a lawn freshly mowed

> wood burning on the fireplace
> a pound cake baking in the oven
> roses arranged in a flower vase
> scented candles lighted in a room
> the ocean breeze drifting ashore.

Every time I drive through downtown Orlando and the smell of the freshly baked breads from the Merita Bakery wafts into my car and bombards my senses, I want to roll down my window and eat the air!

Scents trigger memories. Response to an odor involves a mix of biology, psychology, and memory.[3] Advertisers and marketers in the five-billion-dollar-a-year fragrance industry know this powerful connection between scent and emotion. They frequently use this connection in their promotions in magazines that carry perfume-strip advertisements that waft their odor into the noses of unsuspecting readers. No wonder some companies use scented stationery for their mass mailings.[4]

Often a particular scent will cause me to rewind to a moment in time so that I experience again those emotions. When I smell Alpha Keri lotion, I am instantly drawn back in time to Harris Hospital in Fort Worth, Texas where, amidst all the tubes and wires, my premature son was struggling for his life. The neonatal unit covers their preemies in Alpha Keri lotion to keep their skin from drying out and cracking. Whenever I smell that lotion, it still triggers the painful memory of our doctor's solemn words: "Your baby is on 100 percent oxygen. There's nothing more we can do. He may not make it." It causes me to flash back to desperate thoughts of "God, I'm a seminary student serving you—and you are allowing this to happen?"

The scent also transports me back to that morning when I was driving down I–30 to the hospital, pouring my heart out to God—quite honestly, I was a little angry with him—and then God placed it on my heart to start singing the old hymn "Have Faith in God." A short time later, on arriving at the hospital, I was greeted with the words, "It's remarkable! Your son is making drastic improvements!" My thoughts then race to the renewed hope in God that was rekindled when I gently placed that precious, little bundle into his infant car seat to finally make the much-anticipated trip home. All it takes is just one whiff of that lotion, and wham! I'm back in the Lonestar State.

## "God-Impression": The Believer's Fragrance

Fragrances—like the smell of a distinct perfume, firecrackers on the Fourth of July, or the antiseptic odor of a doctor's office—trigger emotional responses in us. So, too, should our Christian presence in the world. If our presence positively reminds people of God, we are then able to make what I like to call a "God-impression" on them. A God-impression is the effect you have on people's opinions about God. As a Christian, you are a walking billboard—an advertisement—for Christ. What your life says about Christ is the God-impression you are making on those who have never connected with God. You will either cause others to say of Christianity, "I want to know more," or you will cause them to say, "Thanks, but no thanks."

> You will either cause others to say of Christianity, "I want to know more," or you will cause them to say, "Thanks, but no thanks."

The quality of its ingredients determines the impression a perfume will make. The best take years to develop and perfect. In making an extraordinary God-impression, it is important that our aroma is of the highest quality based on biblical standards of excellence. If we seek to grow consistently in Christ over the years, we, too, will improve our impact on the market.

When Scripture says that Jabez was "more honorable" (1 Chron. 4:9), it reflects his commitment to saying "yes" even before God asked the question. He was willing and ready to do whatever God required of him. I believe it was his contagious spirit, not his appearance or social standing, that caused him to make a positive impression. "God-impression" was the fragrance Jabez was wearing—which he no doubt splashed on with prayer.

Several years ago, Chicago newspapers carried the story of a busboy in a Chinese restaurant who was sent to a bank to get change for $500. The restaurant needed $250 in coins and $250 in one-dollar bills. The teller grabbed a stack of $100 bills by mistake and gave the young man $250 in coins and $25,000 in bills! The young man noticed the error immediately, but detecting a windfall, didn't say anything. He left the bank with the money and hid it at a relative's home. With some of the money, he went to another bank and got $250 in one-dollar bills. He then returned to the restaurant, thinking he had made a small fortune.

The bank teller, when she discovered her mistake, couldn't identify the person to whom she had given the $100 bills, but she could remember how he smelled. She knew from his scent that he worked in a Chinese restaurant. She not only remembered the aroma, but she was able to connect it with the exact restaurant where the busboy worked. With the police, she located the restaurant and identified the busboy. He was promptly fired and the money was recovered. The bank decided not to prosecute since the mistake was theirs.[5]

Christians, too, are known by their aroma:

> Christ-like attitude
> consistent godly behavior
> encouraging words
> loving responses
> joyful facial expressions
> confident assurance that God is in control.

It's the God-impression they are making on others. It's positive impact in the most genuine sense. When Paul wrote about Christians being the fragrance of God (2 Cor. 2:14–16), he used the scenario of conquering Roman warriors returning from battle victorious. Incense would be burned and freshly-cut flowers would be thrown at the parading soldiers, creating an aroma. It was the smell of victory, of winning, of overcoming. Believers—through their God-impressions—are the determining influence in how the world feels about Christianity.

## What About Bob?

Not long ago I saw once again the hilarious comedy *What About Bob?* which features Bill Murray portraying a superneurotic patient of an up-and-coming psychoanalyst and author (Richard Drey-fuss). This plot thickens as this obsessive patient pursues the doctor when he goes on vacation to his New England summer house, befriends his family, and ultimately drives the doctor mad. Such movie plots stick in my mind and inevitably come to mind at the most inopportune times—usually during drawn-out meetings or boring conferences—causing me to get tickled. This movie title should prompt such a response, but instead it causes me to think about a man named Bob who lives in our city and a friend asking me, "What about Bob? How's he doing?"

A mutual friend of ours had been killed in an automobile accident. Something in the memorial service for this friend connected with Bob, an unbeliever who had never had much use for religion, church, or the Bible. He noticed that although there was great sadness among those who loved and missed him, there was also an air of celebration over the fact that now this Christian man was in heaven. Bob could not quite understand this approach to death.

I attempted to use this experience as an opportunity to reach out to Bob, feeling he could benefit from a friend who understood his confusion and wanted to help him. This, however, was not what Bob thought he needed. When I visited the restaurant he owned, he would not let me talk with him about this. He simply was not interested in joining me for lunch or having me drop by his house to talk. Sensing God was working in his life and not wanting to give up on him, I invited him to our church services. Bob surprised a lot of folks when he actually showed up—and kept showing up—at our church for two years. Throughout that time, I prayed and fasted for him, and I asked God to make his presence known in a transforming way in Bob's life.

Knowing Bob was facing potentially serious surgery, a friend and I went by his house on the Saturday morning prior to his surgery to let him know that we would be praying for him. While Bob was cordial, he obviously did not know how to handle our visit, and the best he could do was to manage some small talk. As we drove away from his house, I told my friend, "I don't think that man will ever come to Christ." (Now that was a fine faith-statement from a man of God!) To my surprise—and to God's glory—the following morning I saw Bob and his wife respond to an invitation I gave to the congregation to surrender their lives to Christ at the end of the worship service.

> ■
> He was drawn by an aroma from on high that had a tremendous impact on his thinking and on his heart.
> ■

He was drawn by an aroma from on high that had a tremendous impact on his thinking and on his heart. Bob followed his nose and gave his life to Christ.

His experience with surgery was an answer to prayer. Bob did not have cancer as suspected, and he soon recovered. Looking back, I think the entire experience smelled a lot like something God used to bring Bob to a point of need. In fact, Bob's wife, Nancy, told me that she had been praying the prayer of Jabez daily throughout the time that she and Bob had been attending our worship services. She believed God was going to do something so big in Bob's life and hers that it would be obviously from him. Nancy now says of this prayer's impact on their lives, "It simply worked."

Through believing prayer, God transformed Bob's life, and he has been a different man since. About four months after his conversion to Christ, Bob and Nancy took my wife, Angie, and me out to dinner at a downtown restaurant full of people who knew him by his former reputation as a nonchurch-going man. As our food came, Bob said, "Let's join hands and pray that God will bless our meal." Before astonished onlookers, we joined hands with Bob and prayed. What a God-impression he made on those in that restaurant that evening!

Bob continues to make a God-impression wherever he goes today. He is truly a changed man. He brings people to church and participates in my prayer group. He is a kinder, gentler man, who is touching other people's lives for Christ. The people of our city look at his new life and ask, "What about Bob? He has changed so dramatically." They are right. Bob caught a good whiff of God-impression, and he's never been the same since. And now *he* is praying the prayer of Jabez.

## Fantastic or Fatal Attraction

None of us gets a second chance to make a first impression. Yet first impressions can be fantastic or fatal and are paramount in our making a God-impression on someone. A corporate CEO remarked, "Most people don't have time actually to figure you out. So their initial perception of you is very important. If you make a bad impression, you have to get over the bad impression. If it's good, you can go on to step two."[6]

Some experts estimate it takes only four minutes to establish a positive or negative first impression.[7] Another CEO says, "In retail, they have what they call a 'twelve-second factor'— that's the time you need to capture a buyer's attention with your product, design, package, color, and positioning. The same time limit applies to making an impression as an individual."[8] Still another CEO declares, "You have approximately three seconds to establish your presence. Two seconds to size up the situation and how to approach it, then one second to correct yourself if you're wrong."[9]

How exciting! If any of these time frames are anywhere close to being accurate, it means I have the opportunity to make a God-impression while. . .

> standing in line at Kmart
> pumping gas at 7-Eleven
> buying stamps at the post office
> making a deposit at the bank
> renewing my driver's license at the DMV.

It brings new purpose—and an expectant joy—to being told to wait in line! I must confess, however, that I am not sure I am ready to start praying, "The longer the lines the better, God." I admit I can get a tad frustrated when standing in the ten-items-or-less line and the person in front of me has eleven or more items in the cart. (I know this, because I counted!)

Holiday Inn, when looking for five hundred people to fill positions for a new facility, interviewed five thousand candidates. They excluded all candidates who smiled fewer than four times during the interview. This applied to people competing for jobs in all categories.[10] While you are probably not presently interviewing for a job at Holiday Inn, you are constantly under the microscope by those who are searching for God. Better be sure that what they see looks like authentic Christianity and sounds like a relevant faith. You cannot "clock out" on living your beliefs as you would in punching a time clock at work. The clock is always running with no coffee breaks.

Recently I had the privilege of finally meeting two heroes of mine while attending a conference where both were program speakers. Prominent Christian leaders, both men have had worldwide impact. The first "hero" I met while dining with a couple of friends. We were enjoying our meal, when—to my surprise and delight—this guy walked over to our table and sat down next to one of my friends. He struck up a conversation with our mutual friend.

Within moments of his joining us, I heard him say something very inappropriate—and actually quite shocking. I was not trying to eavesdrop, but I could not help overhearing what this guy had—rather loudly—said. I couldn't believe my ears! Surely he didn't say what I thought he said. I must have been mistaken.

But I wasn't. Disappointingly, I soon heard him repeat himself—even more boisterously. A thousand admiring thoughts within me had their funeral in that moment. I'm sure I heard taps playing as he walked away from our table. I was disillusioned—to say the least—since this was the first time I had gotten up close to this "hero."

Such fatal first impressions are hard to shake. I continue to pray for this man and respect what his ministry is doing for Christ; however, I no longer think of him in quite the same way. Am I being too hard? Possibly so, but I am trying to share my feelings honestly regarding this fatal encounter, as I believe that those who are without Christ evaluate Christians in much the same way when we say such things that discredit our testimony.

Contrast that fatal first impression with an experience that occurred a short time later. I had the opportunity to visit briefly with Dr. Stephen Olford. I was thrilled to have the opportunity to finally meet this man, whom I had admired for years. I was not disappointed in the man or his witness. I found that he was everything I had hoped he would be—and more. He was godly, kind, and humble. I left our visit thanking God that I had seen a credible example of truth and grace. It underscored in my thinking the importance of first impressions, for in just one instant an impression—either fatal or fantastic—is made fatal or fantastic for the One whom we represent.

Each time I explore the first book of Chronicles, I am fascinated by the genealogies. The first nine chapters, which I have dubbed the "Begat Chronicles," list characters whose names sound as if they could be people from my small hometown in Arkansas. Among all those begats you'll find Eber, Jetur, and good 'ole Ezer.

What is it, then, that made Jabez stand out from all the rest? He was a different breed of individual who made a God-impression on his world. He's only one of a handful of people in all the "Begat

Chronicles" mentioned by more than his name. He was more honorable than the people around him (1 Chron. 4:9). I don't mean different in a weird sort of way—a "look at that fanatic" way—but in a "hey, that guy's got something I want" kind of way. To put it in contemporary vernacular, Jabez wasn't a part of an organization called "Geeks for God" or "Dweebs Making a Difference." His kind of faith was not a God-turn-off. His God-fragrance has lasted for centuries. The world was not then—and is not now—turned off by authentic faith in God.

## A Nose That Knows

Anne Gottlieb has a nose that knows and is insured for a substantial amount. She works as a fragrance consultant whose nose for a winning formula has put her at the top of her profession. Gottlieb rose to fame when a friend asked her to help a small design company with its first scent. The company was Calvin Klein and the scent was "Obsession," the first of many blockbusters. Now the fifty-three-year-old American mother of two is an olfactory chameleon, responsible for a myriad of sweet-smelling fragrance blockbusters that earn the perfume industry more than one billion dollars a year. Because she hasn't signed an exclusive deal with one perfume house, she has become a walking-talking insurance policy against her clients' developing a scent similar to another company's scent.[11]

> Jabez wasn't a part of an organization called "Geeks for God" or "Dweebs Making a Difference."

Early in the history of the fragrance industry, formulas were closely guarded secrets, trusted to few because formulas could not be patented. The only way to prevent them from being copied was not to divulge the ingredients. In this way the secrecy of the formula was more or less protected.[12]

Christianity's fragrance formula is handled just the opposite. Rather than being a guarded secret, Christians should want to share with everyone the news of the fragrant life. In fact, Christ mandated it. Unlike fragrances on the market today, this one is patented. "God-impression" cannot be reproduced by anyone other than God himself in the life of the believer. The ingredients of its precious formula are found in God's fragrance book, the Bible. Yet many would like to pass off inferior copy-cat or impostor products for the authentic fragrance of Christianity.

More than one thousand body fragrances exist in today's market[13] and over five thousand different chemicals are used in fragrance products, with some perfumes containing as many as six hundred individual chemical ingredients. Of the 150 highest volume chemicals used in fragrance products, more than a hundred are known to be toxic, with the effects of many fragrance chemicals on human health still largely unknown.[14] On the world's spiritual index we can spot toxic sensations and beliefs that knowingly target and seductively entice far too many unsuspecting spiritual fragrance consumers. The competition—packaged as seemingly innocent as psychic hotlines, L. Ron Hubbard's *Dianetics*, James Van Praagh's books on communicating with the dead—is vying for people's attention and trying to win noses—and hearts—even though they produce adverse effects on people's spiritual well-being.

Of all of God's creatures, humans have the poorest nose. We have virtually lost the sense of smell.[15] While such a generalization should be taken with a grain of salt, it does have a direct correlation to fallen humanity's spiritual plight. With the introduction of sin and its detrimental influence on our ability to discern, we are too often duped by inferior counterfeit spiritual fragrances.

"God-impression," while desperately needed by a scent-challenged world, can only capture the attention of the world if it's taken out of the box and sampled. If we, as Christians, are going to influence people genuinely to embrace Christ, we must offer them more than the God-talk that takes place in the confines of

> **The world will only be touched by lives that are passionately lived for Christ—24/7.**

our churches. The world will only be touched by lives that are passionately lived for Christ—24/7—and splashed on liberally so that the true "God-impression" permeates the very air that they breathe.

As believers, we must pray for wisdom and discernment for we, too, can easily be misled. We must always remember that our experience does not sit in judgment on the Bible; rather, the Bible sits in judgment of our experience. We must keep our noses in God's Word so that we will be able to sniff out a counterfeit fragrance or a spiritually offensive odor when we encounter one. Our being able to do this effectively may be a problem if we, like 82 percent of Americans, claim that the "Bible verse" we most often quote is "God helps those who help themselves"—a Thomas Jefferson quote (which, by the way, is not found in the Bible!).[16]

## Scratch and Sniff

A Nike television commercial for hiking shoes was shot in Kenya using Samburu tribesmen. The camera closes in on one of the tribesmen who speaks in native Maa while the Nike slogan "Just Do It" appears on the screen. Lee Cronk, an anthropologist at the University of Cincinnati, says the Kenyan is really saying, "I don't want these. Give me big shoes." Says Nike's Elizabeth Dolan, "We thought nobody in America would know what he said."[17] There must be no contradiction between Christians' lipping it and living it. There's always someone in the world who is listening to us, as Christians, and interpreting our actions to see if they match our words. When our lives reflect consistency, it is a match made in heaven that ignites authentic interest in the things of God.

One Sunday as I preached the message "Making a God-Impression," a waitress who had waited on my family and me the day before sat in the congregation. She did not know I was a pastor until she saw me preaching that morning, and she only knew me as the guy whom she had served. As she listened to my sermon on making a God-impression, she weighed the words in the message with the behavior she saw in me on Saturday. Guess which message spoke more loudly. You've got it! She had already done the scratch-and-sniff test the prior day. What was her impression? She commented to her friend who brought her to the service, "By the way, your pastor and his family came into my restaurant yesterday. They, in fact, made a God-impression on me."

I would like to tell you that I always make a God-impression on others, but if I did my nose would start growing. One day an older friend and I were in Braum's Ice Cream Shop enjoying an ice-cream cone when a mentally challenged woman started pointing at me and hollering, "That's my pastor, that's my pastor!" She eventually exited. The place was full of people who no doubt were blinded by the blush on my face. My friend didn't know what was going on, and so I tried to whisper to him what that scene was all about. Since he was hard of hearing, I was forced to speak more loudly. Still, I could not make him understand. Finally in a too loud voice I said, "George, she's crazy!" He heard me that time, but, unfortunately, so did everybody else in the shop.

> ■
>
> The percentage of Americans who say they feel the need to experience spiritual growth has risen sharply, up twenty-four points, in just four years.
>
> —GEORGE GALLUP JR.[18]
>
> ■

I will never forget one particular woman staring holes through me, giving me the "angry eyes"—like the kind of angry eyes that *Toy Story 2*'s Mrs. Potato Head reminds her husband to pack for his trip. Well, this woman in the ice-cream shop definitely had packed—and was wearing—hers! I asked her what was wrong. She replied, "I don't think a pastor ought to be talking like you talked about that poor lady." Ouch! That really hurt. I

> ■
> **Twinkie saints won't satisfy the world's search for a real God-experience.**
> ■

definitely made no God-impression—just a God-turn-off—that day.

The atmosphere is right to make God-impressions. A *New York Times* lead story stated, "Now, even people without faith are looking for God."[19] Martin Marty, professor of modern Christianity at the University of Chicago, was asked if he felt the modern soul fascination was authentic. "The hunger is always authentic," he answered. "It's just that you can feed it with Twinkies or with broccoli."[20] Twinkie saints won't satisfy the world's search for a real God-experience. They are looking for authentic Christianity. You can better believe that those without God have their spot-a-fake antennae on looking for fakes and flakes, all the while desiring a genuine encounter with God.

## Get a Whiff of This

In the movie *Muppets from Space*, after announcing to the world on Miss Piggy's talk show that "we are not alone in the world," Gonzo becomes the target of paranoid government operative, K. Edgar Singer. While being held for interrogation in the secret government compound, Gonzo is asked, "How do you smell?" Singer, of course, was referring to the fact that Gonzo has no nostrils. Gonzo's roommate, Rizzo the Rat, responded as if Singer were referring to Gonzo's body odor.

If I were to ask you how you smell or if you are making a God-impression on others, how would you respond? Suppose your name was tossed out in a word association game around those who don't know God. What would be the first word out of their mouth, indicating their immediate impression of you?

If you do not feel as if you, as a Christian, are making the God-impression you desire, let me offer some helpful suggestions. First, work on your "A.Q." (that is, attitude quotient). You need to choose to have a great attitude no matter what kind of "terrible, horrible, no good, very bad day" you might be having.[21] You must guard against being like the man who was told, "Have a good day," and responded, "No, thanks, I have other plans."

My mother sent me a greeting card bearing the famous quote of Henry Wadsworth Longfellow: "Into every life a little rain must fall." When I opened the card I read, "Followed by large hail and damaging winds." Some people live with that sort of expectancy— anticipating that the worst is going to happen. Murphy of Murphy's Law seems to be their adopted twin. While followers of Christ may not be able to control what happens to them, they can control— through God's strength and power—what happens inside of them and how they respond to it. Bad attitudes on the part of Christians could possibly be the "Number One God Turn-off."

Having a sense of humor is another great way to leave a God-impression on others. If you go around looking as if you have just sucked buttons off a sofa,[22] you won't give off a very good aroma. A sense of humor has helped me in some tough situations. At one of our Wednesday evening services a man sat in the second or third row of the church. I said something that made him laugh so hard his upper plates shot out of his mouth and across two pews, where they landed at the altar by my feet. No one except me saw what happened. My only salvation was to think of a quick joke and tell it. As I recall, my joke wasn't all that funny, but I needed to tell it, as I was tickled to death. Oh, what a relief it was to laugh!

Some individuals seem to enjoy living under a dark cloud rather than stepping out into the sunshine. They see a cloud behind every silver lining. Some of them sat in the audience at a church where I was speaking. The bored and uninterested expressions on their faces revealed I wasn't connecting with them. Mid-message I walked over, picked up my guitar, and began singing: "Gloom, despair, and agony on me, deep dark depression,

> ■
> Some
> individuals . . .
> see a cloud
> behind every
> silver lining.
> ■

excessive misery...." The congregation erupted in laughter. Finally, they came out from under their cloud and actually acted excited about our worshiping together. Jokingly, we declared the gloom and despair song our theme song for the revival services. A ho-hum impression was turned into a God-impression.

Likewise, kindness leaves a God-impression. Being unthoughtful, rude, untactful, obnoxious, and intentionally difficult are sure paths to a God-turn-off; however, kindness can lead you down avenues of impact you never before imagined. A friend shared with me the true story of a man who was driving along a rather busy street and noticed a limousine pulled over with a flat tire. He decided to stop and lend a hand. The chauffeur was both surprised and relieved. Together, they quickly changed the flat tire. As the good Samaritan was about to walk away, a back window in the limo lowered. Donald Trump stuck his head out and said to the man, "Thanks very much. My wife and I really appreciate your help."

"Aw, it was nothing. Glad to help," the guy replied.

Trump then asked if there was anything he could do to express his appreciation—anything. The man sort of blushed and said "no."

As he turned toward his car, another attempt followed. "Wait! Isn't there something we could do to show you how grateful we are? We'd really like to express our appreciation," Trump insisted.

The man paused, turned around, and answered, "Tell you what. Just send my wife a bouquet of flowers. She'll never believe Donald Trump personally sent her flowers!"

Trump nodded and agreed to do just that. The man left her name and their address before leaving. Several days later their doorbell rang. The man's wife was given a huge vase of orchids—which absolutely stunned her, especially when she saw that they were from Donald Trump—and a small envelope. Inside the envelope was written the message, "We hope you enjoy the flowers. Your husband helped us out the other day, and we wanted to express our gratitude. In addition, just wanted you to know we also paid off your mortgage." The impact of a deed of kindness can be great.

## Right Under Our Noses

A good perfume has been traditionally formulated to last six to eight hours. It must make an immediately powerful first impression as it comes out of the bottle. It must develop a reaction after introduced to the skin and then linger with a quality fragrance. When this is accomplished, the perfume then makes an impact that is immediate and long lasting.[23]

Some companies boost productivity by introducing scents into the workplace. According to research, a room's scent can profoundly affect a person's concentration, mental alertness, and clear thinking. People worked 33 percent more efficiently in rooms scented with almost any pleasant aroma. In fact, some smells are super-powerful; for example, a lemon scent diffused into a work environment reduced typing errors by more than 50 percent.[24]

Scent impacts worship. When the scent of God's people engaged in passionate worship penetrates the atmosphere, it has a profound effect on all who worship. It fills the service of worship with the obvious presence of God, arresting people's attention and causing them to look up. It invites people to think about their relationship to God and their witness for Christ. That kind of scent-invoked atmosphere leaves a lasting impression.

As Christians we should leave a lasting impression on those with whom we come into contact. Our competition includes all those -isms, schisms, and spasms that are a "different gospel" (Gal. 1:6). We have to leave an immediate and powerful first impression—even if we have only a few moments contact and will never see the other person again. We should strive to make the other person pause and consider God.

The Research Institute of America conducted a study for the White House Office of Consumer Affairs in which they found the average business will hear nothing from 96 percent of unhappy customers who receive rude or discourteous treatment. Ninety percent who are dissatisfied with the service will not come back again. To make matters worse, each of those unhappy customers will tell his or her story to at least nine other people, and fourteen percent of those unhappy former customers relate their stories to more than twenty people.[25]

People who have formed unfavorable impressions of Christians are just as likely to stay away from church and to tell others about their bad impressions. That is why making a positive and lasting God-impression—everywhere we go—is so important. People may not remember our names, but as they look back in life's rearview mirror, they will recognize the lingering scent of a God-impression.

Bloomingdale's introduced a limited-edition fragrance called "Moi," developed for the Muppets's very own Miss Piggy, who offered some advice for perfume shoppers: "It is moi's duty, as the embodiment of the epitome of glamour and impeccable taste, to offer assistance."[26] Christian, we must each realize and proclaim, "It's moi's duty to make a God-impression."

## Heaven Scent

Throughout biblical times scents have played an important role. The ancient Hebrews used fragrances to consecrate their temples, altars, lamps, and priests. By the first century A.D., Rome was consuming more than 2,800 tons of imported frankincense and 550 tons of myrrh per year. In fact, Emperor Nero spent the equivalent of $100,000 to scent just one party he threw! The New Testament records the use of fragrance in the life of Christ. Frankincense and myrrh are prominent in the story of his birth (Matt. 2:11). Later in his life and ministry Mary Magdalene anointed his feet with the costly perfume, spikenard (John 12:3–4). When Jesus died, about seventy-five pounds of a myrrh and aloes mixture was used in his burial preparation (John

> When we possess Christ, we become his Chanel No. 5 or his Armani for the world.

19:39–40). Even the Greek word for Christ means "anointed."[27] No wonder when we possess Christ, we become his Chanel No. 5 or his Armani for the world.

People have come up to me and asked, "Do you mind telling me what kind of cologne you are wearing?" They didn't know what it was, but they knew they liked it and wanted some of it. That's what happens when you smell like Christ. "What's different about you? What is that you are wearing?" "Oh, it's called 'God-Impression.'"

You carry with you impressions—the smell, the odor—of where you have been.

> If you have been in a smoke-filled room,
>     you are going to smell like smoke.
> If you have been around food preparation,
>     you are going to smell like food.
> If you have been working with floral arrangements,
>     you are going to smell like flowers.
> If you have been working around oil and grease,
>     you smell like—pardon the pun—the pits.
> Likewise, if you have been with Christ,
>     you should smell like him.

When you possess a genuine relationship with the Anointed One, Jesus Christ, you begin taking on his distinctive fragrance. You acquire this aroma when you spend time with God through prayer and reading the Bible, worship and fellowship with other Christians, and seek to do your heavenly Father's will. After a while, heaven's scent becomes your own. In fact, may I be so bold in suggesting that if you would attempt *The Prayer Experiment*, your aroma could change in thirty days.

Pause now. Pray the prayer of Jabez; however, before you do:

1. What are the missing ingredients in your life that keep you from making a God-impression? Ask God to richly supply those ingredients to you.

2.  Think of those individuals on whom you are most likely to make a God-impression because of your relationship to them. Pray for them, as well as for your potential impact on their lives.
3.  Pray that you will be put in those places where you can make a God-impression today.

> Lord, bless me indeed. . .
> Do something so big in my life that it is obviously from you.
> Increase my influence and opportunities for you,
> And give me a sense of your continual presence and direction.
> Protect me, and keep me from falling into Satan's traps. Amen.

If you do not want to limit God's awesome opportunities in your life, you may want to continue the experiment.

# 8

# Why Your Opportunities May Be Limited

*Increase my . . . opportunities for you.*

Can't you see it? Maybe not, if you are one of the 71 percent of adults ages eighteen to forty-nine and one of the 90 percent of adults age fifty and above who require some type of corrective lenses to better see things.[1] Yet many people with 20/20 ocular vision are either spiritually blind or vision-impaired. Although blind from the age of two, Helen Keller arrived at the conclusion that "the only thing worse than being blind is having sight but no vision." Many Christians have limited opportunities because they have a limited vision of what God can do in and through their lives.

## Visually Impaired

A man was handed a great opportunity, but his vision was limited. His friend Walter was taking him for a ride in the country. The two men drove off the main road through groves of trees to a large uninhabited expanse of land where a few horses grazed and a couple of old shacks remained. Walter stopped the car, got out, and started to describe with great vividness the wonderful things he was going to build. He wanted his friend Arthur to buy some of the land surrounding his project to participate on the ground floor of an investment rich with potential. But Arthur thought to himself, *Who in the world is going to drive twenty-five miles for this crazy project? The logistics of the venture are staggering.*

Walter explained, "I can handle the main project myself, but it will take all my money. The bordering land where we're standing right now will in just of couple of years be jammed with hotels and restaurants and convention halls to accommodate the people who will come to spend their entire vacation here at my park." He continued, "I want you to have the first chance at this surrounding acreage, because in the next five years it will increase in value several hundred times."

"What could I say? I knew he was wrong," Arthur tells the story today. "I knew that he had let this dream get the best of his common sense, so I mumbled something about a tight-money situation and promised that I would look into the whole thing a little later on."

"Later on will be too late," Walter cautioned Arthur as they walked back to the car. "You'd better move on it right now." And so Art Linkletter turned down the opportunity to buy up all the land that surrounded what was to become Disneyland. His friend, Walt Disney, tried to talk him into it, but Art thought he was crazy.[2] Opportunities to do something big for God aren't usually obvious to many Christians either.

Higher educated Americans are more likely to wear corrective lenses than those who are less well educated: 82 percent of those with postgraduate degrees need corrective lenses, compared to 68 percent of those with only a high school education or less.[3] Perhaps the constant strain of reading and studying weakens their vision. Spiritually, this, too, may be true for many. Logic and reason can easily be substituted for faith. Scholarly pursuits have left many conditioned to believe that "I've got to see it to believe it" is superior to "I've got to believe it to see it" (as faith demands).

Don't misread me. I am an education junkie. I love learning and being challenged to expand my thinking in many disciplines. Although I have earned my doctorate, I don't see that as a "terminal" degree, for I feel as if I have only begun to learn how to learn, and I realize how little I really know. While I know I will be a perpetual student, I realize inherent dangers that accompany increased education. Self-reliance can replace a God-reliance.

## Unchurched by Educational Levels

The more educated people are, the more likely they are to be unattached to a Christian church. Nearly four out of every ten college graduates (37 percent) are unchurched. Among those who went on to receive some graduate education, 39 percent are unchurched. That is significantly higher than the proportion among adults who never graduated from high school and of whom 29 percent are unchurched. (See Fig. 8.1.)

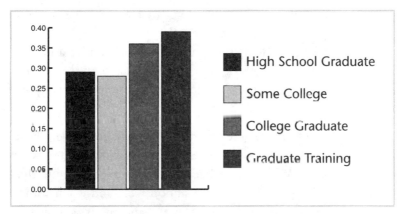

*Fig. 8.1—Ratio of Unchurched People to Educational Levels*

Of those who are unchurched, 62 percent state that a good person can earn his or her way into heaven, 47 percent assert that when Jesus lived on earth he committed sins, and 49 percent define God as other than the perfect, all-powerful, all-knowing Creator of the universe, who continues to rule in his creation today.[4]

Scientists estimate that a single cup of coffee contains enough moisture to blanket an entire neighborhood with fog fifty feet thick. How small an amount of water—spread out so thinly—can hinder our vision almost completely![5] Likewise a little education can cloud our vision. Problems and challenges can do the same. When we possess a fog-focus, we are not God-focused.

## A Flat on the Wheel of Fortune

Would you tell me "no" if I asked if you were a superstitious person? How then would you do on this superstition indicator?

- ☐ Do you have a "good luck" article of clothing that you must wear on game day?
- ☐ Do you have favorite lucky numbers you would play if you were ever in a position to gamble?
- ☐ Have you ever knocked on wood after speaking of fortunate occurrences?
- ☐ Is the number thirteen just like any other number to you, even if it is Friday the thirteenth?
- ☐ Have you ever felt uneasy about walking under a ladder, worried about a black cat crossing your path, been concerned about breaking a mirror, thrown spilt salt over your shoulder, or kissed under mistletoe?

By nature, we all are superstitious to some degree. Even those of us who don't consider ourselves superstitious will often wish others, "Good luck!" We have become conditioned to think that when something good happens, it's good luck, and when something bad happens—or good things fail to happen—it's simply bad luck. While we don't pray, "God, please protect me from black cats, leaning ladders, and broken mirrors," we may ask God to let us win the lottery or the sweepstakes. We speak of odd "coincidences" and "chance" meetings. Our speech and actions might cause some to believe we have more confidence in rubbing a rabbit's foot than in praying to God.

Jabez wasn't counting on good luck in his praying. His prayer did not reflect a belief in coincidences—only in divine control, divine intervention, and divine appointments. Jabez was asking for

God to bring him a breakthrough—a blessing. Living, as Jabez did, by faith has sure God-results because its foundation is the Word of God. Living by chance can make no such claim.

If Jabez—whose name means "pain" or "sorrow"—had been relying on Lady Luck, then prior to God's blessing him, he would have been considered jinxed, a sorry, bad luck loser. But he was far from a flat on fate's wheel of fortune. He was a child of God in whose life the heavenly Father operated and whose faith allowed him to trust in the unseen rather than in appearances. He well understood that if anything good was going to happen in his life, God would have to be in the middle of it. Unlike many of his day, he did not turn to the pagan gods or superstition to improve his fate, but counted on God's control of his life and circumstances.

The Internet contains many websites and electronic bulletin boards that deal with superstition. I visited one of these sites where a guy named Norm was seeking advice about a magazine article on superstition. He wrote, "As an example of superstition the magazine mentions a person who opens the Bible at random and reads the first text he sees, and believes that it gives him the counsel he needs at the moment."

Julie posted the response, "Actually Norm this method of reading the scriptures really works. Leave out the literalism, open your mind and meditate."

Norm asked, "What do you mean 'works'?"

"You open a page, it's text there," Julie answered, "You can read it, and unless you happen to open 1 Chronicles, it's probably something that might be somewhat interesting."[6]

I call this method of seeking divine direction the "flop, stop, and drop" approach. You just flop open your Bible, stop where your finger goes, drop your eyes to the verse on which your finger rests, and presto! You have an IM—Instant Message from God. This superstitious approach can be dangerous. What if the first verse you pinpointed was the verse about Judas's fate: "Then he went away and hanged himself"?[7] Then you flop, stop, and drop on

> ■
> The prayer of Jabez is not a superstitious chant to be recited or a supernatural word-wand to be waved to keep away bad things.
> ■

the words of Jesus, "Go and do likewise."[8] And then you flip and plop your finger on the verse: "What you are about to do, do quickly."[9] You will need "good luck" with this kind of approach. Note to Norm and Julie: Turning to 1 Chronicles—especially 1 Chronicles 4:9–10, where the prayer of Jabez is found—can revolutionize your life.

The universe is not governed by an impersonal fate or luck, but by a personal God. Nothing "just happens." God has a plan for our lives that has nothing to do with luck. His guiding and controlling hand can be seen in the events of our lives—day in and day out—causing things to work together for the good for those who love him.[10] James 1:17 reminds us: "Every good and perfect gift is from above, coming down from the Father of the heavenly lights, who does not change like shifting shadows."

The prayer of Jabez is not a superstitious chant to be recited or a supernatural word-wand to be waved to keep away bad things. For a Christian, even bad things can be God's hidden mega-blessings. What appears to be bad luck may be God's doing something that will bring about the greatest opportunity for growth you have ever experienced spiritually.

## More Than a Blip on Your Spiritual Radar Screen

The weather had been suspect all day; yet, those suspicions didn't become reality until I was five minutes into my message at a church in another state. As soon as I began preaching on the reality of heaven and hell, I noticed several leaders in the congregation getting up, going outside, coming back in, and whispering to the pastor. Trying not to allow myself to be perturbed with all the commotion, I focused even more intently on describing the joys of heaven and the reality of hell. It was then their pastor walked up to the pulpit and said to me, "Excuse me, I need to say something."

My first thought was, *So help me, if that he announces that a little red Honda Accord with license numbers BR–549 has its lights on, I'm going to pull out his tongue in Jesus' name and pray for the battery in the little car to already be dead.*

That was not the case as the pastor announced, "Doppler radar indicates that there is a tornado heading our way. Please exit the sanctuary and go quickly into safer parts of the building." For a moment the people hesitated and looked at me as if it was my fault, as if I had conjured up the wrath of the devil and now he's going to get us through a twister. At that point the sirens in town began blaring at deafening decibels, and the people scurried to safety.

After a short time, the threat had passed. So we filed back into the sanctuary and resumed the worship service. We had been kept safe by God, who displayed his might and power in a number of ways that evening, perhaps the most significant being our seeing a number of people pray to become Christians—perhaps after having hell scared out of them!

The radar, short for "Radio Detection And Ranging," had detected the tornado before human eyes could see it. Radar, however, was not originally invented to detect the weather, but to give advance warning of Nazi air strikes during World War II. Early users noticed that when it rained, the radar screens would be covered in a gray haze. Recognizing this potential to forecast weather, inventors developed the predecessor to today's Doppler radar.[11] What an incredible instrument radar is—as it warns us to prepare and be on the look-out.

God has designed a spiritual radar that is built into, and operating in, the lives of believers who consistently walk in his will following his plan. His spiritual radar goes beyond the National Weather Service warning about a tornado or a thunderstorm, or the local TV weatherman announcing on Christmas Eve that Santa Claus has been spotted on radar. God's spiritual radar is powered by prayer. While we won't have a screen showing blips and UFOs (Unidentified Faith Objects), we will have an inner system that picks up those things that are of God and not of God. This spiritual radar is useful for spotting divine activity and divine appointments as they are happening.

As budding spiritual meteorologists we should learn to recognize such "divine appointments" on our radar screens. They appear as events, often unplanned, when a particular person or circumstance comes across our path, and we are presented with an opportunity to impact or bless someone for God. We should pray for such occasions and expect them regularly.

> ■
> **This spiritual radar is useful for spotting divine activity and divine appointments.**
> ■

That's part of what makes the Christian life so exciting. Contrast praying and being on the lookout for divine appointments with keeping our fingers crossed for a streak of good luck or being surprised by a strange coincidence. Divine appointments are heavenly orchestrated setups as opposed to luck's accidental fortune or coincidental chance. Toss out the four-leaf clover, the crystal ball, and the lucky dice! Power up the spiritual Doppler radar and pray for divine activity to appear on the screen.

## "Coincidences" Happen When We Pray

*The Prayer Experiment* will definitely help you to experience divine appointments in your daily routine as it activates your spiritual radar. Praying this prayer is an effective way of asking God to increase spiritual activity in your life and orchestrate events that will cause people to be directed across your path. The Lord is able to create those circumstances in others' lives so that they are drawn to you as you desire to be used of God to impact the world. William Temple, a man accustomed to praying hours daily, replied to his critics who regarded answered prayer as no more than coincidences: "When I pray, coincidences happen; when I don't, they don't."[12]

Acts 16 records the apostle Paul's "Macedonian call" as he set out for Asia on a missionary journey, yet ran into a roadblock. Satan was not thwarting his zealous efforts, but God was redirecting him to another place, Macedonia. Paul's responding "yes" to God allowed him to encounter Lydia, a praying and searching woman on the side of the river bank in Philippi. As far as Scripture records, she became the first convert to Christianity in Europe. Coincidence? Happenstance? Twist of fate? No way! God orchestrated this redirection in answer to Lydia's prayer and to Paul's seeking to listen to God's voice. The world has never been the same since this divine appointment. Can such amazing appointments happen today? Of course, they can! God has not changed. Has our faith? We must have the faith of Lydia and Paul if we want to see God engineer such opportunities.

Early in the 1900s missionary-evangelist Duncan Campbell attended a convention service in Northern Ireland, when the Holy Spirit suddenly impressed on him the name of the little island of Berneray off the coast of Harris. This recurred three times in the next several minutes. Duncan had never touched foot on the island before, had never corresponded with anyone, and knew no one on the island; yet, he immediately left the service, gathered his things from the hotel, and left for the airport.

> When he reached Berneray, he found that a local elder had prayed all night for revival and that God had told him he would send Duncan Campbell and work through him. The elder had been so sure of God's work that he had already sent word around the island and had announced a service for a few hours after Duncan had stepped on the shore. [The announcement came prior to Campbell's arrival—and prior to the elder's knowledge of Campbell's coming to the island.]
>
> On the third or fourth evening as the people were leaving the church, the Holy Spirit suddenly fell upon them as they reached the gate. No one could move—so mightily were they arrested by the Spirit's power and a tremendous sense

of the presence of God. Duncan called them back into the building, and a mighty movement of God began. All over the island lives were shaken and transformed. Twenty years later Campbell was told that those converted in the revival were still walking with the Lord.[13]

Such divine appointments are still possible today.

God is willing and at work all around you. Prayer helps you to pick up his mighty workings on your spiritual radar screen. Praying the prayer of Jabez can make you more sensitive to God's appointments in your life. Søren Kierkegaard once remarked, "Prayer does not change God, but changes him who prays." Prayer can transform you into a more aware and useful servant of God, better equipped to discern whether the voice inside of you telling you to call someone, to go see someone, to go somewhere is the voice of Thee (God), Me (you), or He (Satan). Through prayer, you will become more willing to respond to God's prompting in your life. Otherwise, without prayer, many of the God-opportunities that come your way will look a lot like aggravating interruptions and mere coincidences.

> ■
> **Prayer is not conquering God's reluctance, but taking hold of God's willingness.**
> —PHILLIP BROOKS
> ■

## Living in a Clock-eyed World

"Time's up."
"Don't waste my time."
"Time out."
"Just killing time."
"Time is money."
"Lost track of time."
"Got time in a bottle."
"What time is it?"

"Time flies even when you're having fun"—or as one frog said, "Time's fun when you're having flies."[14] Our culture is hyper-time-conscious. We meticulously maintain calendars, make detailed schedules to manage blocks of time, measure accomplishments by how well the allotted time segments are used, take appointments seriously, and see promptness as a virtue. We are frustrated when a task takes longer than planned and despise running behind schedule. In fact—according to Zig Ziglar—the average person looks at his or her watch three hundred times a day. (Yet, have you noticed that, when asked the time, most cannot tell you what time it is?)

Contrast our time-conscious approach to living out our days to that of the Indonesian culture. "Wasting time" is a foreign concept as little effort is made to manage the flow of time. "Morning," "noon," "afternoon," and "evening" adequately divide the day. Indonesians explain to Westerners that they live in "rubber time." Appointments, when made, are vague, provisional indications of intention. Harmonious interaction with other people in a flexible, spontaneous, unstructured context is the norm they seek as they focus more on interpersonal skills than on time management principles.[15]

I guess you could label me as a be-on-time-always-keep-an-appointment person. That would make me tend toward the intolerant side of balance. I struggle to keep a smile when someone walks into a scheduled appointment twenty-five minutes late or doesn't bother to show up at all. My problem is filling my schedule so full that I am in a constant race with the clock to keep all these appointments. Such a hectic schedule leaves little time for divine interruptions. With my time-conscious tendencies, I find it absolutely essential to seek to live in an atmosphere of prayer, so that I might be able to sort out the "must do's" from the "should do's," the busyness from the God-appointments.

## Keeping Divine Appointments

When a divine appointment comes your way, you will either seize the moment or blow it. Some of these opportunities only come once and don't last long. Have you ever missed a doctor's appointment? You may have just said to yourself, "Oh well, I'll do better next time," but you may have thought differently when you received a bill for the missed appointment. Missed appointments can be costly—just ask someone who has missed an appointment in court. When you miss a divine appointment, it could cost someone their opportunity to encounter God's offer of salvation, or it could make you miss a great blessing from God. It all boils down to obedience: You must pray and then act on what God has placed on your heart to do.

God undertakes responsibility to work out all the details and the "hows." We are responsible to do as he directs us. He will not do what only he can do until we do all God tells us to do. We can easily get frustrated trying to make sense out of what God is doing. Trust him and his guidance. Sometimes it might not look feasible on paper and may defy understanding. It may not seem logical or reasonable. We may just have a gnawing feeling that we should do something. Perhaps, the Lord has placed a person on our heart and impresses us to pray for this person, go by their home, or write them a note of encouragement. The Lord may even direct us to say or do something for a total stranger.

As a student at Ouachita Baptist University, I often made the one-hour trip to downtown Little Rock to visit a huge Christian bookstore. One day as I was lusting after all the books I wanted, I noticed an older man staring at me. He engaged me in a conversation about books. I could tell this man knew a great deal about Christian writing. At the end of our conversation he said to me, "If you will take me home, I will give you something." Even though that was twenty years ago and I felt safer then about transporting a stranger than I do today, I was still suspect of having this total stranger in my car and going somewhere with him. The inner calm voice of the Holy Spirit said to me, "Go with him. It's all right." I told the gentleman I would be glad to take him home.

This was, no doubt, a divine appointment because as I followed him into his modest apartment near the state capitol, he told mc he had been an editor for the Anchor Bible commentary series and was now going blind. He showed me a biblical library that made me salivate. I will never forget his next words: "God told me to give you my library."

I couldn't believe it. Wow! I asked, "Sir, are you sure?"

He was sure. Because of immediate obedience to God's voice, I learned a great lesson, made a wonderful friend, and now to this day use the books out of his library. I cannot tell you the number of times I have looked back on other incidences that I missed because, at the time, I did not realize they were divine appointments.

## Setbacks May Be Setups

"This is the IRS. Your audit is set up for next month."

"We have found a spot on your x-rays."

"You have cancer."

"You didn't qualify for the loan."

"You can't have a baby."

"The fire burned it all."

"It's a lot worse than we thought."

"I'm sorry. You didn't make the team."

"Here is your pink slip. We are downsizing."

"I'm leaving. I want a divorce."

"The tests on your unborn child look suspicious."

"It's not a carburetor problem. Your whole engine is shot."

"This is not covered by your insurance as it's a preexisting condition."

"You have insufficient funds in your account."

Setbacks—we all have them. They're part of life. When we experience setbacks, we may assume that it's the devil who caused them. Other times, especially when we've been hit hard, we may blame God. "God, why did you allow this to happen? Why don't you do something? Are you punishing me?" Too often we fail to view setbacks as divine setups—opportunities masked to look like hopeless situations that are, in reality, agents for our spiritual growth and occasions for God to be exalted. Setbacks are required curriculum in God's university, not electives. "Setbacks 101" can teach us things that we cannot learn in "Spiritual Mountaintop 101."

As a teenager, I went with a church group on a mission trip to Pennsylvania. We stayed overnight at a church—the females upstairs and the guys in the basement. In the middle of the night the sewer backed up—you got it—in the basement! The next morning Roto-Rooter was called. Soon their man fixed the problem, but I, along with my friends, were still pouting. Such setbacks should never happen to students on a mission trip—and I told God so! Soon, however, my committed spirit of pouting turned into positive joy as I seized an opportunity God himself had orchestrated.

It began when I struck up a conversation with the Roto-Rooter man. I followed him out to his truck as he was leaving and began talking about his relationship to Christ. He looked at me and said, "You know, since I've gotten back from Vietnam I have been searching for something." There beside his white van with its red and blue lettering, I witnessed to him, and the Roto-Rooter guy gave his heart to Jesus Christ. Now, you tell me, was the sewer's backing up worth it? Oh yes, it turned out to be a divine setup. It made me want to pray, "Lord, do it again! But next time, could you let it be a leak in the fresh water pipe?"

The apostle Paul's experience of being stuck in a place called Troas (Acts 16) turned out to be a divine setup. Even though initially it looked like a setback, some eternally significant things happened. Not only did it lead to the conversion of Lydia, but at Troas Paul met Dr. Luke, the man who would be a constant companion, dear friend, great encourager, and personal physician on his missionary journeys—and the man who penned the books of Luke and Acts.

You may discover while praying the prayer of Jabez that you are confronted with what appears to be a setback. Don't believe it! Hang on. Allow God to do what only he can do. If you fail to cooperate with him, you may be walking away from the greatest spiritual blessing that may be right around the corner.

We faced this as a church when the dream of building a needed worship center died—even though we were faithfully praying the prayer of Jabez. From all outward appearances it appeared to be a huge setback; yet, within a month we saw one of the greatest setups by God we could have ever imagined as a church. The setback turned setup as God led us to buy a mall. Today, we would not exchange any building on earth for what God has taught us through a vacated mall.

> If you fail to cooperate with God, you may be walking away from the greatest spiritual blessing that may be right around the corner.

Rewind and replay the following in your mind: "Our God is a turn-it-around God." I'm not suggesting that everything that happens can be labeled as "God did it"; however, I am standing on a promise that no matter what happens, God will in some way, somehow, work through it in such a way as to bring some good out of it (Rom. 8:28). That's why any situation can be a divine setup for something to happen in our lives that will change our lives—or someone else's—forever.

A young man took a shortcut home late one night through the cemetery and fell in an open grave. He called and then tried to climb out—all to no avail. No one was around to hear his cries or lend him a hand. So, he settled down for the night in a corner of the darkened grave to await morning. A short time later another person came the same route through the cemetery, taking the same shortcut home, and fell into the same grave. He started clawing and shouting and trying to get out just as the first man had done. Suddenly, the second fellow heard a voice out of the dark corner of the grave saying, "You can't get out of here." But guess what—he did succeed in climbing out![16] Setbacks often motivate us to see beyond the limits and view the opportunities for change; however, it doesn't always happen on our timetable.

## God Standard Time

God's timing is perfect . . . never early, never late, even if it's 11:59 before he comes through. Remember the saying that timing is everything? Well, for Christians, God's timing is everything—but, oh, how this stretches our faith to the limit! Jabez must have wondered, "Will God ever come through? Will the pain ever end? Will I ever know any of God's blessings in my life?" The Bible says, "God granted his request" (1 Chron. 4:10b), but it was done on God's Standard Time.

Greenwich, a borough in London, England, has been the basis for standard time, called "Greenwich Time." Now there is a new universal time—"Internet Time"—based on the Swatch Beat, the revolutionary new unit of time that makes obsolete all time zones. The Swatch Beat divides up the virtual and real day into 1000 "beats." One Swatch beat is the equivalent of 1 minute 26.4 seconds. That means that 12 noon in the former system is the equivalent of @500 Swatch beats. A day in Internet Time begins at BMT (@000 Swatch beats). Inaugurated on October 23, 1998, Internet Time is the same all over the world, be it night or day. The meridian is marked for all to see on the façade of the Swatch International headquarters in Biel, Switzerland.[17]

There is yet another standard, a more eternal standard, a standard by which you must measure your life: "God Standard Time." God's timing is everything. The birth of Jesus stands as the greatest example of God's precision timing.

> But when the time had fully come, God sent his Son, born of a woman, born under law, to redeem those under law, that we might receive the full rights of sons.
>
> —GALATIANS 4:4

Jesus broke through the world's time zone to arrive at Destination Earth at exactly the right year, month, day, hour, minute, second, and micro-second. He came at a time when the Roman Empire had constructed good roads, assuring that the Good News of Jesus

Christ could travel faster to the farthest corners of the vast empire. By that time most people knew the Greek language, providing a vehicle to communicate the New Testament message to the masses. Christ arrived at a time when the world was spiritually bankrupt, searching for something beyond what they had experienced.

Think about the significance of God's perfect timing. He causes events to happen at just the right moment, even though it often does not seem fast enough for us. In his time, God Standard Time, he acted, intervened, and brought the answer to a world lost and in need. Right where we are, as we surrender to him, he will do it again in our situations. We bear the responsibility to set our lives by his clock rather than by the time on our watches and clocks.

In order to operate on God Standard Time instead of Me Central Time, we must—in faith—do at least three things:

- We must believe that God is at work even when it seems like he isn't. God isn't just idly sitting by doing nothing about our situation as we cry out to him in believing prayer.
- We must believe that God is able to work in our lives. The all-powerful God will work in our lives as we faithfully meet the conditions of his promises given in his Word.
- We must hang on and allow God to come through for us in his perfect time, rather than getting frustrated, taking matters into our own hands, or rushing ahead of God.

David wrote, "Do not be like the horse or the mule, which have no understanding" (Ps. 32:9). This verse is speaking of our need for divine guidance. Horses tend to run ahead while mules tend to lag behind. We must not run ahead of God or lag behind in following his will, but rather should wait to act according to his timing. We must be ready to seize the moment when it comes; otherwise, we may face unnecessary troubles if we don't operate on God Standard Time.

I am fascinated with E-Bay, a site on the Internet—especially the auctioning and buying process. Timing is everything. The seller can post an item to be sold over the course of a set number of days; yet, it is what transpires in the final few minutes that counts. Astute buyers will watch—or use computer software that will do it for them—the countdown clock until there is only five minutes or less left for bidding. Then the sharking process begins. Like sharks circling, waiting for a potential kill, interested buyers patiently wait until almost all the time elapsed; then they go in for the kill by posting what they hope will be the winning bid.

God doesn't operate on the E-Bay system, and you should not either. As you commit to praying the prayer of Jabez, you will become acutely aware of the sense of God's timing in your life. Don't wait until the last minute to post your requests; instead, do your bidding with God in consistent, persistent prayer. You may realize a life-changing divine appointment as you pray the prayer of Jabez.

Pause now. Pray the prayer of Jabez; however, before you do:

1. Ask God to give you a divine appointment today. Begin now to anticipate one.
2. Seek God's wisdom in approaching any setback that may be a divine setup for a blessing.
3. Pause to consider each word in this prayer, realizing it is not simply a recitation of words, but a seeking of God's work and blessing in your life through prayer.

> Lord, bless me indeed. . .
> Do something so big in my life that it is obviously from you.
> Increase my influence and opportunities for you,
> And give me a sense of your continual presence and direction.
> Protect me, and keep me from falling into Satan's traps. Amen.

If you want to discover how to be in a place where God shows up, you may want to continue the experiment.

# ■ 9 ■

# When God Shows Up

*Give me a sense of your continual presence*
*and direction.*

Arriving at the T. D. Waterhouse Centre in the predawn hours gave ticket-mongers only a random chance at being selected in a lottery. What award awaited the winners? The privilege of standing in line at the box office for the possible purchase of tickets for the Orlando concert of 'N Sync. Tickets for this much-anticipated event were sold out in less than thirty minutes, and many of those left standing in line went home empty-handed. Across the country this frantic scene is repeated in venue after venue, wherever this megapopular singing group is slated to appear.

Many might look at this and wonder why people would subject themselves to this kind of anguish. Tens of thousands do it for the sheer opportunity to be present where their favorite band will perform. They are willing to do whatever it takes, be wherever and whenever, and follow whosoever's rules in order to have the privilege of being there when the group shows up. But when the concert is over, those who held the cherished tickets will be left with only short-term memories and outdated souvenirs to remind them of their time in the presence of their idols.

I have often thought about the impact that it would have on the world if Christians displayed this same sort of excitement about

God's showing up in church services and gatherings across the nation. About the time I get despondent over how casual we, as Christians, can be concerning our corporate worship experiences, I quickly remember that even Christ's disciples were not willing to stay awake in the predawn hours to watch and pray for Jesus when he so desperately needed their enthusiastic support for his earthly ministry. This seems to be an age-old problem. I wonder if there are many Christians today who would be willing to do whatever, whenever, and wherever so that they can enjoy the "whosoever" benefits of experiencing the very presence of God. Unlike 'N Sync, Ricky Martin, or Garth Brooks showing up for a concert, when God "shows up" the impact is far greater in potential benefits that will last eternally.

### Looking for God? I Can't Even Find Elvis!

If you've been looking for Elvis, there's a product that may help you. "The Elvis Detector" is guaranteed to detect the presence of "The King" should he come in or near your computer's monitor. Or if you are a part of the crowd who believes that "The King" will show up somewhere sometime, you can purchase "The Official Elvis Scanner," which promises to provide visual proof (à la satellite video cameras) of Elvis's presence within a twenty-mile radius of the area being scanned. I know I can sleep better at night since these inventions have come on the market. No longer will I need to do my 2 A.M. and 4 A.M. Elvis-vigils on the sixth Saturday of every month for the Central Florida Chapter of "The King Will Show Sooner or Later Club"! Now I can be reassured and fully rested to preach on Sundays that follow.

> ■
>
> Who will lead us out of this spiritual vacuum?
>
> —HILLARY RODHAM CLINTON[2]
>
> ■

As ridiculous as all of this is, stories still abound about Elvis's appearances—everywhere: in a small Mississippi town where he supports the residents in exchange for their keeping his presence a secret, at gas stations where he gladly waits on customers, at wedding receptions where he's been seen performing, and even back at Graceland where he secretly resides on the second floor.[1]

And while some people may still be looking for Elvis, others have activated their search engines looking for something that will give them answers to their problems and make some kind of sense out of their lives. There is a spiritual emptiness—a God-shaped vacuum—in their lives that they are trying desperately to fill. As they do, they all too often look for God in all the wrong places.

> *CNN Report*
> *February 27, 1997*
> *Tampa, Florida*
>
> *If you're looking for God, Sumter County, Florida, might be a good place to start. At least that's what the folks at American Family Publishers seem to think. The company earlier this month mailed a sweepstakes notice addressed to "God" to a church in Bushnell, about 60 miles north of Tampa. The message: "God is a finalist for the $11 million top prize."*
>
> *"God, we've been searching for you," American Family wrote in the letter received by the Bushnell Assembly of God. If God were to win, the letter stated, "What an incredible fortune there would be for God!" according to the Sumter County Times, which first reported the divine mix-up. "Could you imagine the looks you'd get from neighbors? But don't just sit there, God." Church pastor Bill Brack said, "I always thought he lived here, but I didn't actually know."[3]*

American Family Publishers is not alone in their search for God. I cannot begin to describe the hopeless pain and the devastating emptiness I, as a pastor, have seen on the faces of distraught individuals who have desperately sought to fill the vacuum in their lives by far less humorous means—by sniffing a white powder, putting a needle in their arms, or trying to find happiness in a bottle. My heart has been gripped time and time again as I counseled someone who was trying to make some sense of the void left in his or her life from a meaningless happy hour rendezvous or "innocent" flirtation-turned-affair. Hearing the successful businessperson describe emptiness at the top of the ladder has confirmed in my mind the foolishness of seeking for fulfillment in power or possessions. Unfortunately, Christianity is often the last resort instead of the first choice in filling the hole in souls of many seekers.

The supernatural and paranormal—not necessary in the realms of Christianity—does, however, fascinate and draw people. In his thought-provoking book *High Tech, High Touch*, John Naisbitt addresses this fascination. "People are trying to find something higher, deeper, greater, more profound. Something that unites them with something bigger than just who they are."[4] An ordinary glass-paneled office building overlooking a parking lot in Clearwater, Florida, became a shrine when late in 1996 some palm trees in front of the building were cut down. Appearing on eleven glass panels was a rainbow-colored image that some say had an uncanny resemblance to the Virgin Mary. Initially as many as eighty thousand people a day flocked to see this apparent miracle.[5]

An inordinate number of reports circulate worldwide recounting "supernatural signs and miracles": icons that weep and bleed, apparitions of Jesus in the night sky, a nun who claims Jesus has met with her every Thursday since 1987, and healing waters from a well in Tlacote, Mexico, that was accidentally discovered when a sick dog recovered soon after drinking some of it.[6]

But not only do the unchurched search. Half of the adults who regularly attend church services admit that they haven't experienced God's presence at any time during the past year.[7] Their search engine is still running as they seek what they do not normally experience in worship: an awareness of God's presence. When asked if it is unusual to experience his presence at a church worship service, 71 percent of respondents to a Barna Group survey indicated they never experience God's presence, 2 percent rarely, and only 8 percent sometimes (see Fig. 9.1).[8]

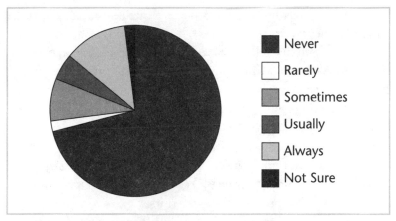

*Fig. 9.1—Experience of God's Presence in Church*

## Jolt Cola Generation

The infomercial offers real-life testimonials telling how a microwave dryer can dramatically reduce the time needed for this household chore. In an instant you can dry that article of clothing you forgot to launder—all with more energy efficiency and cost effectiveness than former clothes dryers. Think about the possibilities: While drying your jeans, you can pop a packet of Orville Redenbacher in one pocket and a Jenny Craig meal-in-a-box in the other. In just two minutes and forty seconds, with the microwave dryer on Power 7, you can have dry jeans, delicious popcorn, and a slimmer you! Sounds too good to be true? It is.

We are suckers for easy answers, crying out for quick fixes to complex problems and Band-Aid solutions for deep emotional injuries. Witness our phenomenal demand for miracle drugs, overnight-success vitamins, fast-yet-healthy food, self-help books, and motivational seminars that promise a few easy steps to overcoming all of life's problems. The American Academy of Cosmetic Surgery, the nation's largest organization representing cosmetic surgeons, reports there has been a 1,279 percent increase in tummy tucks, a 606 percent increase in facelifts, an 837 percent increase in liposuction, and a 375 percent increase in hair implants, all within the last decade.[9]

The instant fix only creates a desire for gotta-have-more. Forty-three-year-old Cindy Jackson, although born in the United States, declares herself to be "made in Britain." She has endured twenty-nine surgeries in the United Kingdom over the last decade to transform herself from what she saw as a plain-Jane farm girl to a beautiful Barbie look-alike. All of these appearance-altering operations are not enough for this Mensa member. Cindy plans on having more plastic surgery because the combo of beauty and brains are not enough to satisfy her thirst.[10]

Ours could be labeled the "Jolt Cola Generation" because we crave that immediate surge of energy, happiness, and answers. Two college students were so "overcome with the power of Jolt" (their own words) that they created their own *Jolt Drinker's Anthem* to tout this espresso of soft drinks:

> Jolt is great. This I mean.
> It loads your brain with sweet caffeine.
> Pick some up at your local store.
> I guarantee you'll be back for more.
>
> Colas come and colas go,
> But godly Jolt will ever flow.
> Those fools drinking Pepsi, Coke, and other
> Should take up their drinks and go crying to mother.
>
> If a test is tomorrow and you need to cram,
> Slam down a Jolt and pass that exam!
> I wouldn't laugh at the Almighty Drink.
> You might need this cola more than you think.[11]

"Almighty" Jolt Cola and other soft drinks are far from the only things dispensed in vending machines around the world.[12] The list of items sold in vending machines is limitless and is indicative of the world market's demand for quick and easy. I believe sometimes we view religion as a vending machine product.

If we can just pray a prayer, name and claim what we desire, drop some quarters in God's vending machine, then we can get the instant spiritual high we desire. We sing, "Give me that vending machine religion . . . it's good enough for me."

## Cafeteria Christianity

The current religious climate might be characterized as "Cafeteria Christianity," where people pick and choose what they want rather than what they need. This pick-and-choose approach to faith—the desire to take from it "all that is wonderful and good"—will likely continue in this new century. Many predict the same consumeristic and experiential approach popularized via Eastern mysticism will be brought to the traditional spiritual teachings of the West.[13] Though most Americans believe in God, a *Newsweek* poll estimated that only 60 percent "think a person needs to believe in God in order to experience the sacred."[14]

Thirsty souls need more than vending machine beverages and cafeteria lines to satisfy their insatiable longings. The world is crying out: "Can God.com connect me with the supernatural?" In an attempt to make a high-speed modem connection with God, they almost frantically plead, "Is there some seminar I can attend, some place I can go, some trip I can take, some tape to which I can listen, some magic

■

**SOLD IN VENDING MACHINES**
Underwear, blue jeans, pajamas, computer software, inkjet cartridges, CDs, raw eggs, sushi, fresh steaks, dried squid, live shrimp, emu, bread, peeled fresh fruit, pizza, French fries, comic books, business cards, worms, frogs, leeches, beetles, watches, flower arrangements, poetry, paintings, sculpture, gasoline, video rentals, tennis balls, cellular phones, insurance, hunting permits, temporary tattoos, binoculars, super glue, pet shampoo, snow globes, Bibles, marijuana, holy water, pet rocks, and air.

■

words I can recite, or just somebody—anybody—who can put me in touch with God?"

This kind of desperate search can prove negative when it fails to cause the seeker to log onto real Christianity. Tragically, too many go to dangerous spiritual sites when searching out the supernatural. They mistake religious fluff for authentic faith. Many contradictory paths do not lead to the one true God. Yet searches can carry potential for positive results when Christians get "online" with their lives and witness and begin sharing the life-transforming message of the Gospel to those whose search engines are on. What a tremendous opportunity exists for authentic revival in this spiritually inquisitive age.

> ■
> The world is crying out: "Can God.com connect me with the supernatural?"
> ■

Jabez, too, was searching for something; yet, he didn't go for the quick-fix. Instead, he went for the real thing, seeking for the sense of the presence of God in his daily life. He cried out, "Let your hand be with me" (1 Chron. 4:10). While God was with Jabez at all times, Jabez desired the sense and manifestation of God's presence in his life. More than a warm, fuzzy feeling, Jabez wanted to live in the reality of God's presence. When that is experienced, no other substitute will ever do. Sensing God's presence is based on saying "yes" to God. The actual presence of God, however, is God's responsibility—whether one feels it or not.

Jabez needed for God to show up so he could face the challenges of life, have a greater impact for God, and overcome Satan's strategies on his faith. He simply wanted to live in the reality that God has shown up. He was praying, "God show me the way. God, I'm stopping to ask you for directions." (This was quite a miracle for a man!) He handed God the remote control of his life, a prerequisite for God to show up. His prayer experiment worked— not overnight, not at Instant-Messaging speed—but it worked. It can, too, for others with their search engines on.

## God, Just Dew It!

Pastor and friend O. S. Hawkins asks the question, "Does dew rise from the ground or fall from the sky?" It does neither. Surprised? When the atmospheric conditions are right, it just shows up. During clear, calm nights after sunny, warm days, the ground radiates back to the atmosphere its heat stored from the daytime. The air on the ground will cool off rapidly. If the air is calm and moist enough, it will be cooled by contact with the ground, reach its condensation point, and form dew on plants, grass, and other objects.[15] When the spiritual atmospheric conditions are right, God "shows up." God promised: "I will be like the dew unto Israel" (Hosea 14:5). As Christians, we too must pray, "God, dew it again."

*Touched by an Angel*, a popular CBS television series, has had a significant—albeit eschewed—impact on American popular thinking concerning spiritual matters. A much greater impact, however, occurs when people are "touched by an atmosphere" where God shows up. Jesus told his followers, "For where two or three come together in my name, there am I with them" (Matt. 18:20). This verse has been a popular proof-text for Christians claiming God's presence, just because two or three of them decide to get together. However, this is not an automatic promise of a genie offered unconditionally to everyone when they rub the magic lamp of prayer. We need to examine the necessary conditions for Jesus' showing up.

First, two or three Christians must meet "to do God." This is far more than our meeting "to do lunch." Instead, we should purpose to encounter or worship God in a genuine way. As part of his family, we can be certain our heavenly Father will show up as we fulfill his conditions.

The second necessary condition for Jesus' showing up is that we must gather "in his name." This means that when we meet to worship under the authoritative name of Jesus Christ, we should be ready to hear from God, obey, and do whatever our Lord asks. Jesus' name is synonymous with his person, his presence, and his power. His name is the "name above every name" at which "every knee should bow" (Phil. 2:9–10) and the name by which we are saved (Acts 4:12; Rom. 10:13).

We should...
      bless
        praise
          exalt
            magnify
              glorify
                rejoice
                  exult in
                    thank
                      hallow
                        fear
                    love
                      remember
                  proclaim
                declare
            wait on
          walk in
        desire
      seek...
            the name of our Lord.[16]

When we seek to encounter God, we place our feet in another world as we leave behind the secular and step into the sacred. When we seek to gather in his name, therefore, we cannot just wake up, clean up, get up, eat up, dress up, go up, tell the world to "shut up," blow up, turn up, and expect God to show up. Our expectations must be tuned to—and our hearts prepared to—encounter the One who is Wholly Other and Holy Other. We must be prepared to leave behind our selfish pursuits and seek God with all of our hearts.

In the book *Shopping For Faith*, a young accountant from Pittsburgh shares, "If all the gospel of Jesus Christ is going to do is change my Sunday schedule, then I'm not interested. I want something that is going to change my finances, my sex life, the way I work, the way I keep my house, and the way I fix my yard."[17] People come with an agenda to church. If the worship experience there does not meet their expectations, they may be like the person William Hendricks quotes in his book *Exit Interviews*: "You know what I would rather do? Sleep, read my Sunday paper. Oh, I love reading my paper on Sunday morning. I hate anything to interrupt that. And I gotta tell you ... church wasn't giving it to me, not to get me away from my paper on Sunday morning."[18]

Our thinking must change if we are truly to encounter God in our time of corporate—as well as private—worship. God doesn't have to meet our conditions; we have to meet his conditions if we want him to "show up." We must tune our hearts to receive him. We must practice the presence of God. Centuries ago, Brother Lawrence wrote of this practice:

> I know a person who for forty years has practiced the presence of God intellectually, but gives it several other names. Sometimes he calls it a simple act or a clear and distinct knowledge of God. At other times an indistinct vision or a loving gaze, a sense of God. Still other times he calls it a waiting on God, a silent conversation with God, trust in God, the life and peace of the soul. Finally this person told me that all of these [are] expressions for the presence of God. By force of habit and by frequently calling his mind to the presence of God, he has developed such a habit that soon as he is free from his external affairs—and even often while he is immersed in them—the very heart of his soul, with no effort on his part, is raised up above all things and stays suspended and held there in God.[19]

## The Upstairs Came Down

A young boy from a small rural area visited a large city and took his first elevator ride. Attempting to describe the experience to his mother, he said, "I got into this little room and the upstairs came down!"[20] That boy's description of an elevator ride is also a wonderful definition of prayer. Heaven comes down when Christians get serious about talking and listening to God.

"The whole reason why we pray," says J. C. Ryle, "is to be united into the vision and contemplation of him to whom we pray." Here's our family secret: When we pray to God, we encounter his presence. "Come near to God and he will come near to you" (James 4:8).

> Praying without being specific is like pulling up to a Taco Bell drive-through window and saying, "Please give me Mexican food."

Jabez is known for only one thing: He prayed. That's what it took for heaven to come down and God to show up in his life. Jabez made four targeted, specific requests of God in prayer (1 Chron. 4:10). If we fail to pray specifically, we too might miss the answer when it comes. Praying without being specific is like pulling up to a Taco Bell drive-through window and saying, "Please give me Mexican food." We might be disappointed when we don't get what we desire. Even the Chihuahua in their commercials is specific when he asks for "gooey cheese."

Over the years I have listened to many prayers—most sincere—that have been prayed on auto-pilot. If I were to compose a nonspecific, going-through-the-motions, general prayer composed of lines from rote praying, it would read: "Lord, lead, guide, and direct us. Bless the gift and the giver. Help the hungry, the hurting, and the homeless. Bless all the missionaries. Save the lost, heal the sick, and comfort all those in sorrow. Bless this meal to the nourishment of our bodies. And give us all a good day. Amen."

Jabez's specific praying must have been prayed in faith and with a right motive. He had a big faith in a big God and he dared to pray a big prayer. Faith is not just believing that God *can*—surely he can! It is the belief that he *will* when you stand on his Word. Jabez's request for more real estate obviously had a pure motive. He sincerely desired to make an impact for God—the more land, the more influence. Like the Energizer Bunny, he was persistent as he kept going, and going, and going, knocking on heaven's door. What God did for Jabez, he will do again when asked with persistent belief accompanied by proper motives.

> You do not have, because you do not ask God. When you do ask, you do not receive, because you ask with wrong motives, that you may spend what you get on your pleasures.
>
> —JAMES 4:2B–4

The praying of my congregation in Florida has dramatically changed since we have begun praying the prayer of Jabez. We have experienced a new sense of expectancy in our praying. Whenever God-sized challenges emerge, our people instinctively suggest that we "Jabez it" until the answer comes. The church has begun to view trials as an alias for opportunities—opportunities to increase our impact and influence for God. We further realize that some of God's choicest blessings come through adversity. I think all of us who have prayed the prayer of Jabez have taken on Jabez's name as God has taught us that pain and sorrow are part of what he employs to make us useable. We have further come to believe that once you start praying this prayer, it has long-lasting effects, like a time-release capsule.

"What have I gotten myself into?" is a common comment I hear from people praying this prayer. There seems to be a pattern of God's using adversity to bring blessing. Some dear friends of mine in the ministry began praying this prayer, and adversity hit them almost immediately. On the same day doctors informed them that the wife had lupus and their teenaged son had rheumatoid arthritis. As I discussed with them all that was going on in their lives, the wife looked at me and said, "I like you in spite of that prayer." I have heard those words many times before, and I empathized with them. Nevertheless, I rejoiced with them when they went on to share how God was honoring their prayer to be used by him to impact their world and how he was blessing their ministry in unbelievable ways.

## Rolling Out the Welcome Mat

Welcome mats can tell a lot about an individual. When I visit a home for the first time, I feel good about seeing a mat with a big "Welcome" pineapple (the southern symbol of hospitality), or the slogan "Backdoor friends are the best" on it. I think to myself, "These people are trying to be warm and inviting." Whenever I have visited the apartments of college students or young singles, I have gotten a kick out of seeing some of the cartoon characters that grace their mats, as well as humorous greetings, such as "Hi, I'm Mat!" and "Welcome Back, Mat!"

Some people have taken up their welcome mat and replaced it with one that is much less inviting, one of a line of mats that rudely bears the ungreetings: "Go Away," "Unwelcome," and "Don't bother me!" Some people just don't buy into the idea that the "welcome mat is always out." In fact, I learned of one man who boastfully declared, "I even cut the tail off my dog. I didn't want anything welcoming my mother-in-law."

For God to show up in your times of prayer and worship, you must roll out the welcome mat of your life. Warmly greet God as you bid him to come and inhabit your praise and acts of devotion, making certain that you possess the attitude that God is truly welcome to do anything he wants in your life. What are some welcome mats you can place before him?

Use the welcome mat of the fear of God. It is the sense of his awesomeness and majesty. He is not the "Man Upstairs" or "The Big Dodger in the Sky." Nor is God the *Star Wars'* cosmic Force that may be with you. Nor does he look or act like a cigar-smoking George Burns, who played "God" in the movie *Oh, God.* Heaven forbid that anyone should think of God as he was portrayed in the short-lived NBC animated television series, *God, the Devil, and Bob,* in which he is a beer-swigging, bearded, old hippie deity with a girlfriend. Rather, we should view and approach God with reverence, a set-apartness from everyone else, as an all holy God. The loss of the fear of God in our society may be the reason many never experience him—even in church.

Also use the welcome mat of surrender, where you wave the white flag of your life to God saying, "Lord, I surrender it all. Anything, anytime, anywhere ... the answer will always be 'yes.'" Once you have surrendered your life, he begins to point out areas in your life that are unpleasing to him. When God shows up, he shows us our sins and confronts us with conviction that demands we radically deal with it by exercising repentance.

It is not just being sorry we got caught, but being sorry over breaking the heart of God—who demonstrated the seriousness of that sin by nailing his only Son to a Roman cross. It is confessing your sin: not excusing, justifying, or blaming someone else. It is doing a 180 and turning away from your sin and walking in paths of obedience. Tolerating sin in your life guarantees that God won't show up. Sin grieves the Holy Spirit, who brings the sense of God's presence to you. You may be wondering whether this process is painful. Oh, yeah—but the results are simply out of this world.

A. W. Tozer writes of this surrender leading to a life lived in the glorious knowledge of God's presence:

> The Presence and the manifestation of the Presence are not the same. There can be one without the other. God is here when we are wholly unaware of it. He is manifest only when and as we are aware of his presence. On our part, there must be surrender to the Spirit of God, for his work is to show us the Father and the Son. If we cooperate with him in loving obedience, God will manifest himself to us, and that manifestation will be the difference between a nominal Christian life and a life radiant with the light of his face.[21]

> If we cooperate with him in loving obedience, God will manifest himself to us ... the difference between a nominal Christian life and a life radiant with the light of his face.
> —A. W. TOZER

## Scripture-Smoking Pagan

Gaylord Kambarami, the General Secretary of the Bible Society in Zimbabwe, tried to give a New Testament to a belligerent man who insisted he would roll the pages and use them to make cigarettes. Mr. Kambarami said, "I understand that, but at least promise to read the page of the New Testament before you smoke it." The man agreed and the two went their separate ways. Fifteen years later, the two men met at a Methodist convention in Zimbabwe. The Scripture-smoking pagan had found Christ and was now a full-time evangelist. He told the audience, "I smoked Matthew, I smoked Mark, and I smoked Luke, but when I got to John 3:16, I couldn't smoke anymore. My life changed from that moment."[22]

While almost every household in America (92 percent) owns at least one copy of the Bible—with the typical count being three Bibles per household[23]—less than four out of ten adults (38 percent) read the Bible during a typical week.[24] Fred W. Cropp, president of American Bible Society, received a letter asking the question, "What do you recommend for keeping the leather on the back of Bibles from getting stiff, cracking, and peeling?" His reply was, "There is only one oil that is especially good for treatment of leather on Bibles. In fact it will insure your Bible will stay in good condition. It is not sold, but may be found in the palm of your hand."[25] While it's good for Bibles, it's even better for keeping you in a great spiritual condition. The Bible must become more than just an information book. It must become a daily life-transformation book.

People are hungry to know how a first-century book can work in a *USA Today* world.

- They view CBS, ABC, NBC, and CNN and often get discouraged.
- They listen to Jerry Springer, Ricki Lake, and Jenny Jones and are often left disillusioned.
- They pick up the *Wall Street Journal*, *Time*, and *Newsweek* and are often left confused.

- They tune into Jay Leno, David Letterman, and Comedy Central and often still feel sad on the inside.

But when they open the Bible with an intention to act on it—not to just read it or hear it—they experience God. God shows up. In fact, the Bible is the only book where the Author is guaranteed to show up when it is read with eyes of faith. "Oprah's pick" can't offer that promise. Jabez simply stood on God's promises. He well understood God's Word to bless those who kept his vows (Deut. 28:1–2). He, like Jacob at Bethel (Gen. 28:20–22), sought God's blessing on his people.[26]

Our world is caught up in the "gotta have the right feeling" syndrome, which supercedes biblical faith. Feelings too often drive our actions. This, however, is not the way to experience God's presence. A more accurate formula which should govern our understanding would be:

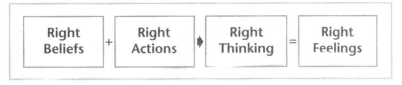

We, as Christians, must experience God, not based on our feelings but on faith and centered in the truths of God's Word. Then only we can truly "feel" a sense of his presence in our lives.

## Spiritual Fatigue Syndrome

Stress! The clock is too tightly wound.

Worry. No white space on the calendar. Arghh!

Can't sleep, yet constantly tired.

Tense. Can't eat 'cause something is always gnawing on the inside.

Anger flashes.

Chronic aches and pains hold captive the pushed-to-the-max body.

Dissatisfaction.

Feelings of inadequacy and self-doubt hinder the superhuman from doing all that could possibly get accomplished if only. . .

Sound like anybody you know? I bet! In fact, with book deadlines, speaking engagements, church duties, family obligations, and community involvement, I can better identify these telltale signs than I am comfortable to admit. We often bring the stress on ourselves. Of course, it's always for "good and noble" reasons that we take on more than is humanly possible to manage.

Stress eats our lunch and spits it right back at us. It makes us less productive and often ill. Forty-three percent of all adults suffer adverse health effects because of stress. Seventy-five to ninety percent of visits to primary-care physicians are stress-related. In fact, job stress is said to be responsible for more than half of the 550,000 workdays lost annually because of absenteeism and is estimated to cost U.S. industry $300 billion annually.[27]

The signs of stress are not just visible on the job and on our health, but also in our relationships—especially our relationship with God. We get to the point that we are not really experiencing joy and peace—or even communication—in our relationship with God. Worship becomes rote or nonexistent. Even though we are on overdrive, we are not moving any closer to God. He is no longer showing up in our everyday lives. We are left empty in spite of all that we are doing and experiencing.

Many of us suffer from an extreme case of Spiritual Fatigue Syndrome. The symptoms include being too stressed, too busy, and too tired to get in touch with God. It's not that we don't want God to show up—for the most part, we aren't antagonistic. We just don't have the time or energy to pull off what it takes to maintain a relationship with him. The job, housework, yard work, grocery shopping, meals, laundry, school, volunteerism, ball games, recitals, proms, phone calls, e-mails, voice-mails, marriage, parenting, and even church work cause us to wonder how God could have ever taken a day off. It's like there is "call block" on our encountering God.

Chronic Fatigue Syndrome, a condition that affects one's immune system and whose symptoms include prolonged fatigue, muscle pain, and forgetfulness, has been estimated to occur in four to nine of every hundred thousand American adults. No known cure exists for CFS, which seems to affect a higher percentage of over-thirty Caucasian females with advanced education than any other segment of the population.[28]

While statistics are not documented for the occurrence of Spiritual Fatigue Syndrome, it is known to strike equally all segments of the population, but it does have a proven cure. To realize a total cure, sufferers of this debilitating syndrome must rearrange daily priorities and place meeting with God as the priority appointment in their daytimers and Palm Pilots. Their preoccupation must be with him rather than with all that has to get done in a given day. Jesus promises that if we will do that, everything else will fall in place.

> Seek first his kingdom and his righteousness, and all these things will be given to you as well.
>
> —Matthew 6:33

## Lowering Your Cholesterol Count

"Hey, Mikey!" Life Cereal's parent company, Quaker Oats, launched a daring marketing campaign in the fall of 1998. Residents of Lafayette, Colorado, were asked to try an experiment designed to prove eating oatmeal everyday for thirty days would reduce their cholesterol and their risk of heart disease. The town took the challenge, and at the end of thirty days ninety-eight out of a hundred of Lafayette's participants experienced lowered cholesterol. One of its citizens commented, "I think the best part is sharing with others how a simple change by eating oatmeal has made an improvement in my life. That's what it's all about."[29]

Trying *The Prayer Experiment* may not show up in your cholesterol count; it will, however, allow God to show up in your personal

Christian walk and worship. If you suffer from Spiritual Fatigue Syndrome, then claim the promise of God's Word to seek him first as you diligently pray the prayer of Jabez for thirty days.

Pause now. Pray the prayer of Jabez; however, before you do:

1. Think of someone you know who is searching for God in all the wrong places. Commit to praying for that person, as well as being used to help direct that individual's attention in a Godward direction.
2. Extend now a welcome mat in your life to God.
3. There is a difference between God's presence and the awareness of his presence in your life. Seek to know both today.

> Lord, bless me indeed. . .
> Do something so big in my life that it is obviously from you.
> Increase my influence and opportunities for you,
> And give me a sense of your continual presence and direction.
> Protect me, and keep me from falling into Satan's traps. Amen.

If you want to know how to experience God's hedge of protection in your life, you may want to continue the experiment.

# ■ PART FOUR ■

# Impact . . . Your Assurance

*Protect me and keep me from falling into Satan's traps.*

# Posting God's "Keep Out" Sign

*Protect me.*

I received a telephone call this morning from a woman whom my wife, Angie, and I had visited less than a week ago. She and her husband are great people, yet are facing some significant struggles. During our two-hour visit in their home, I felt strongly that I should share with them Jabez's prayer in 1 Chronicles, writing out the paraphrased prayer and asking them to commit to praying it for thirty days. Together, we prayed the prayer, and then Angie and I left.

When this woman called today, she shared how this prayer had already been used in her life. "I thought you would want to hear what happened," she said. "As we were praying the prayer last Saturday morning, my son—who is visiting in Kansas—and his friend experienced a terrible accident. En route to a tennis match, he lost control of the truck he was driving and demolished it. As the paramedics came upon the scene, they commented that they couldn't see how anyone could survive this crash. Certainly the occupants of the crushed truck were dead. But they soon discovered they were not. So the paramedics immediately rushed them to the hospital to have them checked out. Amazingly both boys walked out of the hospital the same day, unhurt."

This woman had made the connection between our praying in Florida and her son's being kept safe on a highway in Kansas. Just minutes before this accident occurred, we had prayed for their family, "Protect them. . . ." I cannot begin to tell you the significant number of testimonies I have received from individuals, couples, and families who have seen God's hand in keeping them safe from tragedy or harm and who connect his divine protection with their praying this prayer in faith. It makes me stop and wonder, "What if they had not prayed?"

## What in the Steal Is He Trying to Devil?

Over one and a half million cars are stolen annually in the United States. Millions more are vandalized or stripped. Vehicle theft is the most costly property crime in the United States, with a staggering estimated cost of eight billion dollars annually.[1] The National Insurance Crime Bureau (NICB) reports that if vehicle theft were a legitimate business, it would rank fifty-sixth among the Fortune 500 companies.[2]

> **NICB Report**
> ## Top 10 Vehicles Stolen in 1998
> 1. Honda Accord
> 2. Oldsmobile Cutlass
> 3. Toyota Camry
> 4. Honda Civic
> 5. Ford Mustang
> 6. Chevrolet Full-size Pickup
> 7. Toyota Corolla
> 8. Cadillac Deville
> 9. Chevrolet Caprice
> 10. Jeep Cherokee

Many cars today are stolen simply for the parts. No car is too old, too rusty, or too ugly to be stolen. While a car may be considered by its owner to be too ordinary to be stolen, a thief may have his eyes on it simply because a car theft ring has a ready market for its parts. Many disassembled cars are worth three times their retail value. Jesus warns his followers that Satan is out to steal and destroy not automobiles, but far more valuable human beings of all makes and models (John 10:10). Like a car thief searching for all models to sell to chop shops, Satan has fixed his eyes on a variety of people to tear apart and offer them to the highest bidder.

The last "amen" had been said as we concluded an evening worship service where we had just experienced God's presence in a powerful way. As the people were leaving, they continued to visit with each other inside and outside our worship center. Only a few minutes had elapsed before one of our men rushed back inside to inform me of a problem. "Did you hear what happened?" he asked.

"No," I said as a sickening feeling came over me about what I might be told.

"Well, you know the Hunters?" he continued.

I nodded and said, "Yes. Jan is my prayer warrior, and they are dear friends."

"Well, you know their new car? It's sitting on the pavement with two of the tires—wheels, everything—gone!"

While we were worshiping, professional thieves were at work. Most likely in less than three minutes they had jacked up the car, taken the wheels, and slipped away undetected. Realizing that only material property had been robbed, this godly couple said about this unfortunate incident, "Thank God it didn't happen to someone who wasn't a Christian and was visiting our church."

Those thieves were not the only ones working while we were worshiping. Satan was aggressively at work as he is every Sunday, Monday, Tuesday. . . . He could easily be charged with grand theft when it comes to what he has robbed from unsuspecting, unprotected, unprepared Christians. He is always on the prowl and ready to heist our. . .

Cheerfulness—Satan wants to steal our joy.

Contagiousness—Satan wants our faith to be unattractive.

Confidence—Satan wants us to doubt God.

Convictions—Satan wants us to stand for nothing.

Compassion—Satan does not want us to care.

Commitment—Satan wants us indecisive.

Character—Satan does not want us to grow in Christ.

Certainty—Satan wants us unsure of our salvation.

His method of operating is to take these things from us so that we will lose our impact and influence for God.

Over a period of years I have served in some difficult churches—churches that have experienced splits, immorality in leadership, and other malignant issues that were swept under the rug until after I arrived. These years of don't-deal-with-it-or-you-will-hurt-people's-feelings issues became perfect platforms for Satan's attacking the big three have-to-haves in my life: joy, peace, and integrity. Surviving as the leader in those no-win situations became a lonely time, a time when even God seemed distant.

I could share many painful—and embarrassing-to-recall—memories of those pastorates. One such incident followed a difficult church business meeting where we had dealt head-on with some tough congregational issues. I tried to handle things in a way that would be least divisive to the church body, yet accomplish what we needed to do. When the meeting dismissed, a man who had determined he didn't like me from Day One made a statement he intended as offensive: "You should have been a politician. Why don't you go and run for governor?" He then turned on his heels and marched off.

How Satan used this golden opportunity to go after me—then a young pastor with a much shorter fuse than I have today. I am ashamed to say I charged after that man. By the time I caught up with him at the back of the worship center, my temper was flaring and my fist was raised in his face. To be honest—and I'm embarrassed to admit it—I wanted to deck him, though of course I didn't. The only one shamed and hurt was a young pastor who should have known better. Gone was my joy, my peace, and my integrity—all robbed from me.

I still struggle with my sinful nature, especially in these three areas of my life. And while Satan knows well how to pick up on my struggles, I am learning better every day how to guard and to post a "Keep Out" sign over these precious treasures. I have installed some new alarms in my life—learning to listen to God's voice, daily being under the control of the Holy Spirit, and consistently spending more time with God in prayer—which have effectively served as a warning system when Satan was about to rob me.

## Back Off, Jack!

Where did I leave my car? Carrying some packages and fumbling for my keys, I searched the massive shopping mall parking lot for my vehicle. I thought I left it over there. Cutting across the rows to get to my car, I heard something like, "Hey, back off, Jack! You're standing too close." Now I am normally an easy-going guy, but my lack of love for such shopping excursions had left me frustrated to the point I was not in the mood to be spoken to in that tone of voice. Yet, as I looked around, I couldn't identify my antagonist. Was it a mad church member hiding behind a car for a chance to tell me off? I'm looking, but . . . no. Was it the lady who wanted the tie I bought and now she was trying to scare it out of me to get it for her husband? Still looking, but . . . no. Was it my dentist who was still upset I cancelled my appointment earlier that day on short notice? Again looking, but . . . no.

Once again I heard the irate voice, and as I turned, I realized that it was just a car—albeit a car with a serious attitude. I couldn't believe my ears! This bully piece of metal was provoking a confrontation with me. I was ready to give this hi-tech smart aleck a piece of my mind, when it, too, has apparently had enough of me. As its lights began flashing, I realized that the countdown had begun and I was only seconds away from enduring an ear-splitting, high decibel, siren-blaring scolding. Embarrassed that I had been pushed around by a macho car, I quickly escaped to the safety of my wimpy mute-mobile. As I recovered in the safety and serenity of my automobile, I wondered, "Is a new shirt and tie worth it?"

Statistics show the chance of our car being stolen or broken into is one in forty. One vehicle is stolen every twenty-one seconds in the United States, with older model cars being stolen more often than newer models. Unfortunately, the recovery rate remains around one in two stolen cars returned to their owners. Auto theft can happen to anyone, anytime, anywhere. While there is no way to absolutely prevent a car from being stolen, security systems in automobiles can be a deterrent.[3] In the early 1990s the talking car alarm was a popular crime deterrent—and a major annoyance to those parked or walking near a vehicle with one activated. Since that time more technologically advanced, state-of-the-art alarm systems have captured the market.

Believed by many to be the oldest book in the Bible, Job offers the first record of a talking alarm. We see it activated in a conversation between God and Satan when God warned Enemy Number One to back off on trying to rob certain areas of Job's life.

> Then the LORD said to Satan, "Have you considered my servant Job. There is no one on earth like him; he is blameless and upright, a man who fears God and shuns evil."
>
> "Does Job fear God for nothing?" Satan replied. "Have you not put a hedge around him and his household and everything he has? You have blessed the work of his hands, so that his flocks and herds are spread throughout the land. But stretch out your hand and strike everything he has, and he will surely curse you to your face."
>
> Then the LORD said, "Very well, then, everything he has is in your hands, but on the man himself do not lay a finger."
>
> —JOB 1:8–12

Satan's efforts to rob Job of his righteousness were frustrated since he couldn't get to Job because of a protective hedge God placed around him. In essence, God was saying to Satan, "Back off! Don't mess with my servant. Beware if you attempt to get too close."

As I was visiting some church members in their home, I noticed the family dog ran freely in the front yard, without any restraining leash or fence. "That is one well-trained dog," I thought. But later I discovered what I could not see: They had installed an invisible fence that electronically "reminded" the dog that there were boundaries. While others—not even Mrs. Job or Job's three buddies—could not see God's hedge of protection around Job, it was there and reminded Satan of his boundaries on Job's life.

Seeking God's protective hedge is what Jabez must have had in mind when he prayed, "Let your hand be with me, and keep me from harm" (1 Chron. 4:10). He understood that with great blessings come great temptations. The times we are most victorious are often the times we are most vulnerable. We tend to drop our guard spiritually when we have experienced personal victory. Jabez understood and feared this danger.

> The times we are most victorious are often the times we are most vulnerable.

Although the devil cannot read our minds, he is a good observer. He knows exactly when and how to attack. He is always looking for an opportunity to strike. In one unguarded moment, he moves in, and it's too late. Regrets come, remorse fills the heart, and while forgiveness is available through repentance, the consequences can no more be stopped than a driver trying to stop an eighteen-wheeler on a dime while doing a hundred miles per hour. We must be proactive in trying to stop Satan before sin gets out of control in our lives. Daily we must activate God's antitheft protection, as well as warn Satan to back off whenever we sense he is approaching us.

### "Don't Forget to Set the Alarm"

"Don't forget to set the alarm" was one of the last things that I said to my son before I went to bed. And Will did—but with the wrong code. He set the sensory alarm that detects even the slightest motion. Awakened in the wee hours of the morning, I got up to ... well, you know what we do when we get up at that time of the morning. Still three-fourths asleep and trying not to wake up all the way, I stumbled into one of the rooms protected by a motion sensor. When I did, I was instantaneously startled out of my stupor by bells ringing, whistles blowing, sirens blaring, and the dog barking. I know I must have jumped at least seven feet in the air, and I had no idea what was happening.

In a flash, everyone in the household came running and yelling, "Dad! Jay! Dad! What's going on?" The phone then rang! It was the security company asking, "Is everything all right?" "No!" I exclaimed. "Sir, what's your password?" they requested. At that point, I still had not completely regained my capacity to think or reason, so I muttered, "It's uh ... Oh! It's 2 A.M.! Wait a minute. It's 253–56–44... no that's my Social Security number. What do you want to know?" Well, that was not the response they wanted, for they will only accept one password. As they were ready to summon the police, I remembered! Praise God, I remembered! The password finally came out of my mouth, and all was well— that is, except my son!

Every Christian has access to God's monitored security system and should remember to set it for protection against Satan and his schemes. In the book of Job, we are given the family security code to activate the system:

1  Be Right With God. Like Job, we should have a heart for God, a passion for God, and a reckless abandon to God (Job 1:1).

12  Be Morally Pure. Like Job, we should have a pure heart that refuses to allow immoral thoughts and actions to seize us (Job 1:1).

1    Be Honest. Like Job, we should tell the truth and be transparent, striving not to be a hypocrite (Job 1:1).

18    Be Awestruck. Like Job, we should have a holy fear of God, a sense of deep reverence and awe at his power and majesty (Job 1:1).

13    Be Avoiding. Like Job, we should avoid anything that even has the appearance of evil (Job 1:1).

14    Be Responsible. Like Job, we should assume responsibility to pray for the people around us and remind them of God (Job 1:5).

15    Be Praying. Like Job, we should pray as a way of life, abiding in prayer and not just praying in emergencies (Job 1:5).

23    Be Ready. Like Job, we should prepare ourselves for Satan's attack (Job 1:5).

15    Be Worshiping. Like Job, we should praise God even when our world falls apart (Job 1:20–21).

14    Be Believing Anyway. Like Job, we should believe God no matter what the circumstances (Job 1:22; 13:15).

The numbers above correspond—in order—to the letters of the alphabet. When we enter in these numbers, it spells:

A   L   A   R   M       N   O   W       O   N.
1   12   1   18   13       14   15   23       15   14

I am grieved every time I learn of another pastor who has fallen into immorality. I find it heart-wrenching each time I consider the sad number of married pastors and other Christian leaders who have destroyed their marriages and ministries going after "the woman of their dreams"—someone they have met in an Internet chat room, worked beside on a mission trip, helped in a counseling situation, or been with on social occasions with their spouses.

I have listened with saddened amazement as some have explained how they became hooked on pornography and thought they could defy the odds by handling it without affecting their marriages or their lives. None of these incidents happened all at once, but through a gradual slide into sin. Little by little the guard was let down, the hedge weakened, and then—in what seemed like an instant—the "man of God" fell. He was no longer able to resist Satan.

As I think about the enormous gravity of ill-chosen, selfish decisions, my heart aches and I cry out to God, "Please, Lord, don't ever let me get calloused to hearing and being affected by this. Please keep me from falling into Satan's traps." I constantly pray, as did Job, that God will put a guard over my eyes—and my heart.

> I have made a covenant with my eyes not to look lustfully at a girl.
>
> —Job 31:1

I have come to realize that I cannot take my moral integrity, my fidelity to my wife, or my commitment to God for granted. It is something at which I have to work—and about which I have to pray constantly, throughout each and every day. I know I cannot compromise on even the smallest things for fear I will give Satan a foothold—if just a point of entrance—in my life. I must constantly be diligent about setting God's alarm in my life.

One other thing must be said about setting God's alarm system. In the New Testament, we are also given a family password. Without it, there is no true security. With it, we can feel safe. The password? J-E-S-U-S. That's the only one God will accept. For when we pray in his name—through the power of his sufficient strength—we can be kept safe from the Evil One.

## Response Time

Before our church moved to the mall, our staff constantly received calls in the middle of the night because the sensitive security system on our old church property had been set off. Most of the time it was a false alarm; however, on this one occasion it had been activated by someone who had broken into our facility. When one of our staff members responded to the alarm and rushed to the church, he was met by an officer with the police K–9 unit. The investigating officer opened one of the doors of the church and called out in a loud voice, "If anyone is in there, come out now or I will release this dog."

Silence. Not wanting the individual to escape, he released the dog and within a few minutes a loud cry came from the sanctuary, "Help! Get this dog off of me!" The dog had done what he had been sent to do and had caught the perpetrator by the seat of his britches. Now this apprehended burglar was more than eager for the officer to come and rescue him—even if it meant arresting him. Because of the effectiveness of the alarm system and the police's quick response time, it all worked out in the end . . . literally.

It only takes seconds for a burglar to break into a home or non-residential property. The Federal Bureau of Investigation reports that while the nationwide burglary rate is the lowest in more than two decades, still there is an approximate three billion dollar loss nationally experienced by burglary victims each year, with the average dollar loss per burglary victim being around $1,300.

This FBI study shows that 65 percent of all burglaries involved forcible entry, with two out of three burglaries being residential. Fifty-three percent of all burglaries occur during the daytime and 47 percent happen at night. Adults were involved in 81 percent of all burglary offenses, with the remaining 19 percent involving juveniles. Eighty-one percent of the burglary arrestees in 1998 were males, and sixty-four percent were under twenty-five years of age.[4] Although there is an eight-year steady decline in burglaries, there is an increase in individuals protecting their homes and businesses with electronic security systems. While security systems are not fool-proof, they can deter or stop the amateur and slow the professional.

Sometimes Satan hits without any advanced warning. It may be a temptation that comes upon us, and we only have a few seconds to determine what we are going to do. It may be a trial of some kind, where in a moment we must decide whether to thank God for it or to step out of his will. According to our response time—the time it takes us to turn it over to God and do the right

> ■
>
> **Prior to stepping out of our homes and into the world each day, we need to set the spiritual alarm on our lives.**
>
> ■

thing—we will either successfully thwart Satan's attempted theft or be robbed of the joy of experiencing Christ's overcoming power and grace. Prior to stepping out of our homes and into the world each day, we need to set the spiritual alarm on our lives. We can do this by spending time with God: praying, getting into his Word, seeking his guidance, and recommitting ourselves to serving him that day.

As a pastor, I am most vulnerable to Satan's attacks in the twenty-four hours following the times I have preached or spoken to a group where God has visibly blessed those efforts. I can identify with Elijah, who after seeing the power of God displayed in a mighty way on Mount Carmel, ended up fleeing to Horeb to escape attack and to await the voice of God (1 Kings 18–19). I don't exactly know what happens inside of me, except that I expend so much of my energy and my emotions when I do preach or speak that I have little reserve to fight the enemy.

I am not alone in this experience. While I was in seminary, one of my preaching professors took a stress test while he was preaching. It showed the same impact for every sermon he preached, as if he had engaged in eight hours of strenuous manual labor. As I look back on that test, from my current perspective of having preached for a number of years, I'm not surprised because it resonates with my own experience. When I preach or speak multiple times in a day, I am left with an empty tank, providing an opportune time for Satan to try to steal my joy. Until I can get refilled and recharged—which usually takes about a day—I must constantly fight depression, doubt, and irritability. I immediately have to set the alarm in my life by allowing only trusted people close to me during those times to pray for me, encourage me, and help protect me from Satan's attacks. That's when I need the body of Christ to minister to me the most.

Knowing this, Satan doesn't miss a beat. He always attempts to surround me with people who have a negative spirit or those who have not been able to catch me any other time during the week. Now is their opportunity to tell me what's wrong, what I need to do, what our church needs to do, or whom I may have offended. Having just poured out my heart and seen many lives touched and having experienced God—wham! Like two tons of bricks dropped on me, I'm hit with eternally insignificant issues. Don't get me wrong. It's not that I don't care about these things. It's just that I am drained in every way and not at my best to handle them.

I have discovered that after I'm exhausted from preaching or speaking, I first need physical rest and then emotional rest, in addition to my need for the spiritual renewal of entering into God's presence and letting him minister to me. If I don't respond immediately to all that is crying out within me to back off and get with God, I'm in trouble. I also desperately need a quick response time from God in restoring me and refreshing my spirit.

## The Edge with the Hedge

Throughout Great Britain and continental Europe amazing hedge rows have been growing and groomed over the centuries to define property boundaries, confine or exclude animals and people, as well as to enhance the beauty of the property. Most of these living hedges were designed to be impenetrable, with some growing to a height of 15–20 feet. Hedges grow from a variety of trees and shrubs—some thorny, some flowering, some evergreen, some slow-growing—and take between five to seven years for these plants to reach the height of a fence-sized barrier. Hedges require care and trimming to continue to serve their designed purpose.

God's hedge of protection in the Christian's life provides proof that a sovereign God loves and cares for his children. As beautiful to behold and as lovely to observe as established hedge rows is

God's hedge about those whom he calls his own. More effective than any living hedge is the Father's security in the life of obedient believers. Some doubt this, however, for they see:

- Christians suffering with illness and wonder where God is
- Christians losing loved ones and wonder where God is
- Christians experiencing hard times and wonder where God is
- Christians enduring divorce and wonder where God is

Exactly where is God with his spiritual, physical, emotional, mental, social, and relational protection when these things happen to believers? Many find it impossible to see the hedge for all the trees.

Let's begin with the issue of faith. As Christians, we serve a sovereign God, who remains in control. We accept this by faith even though we don't always understand it—in fact, most of the time we don't understand it. Jesus recognized this and consequently reminded his followers that a sovereign Lord watches over us and cares for us.

> Look at the birds of the air; they do not sow or reap or store away in barns, and yet your heavenly Father feeds them. Are you not much more valuable than they?
>
> So do not worry ... but seek first his kingdom and his righteousness, and all these things will be given to you as well.
>
> —MATTHEW 6:26, 31, 33

King David was able to sleep in the midst of his enemies because he knew that God's providential control and protection made him "dwell in safety." No wonder he could say, "I will lie down and sleep in peace" (Ps. 4:8). Many psalms are an encouragement for us to trust God rather than to fear, because the Lord keeps and protects his people. For example, Psalm 91:1–5 speaks of not fearing "the terror of the night, nor the arrow that flies by day":

He who dwells in the shelter of the Most High
   will rest in the shadow of the Almighty.
I will say of the LORD, "He is my refuge and my fortress,
   my God, in whom I trust."
Surely he will save you from the fowler's snare
   and from the deadly pestilence.
He will cover you with his feathers,
   and under his wings you will find refuge;
   his faithfulness will be your shield and rampart.

The early American Indians trained young braves in a unique way. After he had learned to hunt, scout, and fish, the young brave was put to one final test on the night of his thirteenth birthday. He was placed in a dense forest to spend the entire night alone. Until then, he had never been away from the security of the family and the tribe. But on this night, he was blindfolded and taken several miles away. When he took off the blindfold, he was terrified, realizing that he was in the middle of a thick woods. All night long, every time a twig snapped, he visualized a wild animal ready to pounce. After what seemed like an eternity, dawn broke, and the first rays of sunlight entered the interior of the forest. Looking around, the boy saw flowers, trees, and the outline of the path. Then, to his utter astonishment, he beheld the figure of a man standing just a few feet away, armed with a bow and arrow. It was his father. He had been there all night long.[5]

Our heavenly Father keeps watch over us, his children. If we genuinely believe that all good things are caused and protected by God, then we must give thanks and say, "Praise the LORD, O my soul, and forget not all his benefits" (Ps. 103:2). Likewise, we also remember the instructions to "give thanks in all circumstances" (1 Thess. 5:18) as we express our confidence in God's sovereign and wise control over anything that would touch our lives.[6]

The teaching leader of Bible Study Fellowship shared with the group with which my wife was involved a story of a mother who prayed each morning for a hedge of protection to be about her daughter while at school and with friends. At her daughter's ten-year class reunion, a former classmate—a known lesbian—came up to the girl and confessed, "I knew you were a believer in Christ, because every time I tried to approach you, it was like there was a wall around you preventing me from propositioning you. I could only get so close."

As if that were not surprising enough for the woman's daughter to hear, the other woman went on to share, "Since our graduation I have become a Christian. I have come to understand that you had a hedge of protection around you." Because this faithful and believing mother prayed for her daughter's well-being and protection, her daughter was given an edge over the enemy. What a convicting challenge for us who are parents!

## Wanted: Experienced Hedge Work Supervisors

Jabez understood a principle that we likewise should examine and embrace. He was called "honorable" not because he had attained an influential or important station in life, but because he was obedient in living out his deep faith in God. Therefore, when Jabez asked for God's protection—"and keep me from harm" (1 Chron. 4:10)—he could feel confident in making such a bold request because he had done those things in his life that made honoring such a request reasonable and expected. His lifestyle of careful and godly choices put him in a position where he did not have to suffer the consequences of poor behavior.

If we, like Jabez, obediently follow the teaching of Scripture, we must position ourselves to ask for God's protection in all areas of our lives. The Bible teaches that our bodies house the Holy Spirit; therefore, we should avoid putting anything in our bodies that would tear them down. If we act on that principle, we will live healthier lives.

The Bible teaches that bad influences corrupt good morals (1 Cor. 15:33); therefore we should choose our influences wisely. If we do, we avoid a spiritual downhill spiral. The Bible teaches to avoid sexual sin (1 Cor. 6:18); therefore, we must keep ourselves sexually pure. If we do, we avoid guilt, embarrassment, possible diseases, unwanted pregnancies, and the potential for an unhappy marriage. God's way works and adds protection to our lives. If we walk down this path, we should be able to see tangible evidence of God's protective hedge about us.

What do I mean? Consider one example of God's protective hedge—the Ten Commandments (Ex. 20: 3–17). When God says, "You shall not," he is not trying to rain on our parade, rather, he is trying to protect us. When God warns us not to do something, he does it to keep us from harm, not to make life miserable. Likewise, the entire Bible is not just some kind of rulebook spelling out the do's and don'ts of a godly lifestyle; instead, it is a divine guidebook sharing proven principles for living a joy-filled and blessed life.

How can we prove these principles? Look to medical science and you will find a growing number of doctors are turning to faith as part of the preventive and rehabilitative aspects of healing. Christians shouldn't be surprised. In his fascinating book *The Faith Factor*, Dale Matthews, a medical doctor, presents irrefutable evidence to support biblical principles. He indicates that the more religiously committed we are, the more likely our physical health should benefit. For example, a study in 1972 of 91,909 individuals living in Washington County, Maryland, found that those who attended church once or more a week had significantly lower death rates from the following: coronary artery disease (50 percent reduction), emphysema (56 percent reduction), cirrhosis of the liver (74 percent reduction), and suicide (53 percent reduction).

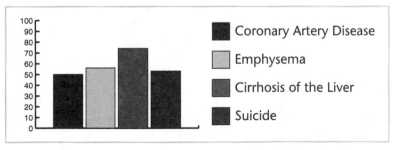

*Fig. 10.1—Lower Death Rate for Regular Church Attendees*

Matthews also cites religion as preventing addictions within adolescents. Religiously involved teens are markedly less likely to use tobacco, alcohol, and illegal drugs. A 1986 study of 16,130 high school seniors found that the students' religiosity was the strongest factor in determining drug and alcohol abstinence or abuse—stronger even than family-related factors, including whether or not the student lived with both parents. A study of 2,278 Americans of all faiths showed that frequency of attendance at religious services was the strongest predictor of marital happiness for both men and women—stronger than education, age, family income, occupation level, and number of children at home. In fact, worship attendance was the only such factor shared by both sexes.

In a 1991 study, adolescents who attended church frequently were significantly less likely to engage in premarital sex, especially if they belonged to conservative denominations. Eighty percent of students attending church three times a week were virgins, compared with 37 percent of those who attended less than once a week. Further studies indicate that religious involvement helps people handle life's hurts in a more positive way. Religious commitment strongly shapes the quality of life along with the feeling of life being worthwhile.[7]

These measurable scientific statistics offer attention-grabbing evidence that God's intervention in the lives of Christians makes a difference. Christians have the edge with God's hedge of protection about their lives. Yes, Christians may well suffer many of the same afflictions and challenges as unbelievers, but the difference is the hope that they have in a God who controls how much, when, and why.

## Hedging Against All Odds

In the world of finance, *hedging* is a way of reducing some of the risk involved in holding an investment. Like an insurance policy, it's a way of insuring an investment against a risk. Among the many ways to hedge against market risk, the simplest though most expensive method is to buy an option for the stock you own to cover general market declines. The best and cheapest hedge is to sell short the stock of a competitor to the company whose stock is held.[8] Some investors hedge to improve or maintain the competitiveness of a company—and add to their bottom line—while prudently positioning the company so that it is not negatively affected by price movements.[9] Their goal is to hedge against all odds.

In our Christian walk, we too need to hedge against all odds. We can ask our heavenly Father to hedge our interests and protect us against Satan's aggressive moves, to keep us safe from imminent danger and potential downfall. We can have confidence that as God protects our interests, he also has control of more than Satan's market share. God controls all options.

- God, not Satan, lifts the hedge. Nothing can touch us until it first passes through God's hands.
- God lifts the hedge to make us more like Christ. God allows us to undergo Satan's attacks in order to chip away at anything within us that does not look like Jesus and to draw us closer to him.
- God lifts the hedge to give us a platform to glorify him. God often presents us with opportunities to be a testimony to others—and even to Satan—of his transforming work in our lives.
- When God lifts the hedge, he never allows us to go through more than we are equipped to handle. God knows our load and time limit, and he gives us the strength and power to bear the load.

Anne and Steve Seaberry, two Southern Baptist missionaries serving in Libreville, Gabon, were awakened in their home by five armed robbers. At first fear seized them, but gradually peace came to Anne when she realized she was wearing a longer nightgown than usual. Bowing her head, she thanked the Lord she was modestly attired in front of the robbers. "God immediately said to me: 'I have gone before you and made sure you were covered. I will protect you and Steve,'" Anne related.

But as the thieves were preparing to leave, one turned in the doorway, pointed his gun at them and cocked it. "Oh, Jesus!" Anne prayed aloud. A bullet immediately fell to the floor. Shocked, the man looked at his gun and realized that was his only bullet. He immediately exited the room along with his companion, presumably to get more bullets.

The frightened couple then began whispering Jesus' name over and over again, until two men reentered the room. Instead of harming them, however, they only tied them up. Closing the bedroom door behind them, the men left the house several minutes later. Anne said, "We know that Jesus protected us. God's grace is sufficient."[10]

Taking to heart and practicing *The Prayer Experiment* can lead you down avenues of faith that will allow you to embrace the understanding and the confidence of the psalmist who wrote:

> I will lift up my eyes to the hills—
>    where does my help come from?
> My help comes from the LORD,
>    the maker of heaven and earth.
> He will not let your foot slip—
>    he who watches over you will not slumber.
>
> —PSALM 121:1–3

Pause now. Pray the prayer of Jabez; however, before you do:

1. Is there someone for whose protection you should be praying today? Be stirred into action by praying the prayer of Jabez for that individual.
2. Think of those areas in your own life where you feel you need God's protection today. Ask the Lord to hedge you in and keep you safe from danger.
3. Activate the alarm system on your life now by praying this prayer.

> Lord, bless me indeed. . .
> Do something so big in my life that it is obviously from you.
> Increase my influence and opportunities for you,
> And give me a sense of your continual presence and direction.
> Protect me, and keep me from falling into Satan's traps. Amen.

If you want to find out how Satan operates and how your faith can defeat him, you may want to continue the experiment.

# Your Faith—A Moving Target

*Keep me from falling into Satan's traps.*

The ancient activity of throwing darts probably evolved from the sport of archery. As early as 1314 we find a reference to "darte," although it probably did not refer to the game we know. The modern game of darts found its beginnings in England and was brought to America by Europeans. Some suggest that the Pilgrims played darts on board the Mayflower as they sailed to this new land. In the 1800s coal miners in working-class regions of Pennsylvania and New Jersey began playing darts. The game was introduced to the Capital District of New York by the men who ran the barges on the Erie Canal. The popularity of darts in America grew during World War I and World War II as people came together in taverns to share war stories and to play games.[1]

Another form of darts existed from the time Lucifer, an angel of God, became Satan, a fallen angel, through his own rebellion. He quickly became the dart champion of the spirit world. The spiritual dimensions of Christianity revolve around a battleground, not a playground. Jabez understood this when he asked God to mega-bless his life. He was certain the enemy, Satan, would not sit idly by without a fight. Jabez recognized that serious prayer invites spiritual warfare. Jabez's last petition, "and keep me from harm" (1 Chron. 4:10), was a plea for divine protection from the fiery darts that were sure to be thrown at him. His faith would be targeted and tempted.

In 1898 an American patented a dart with folded paper flight. Now we know that the best flights in the world are made from turkey feathers. In 1906 an Englishman patented an all-metal barrel.[2] Not until 1969 and the formation of the United States Darting Association were the rules and equipment standardized. Today dart barrels and shafts are made out of a variety of materials: wood, brass, plastic, aluminum, tungsten, titanium, and even gold plate. Satan's designer darts are fashioned out of wickedly constructed circumstances and temptations custom-matched to the intended target. Satan is such a master craftsman that his fiery darts often resemble anything but what they truly are.

## Mr. or Ms. Doubtfire

In 1993 Robin Williams starred in the movie *Mrs. Doubtfire*, playing a divorced dad who so desperately missed his children he was willing do anything—even cross-dressing as a sixty-year-old British nanny—to be with them. Williams, whose character specializes in dubbing the voices of cartoon characters, turns to his brother, a makeup artist, to help disguise him as Mrs. Doubtfire. The disguise is so good that Williams's ex-wife and his three children are completely fooled by the deception.

Consider another doubtfire that is not an act, but comes from Satan's throwing his fiery darts of doubt at the target of your faith. He intends to plant doubts concerning God in your mind:

→ "If God is so good, why did something so bad happen to you?" Dart!
→ "God doesn't hear your prayers." Dart!
→ "Can you really believe what God said in a book written thousands of years ago?" Dart!
→ "Why do those who don't give God a second thought seem to be happier and better off?" Dart!
→ "God plays favorites." Dart!

A dart hits and a doubt-storm erupts. The object of the doubt dart attack is your C.F.S., Central Faith System. Satan does it by casting doubt on God's Word and character. When this dart hits, it leaves a hole in a Christian's faith, which results in prayers that are ineffective.

> When he asks, he must believe and not doubt, because he who doubts is like a wave of the sea, blown and tossed by the wind. That man should not think he will receive anything from the Lord.
>
> —JAMES 1:6–7

The enemy then whispers, "God doesn't care or he would answer your prayers."

This dart has hit me at vulnerable moments in my life. I vividly recall a particularly difficult time in my ministry when I began to question everything that had been previously nailed down in my belief system. For a couple of months, I was haunted by serious questions about God's plan for my ministry that seemed to be leading me into landmines of complex church problems, the love of God I didn't feel, and the presence of God, that seemed a million miles away. I felt as if I had become God's personal punching bag.

While I was ashamed of how I was feeling, I could not hold back these suppressed thoughts and pent-up emotions any longer. I wasn't sure I should tell God about it; however, knowing full well that God knew the doubts that plagued me, I, like Jeremiah, finally broke down and told God how disappointed I was in him. In painful tears, I told him that I didn't think he was being fair. The more I poured my soul out to God, the more I became aware that the real problem was not with God—or even my circumstances; it was with me. I had allowed Satan's insidious doubt dart to convince me I was finished. The moment I begin to get honest with God, I began to understand that I had been duped—lied to by the best. When my eyes were opened to the truth, I began to believe God again and respond in faith. Then the dart was removed.

The doubt dart comes in all shapes and sizes. Some cause you to question your salvation. This paralyzing dart can make you feel you don't measure up, leading to feelings of insecurity in your faith. You feel that what you have done in the past is too bad for God ever to forgive. Satan even throws darts of doubt about how other people see you—and your walk with the Lord:

"He doesn't want to have anything to do with you any longer."
"They think you are a phony and aren't what you seem."
"She doesn't like you."

This missile is aimed as often at new Christians, who are struggling with relationship adjustments, as at mature Christians—even pastors—who are equally susceptible to Satan's mind games.

## Achy Breaky Heart

The title of Billy Ray Cyrus's hit country song, "Achy Breaky Heart," seems to sum up the way many people feel. They have "achy breaky" hearts, a symptom of being discouraged. Discouragement is one of the most dangerous and debilitating darts aimed at our faith. It may manifest itself as being:

down
    depressed
        empty inside
            sensitive to rejection or failure
                disinterested in the things that normally
                    matter most
                lost to the enjoyment of life lived in Christ
            unable to focus
        anxious
    irritable
sad.

This discouragement dart aims to get you to focus on people, circumstances, and things, rather than on God.

As a pastor I have seen a common flight pattern for the dart of discouragement in the lives of Christians. Whenever you allow this dart to stick, you lose perspective of what God is doing in your life. It strikes when people disappoint you, circumstances discourage you, and things fail you. Satan loves to aim his dart at you when you may find yourself thinking, *Christianity is not what it's supposed to be. I didn't sign up for this. The harder I try to do the right thing, the more difficult it becomes. I don't have the same feelings I used to have about God.* Bull's-eye! Satan's subtle strategy is to orchestrate things to discourage you, to worry you, to frustrate you—especially in your prayer life.

> **Satan's subtle strategy is to orchestrate things to discourage you, to worry you, to frustrate you—especially in your prayer life.**

Once your thought life is negatively affected, your tongue will soon follow course. Becoming cynical or sarcastic about matters of faith is the next step. You wonder if the Christian life is worth it. Church is not the same, and it becomes easier to be hypercritical. You begin to distance yourself from the things of God, the very things that could remove this discouragement you are experiencing. At this pace, discouragement's vicious cycle will soon have you in despair. If this dart is not removed, you could become another trophy for Satan—with the inscription, "Defeated through discouragement."

One morning after leading a men's group through the first session of The Prayer Experiment, I returned to my office, and within the hour I found myself dealing with a matter of life and death. Along with the other men I had prayed, "Lord, increase my influence and opportunities for you." I had told the men to expect divine interruptions, but had not given much thought about how this, too, might impact me that very day. I should have seen it coming, as it seems as if God is always making me practice or experience what I preach.

The man in crisis was the picture of confidence, health, success, and family happiness. When he and his family had made our church their new church home, many remarked about his magnetic personality and how much they liked him. Now, just six weeks later, he was sitting in my office, contemplating using a .45 pistol to end it all.

Was this man not a Christian? Oh, yes! He was a Christian with a great testimony of what Christ had done in his life; but he had been hit hard with the dart of discouragement, and it was deeply imbedded in him. As we began extricating Satan's dart, this brother was rescued by his faith in Christ. The discouragement dart was effectively disabled by the readily available power of our Lord. The crisis had past. The note I received from this struggling Christian two days later reflects how God gained the victory over his hellish opponent: "Rev. Jay, yes, God is with you even when you are at the end of the rope."

## Master Illusionist

Although I have never been any good at performing magic tricks, I have always enjoyed watching others do even the simplest tricks. I particularly like those that can be performed on demand, right on the spot. Recently a friend of mine showed me a trick that I was able to learn so well that I can even perform it now long-distance with you. We need no props other than both of your hands.

### The Magnetic Fingers

Clasp both hands together and intertwine your fingers. Squeeze both hands tightly as you slowly count aloud to ten. Now raise your two index (i.e., first) fingers so they are pointing up to the ceiling. They should be about an inch apart. Abracadabra! Your fingers will slowly start moving toward each other. Concentrate. Try to fight it, but they will soon touch.[3] Voila! (They should be touching at this point.) As you look at your hands clasped together with fingers pointing upward, you should also be experiencing a strong urge to say, "Here's the church. Here's the steeple." You may have also noticed that your hands are now in an ideal pray-the-prayer-of-Jabez position.

David Blain has been called magic's "New Prince." Not employing flashy pyrotechnics, gaudy props, or glamorous assistants, Blain has honed in on the streets of New York where he stuns passersby with gob-smacking card tricks and wows television audiences all over the world by levitating six inches off the floor. In an interview with a British journalist, Blain was asked, "But you can't just do magic straightaway, can you? Surely you had to read up on it."

"Yeah, I read a few books," Blain responded. "Uri Geller, Orson Wells, and Jesus Christ are all people I admire for their magic."

"And Jesus Christ? He was a magician?" asked the reporter.

"Of course. He was a great prophet, too, but he was also one of the greatest magicians," replied Blain.[4]

As good as Blain may be, there is still a greater Master Illusionist who has been at it for centuries. Not Jesus, but Satan is the true "Prince of Magic." He masterfully uses his dart of deception to make something appear one way when it is really not that way at all.

The old Lakeland Mall sat vacant for nine years. It served as a picture of neglect, failure, and no future. Approximately 12,675,000 cars passed by that facility over those nine years. I would dare say not one of those passersby looked over at the buildings and said, "You know, that would be a great place for the old downtown First Baptist Church to relocate. They should sell their property and move ASAP!"

When our church bought the mall, we became a laughingstock of our area. Dining out, one of our members overheard someone remark, "Why have those crazy Baptists bought that mall?" This was not an isolated case. We frequently heard things like: "Well you've done it now. You have gone and bitten off more than you can chew." "Look on the bright side ... maybe you can lease some of your buildings to tire stores or telemarketing businesses." So, to capitalize on all the buzz that this faith venture was stirring up, we designed T-shirts for our members with the slogan: "I'm one of those crazy Baptists that bought the Mall."

Appearances can be deceiving, especially when what God has in mind is not obvious. The devil would have had us to believe that it was. . .

> too big
> too much money
> too inconvenient
> too risky
> too "too."

That's the way it looked, but behind those brick walls and stucco God was at work. If we had just trusted appearances, we would have missed God doing a big work.

Things are not always as they appear. When my son, Will, was only three years old, he had a passion for "nummies" (what he called candy and gum) and for climbing. One day, while no one was looking, he climbed until he reached the cabinet where the Children's Tylenol was stored. Believing he had found a cache of nummies he proceeded to devour his find. When my wife discovered him, the evidence was unmistakable. I quickly raced home and asked, "Will, how many little nummies did you eat?" He looked at me proudly and said, "Pise!" (meaning "five"). After examining the bottle, we were pretty sure that he had eaten the whole bottle of Tylenol. After a bottle of syrup of ipecac and a frantic trip to the doctor, Will was fine (although as parents we had yet to recover).

Looks can be deceiving. Satan knows this well as he constantly puts deceptively attractive new labels on old bottles of poison for us. Second Corinthians 11:2–3 warns us of this:

> I am jealous for you with a godly jealousy. I promised you to one husband, to Christ, so that I might present you as a pure virgin to him. But I am afraid that just as Eve was deceived by the serpent's cunning, your minds may somehow be led astray from your sincere and pure devotion to Christ.

## Passion Hustlers

"The first time I looked out of curiosity. It was there, and . . . I don't know. I wondered what it might be like. I thought, 'What harm could there be in just looking?' Besides. . . I'm only human. It's impossible to resist." Weekly I am hearing these words as I listen to stories about men—and from men—who are losing the lust battle. "It's the excitement, the thrill of the hunt that draws me. It's not hurting anyone. I can stop any time."

The birth of the Internet has changed the world of porn dramatically and the lives of many struggling Christians. Internet pornography has gained a stronghold in our society. On the World Wide Web alone, ten thousand porn sites generate one billion dollars annually with thirty-two porn sites being added everyday. Just a click of the mouse on an enticing ad or a provocative word search and there it is! Instantly and privately, what was once considered X-rated and available behind the walls of an adult bookstore now pops up on your computer in your home or office. No longer do people need to sheepishly present the latest "Penthouse" or "Playgirl" to a smirking cashier. It's readily available online. Now your most forbidden fantasy can be generated in the privacy and secrecy of your home. It's easy, inviting, and addictive.

Focus on the Family recently conducted a survey with Zogby International in which they found that one out of five American adults (20.8 percent) have looked for sex on the Internet. It is shocking to think that nearly forty million people could have visited a sexually-oriented Web site. The percentage of those viewing the sex sites was higher among males and young males. Thirty-one percent of men surveyed said that they had visited such sites. Thirty-seven percent of eighteen- to twenty-four-year-olds gave that same response.[5]

In case you are thinking, "He's only talking about non-Christians," you are wrong. Of those who identified themselves as "born again" Christians, nearly 18 percent confessed to surfing for cybersex.[6] This not the only area in which Christians are guilty of moral compromise. In a comparison of the behaviors of Christians and non-

Christians, a Barna Research Group survey found that 76 percent of Christians—as compared to 87 percent of non-Christians—had watched an X-rated movie in the past 3 months.[7] Even more disturbing are stats on the pornography habits of pastors. *Pastor's Weekly Briefing* recently published an article that stated 20 percent of pastors say they use pornography at least once a month.[8]

Christians seem to be living with "eyes wide shut" to Satan's dart of desire aimed at their hearts. It's not just desire for sex, but desire for. . .

> the forbidden
> > the enticing
> > > the thrilling
> > > > the stimulating
> > > > > the "un-have-able"
> > > > > > the "I'm not supposed to ever do this."

"The eyes see it and gotta have it" is referred to in the Bible as "lust of the eyes."

> For everything in the world—the cravings of sinful man, the lust of his eyes and the boasting of what he has and does—comes not from the Father but from the world.
>
> —1 JOHN 2:16

The average speed of a dart hitting a board is forty miles per hour. Far more quick and precise are Satan's darts aimed at your eyes. Satan uses your eyes—which are the gateway to your mind—to go after your thought life. He uses his dart of desire to cause you to be enticed by something you see and then uses the visual image to cause you to dwell on the object of your desire. If you dwell on it long enough, Satan reasons you'll go after it to satisfy the flesh. Satan's goal is to cause you to want to do something with your body that is harmful, will dishonor God, and will discredit your testimony.

This battle came home to me in a disturbing situation that occurred in a church I pastored. We discovered that one of the church leaders who was always present in worship was taking money from the offering plate. His stealing had been going on Sunday after Sunday—for weeks—in order to support a crack cocaine habit. This well-liked and trusted man's addictive desires overcame his desire to do the right thing. He had given in and given up to the dart of desire.

Gaming darts can be of varying dimensions and weights; however, the maximum length may be no longer than twelve inches and the maximum weight can be no more than fifty-two grams. Satan's darts of desire vary as well, and God promises a maximum weight limit on these darts. His rules of play state that the weight of Satan's darts of desire will not be more than we can bear.

> And God is faithful; he will not let you be tempted beyond what you can bear. But when you are tempted, he will also provide a way out so that you can stand up under it.
>
> —1 CORINTHIANS 10:13

## On Pause, On Hold, On Standby

How I hate to be put on hold! When I'm asked, "Could you hold?" I want to respond, "Sure, that will give me a chance to read *War and Peace*, carve the Thanksgiving turkey, put up the Christmas tree, list my New Year's resolutions, and celebrate Easter with time to spare." The ultimate hold is flight delays. On top of the frustration of hurry-up-to-get-there, it is made even worse by the apologetic announcement that the aircraft is "experiencing mechanical problems," the flight is going to be delayed, and your life and plans are put on hold.

According to Department of Transportation guidelines, airlines are permitted fifteen minutes of leeway before a flight is considered delayed. Of the approximately seven million flights in a year, the FAA reports an average delay of fourteen minutes per flight. (I guess that means there's really an average delay of approximately one-half hour per flight, because of the leeway policy.) What causes these delays?

- 75 percent by weather
- 19 percent by air traffic volume
- 2 percent by closed runways or taxiways
- 2 percent by problems with computers, radar, or other control equipment
- 2 percent by other circumstances[9]

My collaborator on this book encouraged me to think spiritually about airline delays. Marilyn mentioned something about my learning to cool my jets, God's sovereign control over flight schedules, and there being a divine purpose even in delays. Then she related an episode of delayed flights and missed connections when she was heading to a meeting in San Francisco. Traveling from the east coast of the United States, she and her family went to catch an early morning connection to a direct cross-country flight. But she discovered it had been cancelled. They were rerouted to another city, and just missed their flight to San Francisco. They then caught a flight to another city and were once again delayed.

At this point, Marilyn's husband, Jon, looked at her and said, "There has to be a reason for all of these delays." Finally, on an airline headed to San Francisco, Marilyn whispered to Jon, "I have a strong sense that we are to be praying for the people below." As the plane was approaching the taxiway in San Francisco, its engines suddenly raced and the plane began ascending again. The pilot made the announcement that they had lost contact with the tower and could not land. At that moment, Marilyn and her family had been protected from the disastrous earthquake that shook the Bay Area on October 17, 1989. The hotel where Marilyn was already to have been in an afternoon conference was severely damaged in the quake that measured 7.1 on the Richter Scale. Her family would have been touring around San Francisco while she worked. God had orchestrated all the delays.

While God will delay things in our lives for our own good, Satan uses his delay dart in the opposite way. While we wait on doing what we know we should, he works against us by throwing this dart that affects our spiritual travel. He often does this by attempting to delay the answers to our prayers. This happened to Daniel. In Daniel 10:1–14, the prophet prayed, and immediately God sent an angel with the answer. However, a strong demon prevented the angel from getting through to this praying man. For ten days the answer was delayed until the archangel overcame the demonic obstacle. Delays are not necessarily God's denials, but they may be Satan's delays designed to confuse you and to shake your confidence in God.

### "Huh, Did You Say Something?"

It happens when I am "in the zone," focused on *Who Wants to Be a Millionaire* or intently watching *The Crocodile Hunter* on Animal Planet. As I become aware of a deafening silence and glance up at my beloved wife, who has been waiting for I-have-no-idea-how-long and apparently hoping to engage in a meaningful dialogue, but who has, instead, been experiencing a frustrating monologue. As I tear my eyes away from the program that has been receiving my undivided attention, I innocently ask, "Huh, did you say something?"

Then . . . then I get "the look," followed by "the question": "Dear, could you please repeat what I have just said to you?" At that point I know I am toast and I begin fervently praying that one of the kids will walk in with a minor crisis or the phone will ring with a call for one of us to interrupt my dilemma.

Like Linus carrying around his security blanket, we men, especially, seem to need to carry around the remote control. Perhaps we are more like Barney Fife toting a six-shooter with one bullet. We are loaded with access to a zillion channels at the speed of touch. We don't even have to engage our brains, just engage our thumbs. The remote control allows us to experience the power of total control. With my trusty universal remote in hand, I feel secure. If I don't like what I'm watching, click! In an instant I can have Cartoon Network as a picture-in-a-picture while I switch back and forth from A & E to ESPN2. Ah . . . I don't have to focus on anything. With one little click I can be somewhere else and forget what is going on around me.

While the television remote has been around for nearly fifty years, it has only been widely used in the last two decades. In 1952, Zenith introduced a remote called "Lazy Bones," which was attached to the television set via a long cable. This wasn't a popular device as there were so few channels to change. Three years later, the "Flash-o-Matic" appeared—a flashlight that when shined toward light-sensitive cells in each of the four corners of the TV would perform different remote functions. This device proved problematic, however, if the television set was placed in sunlight. The sun's rays would play havoc on the operations of the TV.

A group of engineers then developed the Zenith "Space Command," a wireless remote using ultrasonic waves, in 1957. It worked pretty well, except for its functions being affected by clinking metal, such as dog tags, and its high frequencies making dogs bark. In spite of its drawbacks, the ultrasonic remote was used for two decades until engineers discovered the infrared remote control. Now the infrared beam pointed in the direction of the set controls gives viewers—especially male viewers—"be-in-command" power.

> The devil strategically uses the dart of distraction to get at the Christian's faith, specifically targeting the prayer life of a Christian.

As enticing as channel surfing can be, Satan has cleverly come up with even more distracting ploys to take our attention off God. The devil strategically uses the dart of distraction to get at the Christian's faith, specifically targeting the prayer life of a Christian. This dart tends to interrupt divine communication. As you hit your knees, you enter the door of a thousand distractions. That's no accident. The phone rings, your beeper goes off, you suddenly remember something you forgot to do, the doorbell rings, the kids need something, ad infinitum. He also does it through the replay of problems—people problems, work problems, money problems—in our minds as our focus is changed from "up" to "around."

There's another tactic Enemy Number One employs. He attacks someone who is close to you, for if they experience a setback or defeat, it can be used to distract you. Satan is smart. If he can't get you through a frontal attack, he will come through the side door or back door. While you are preoccupied with the other person's problems, zap! Here comes a dart that often sticks better than others. It may be aimed at your children or your spouse. Another may be aimed at a close friend whose marriage is in trouble or whose child is hooked on drugs. This is an effective tactic Satan uses to distract you from the things of God.

## Incoming Scud Missiles

The scud missile, with strike ranges from 100 to 180 miles, was originally designed to carry a 100-kiloton nuclear warhead or a 2000-pound conventional warhead. Its principal threat is its warhead potential to hold chemical or biological agents. This erratic but dangerous ballistic missile proved an important weapon during the Gulf War and Operation Desert Storm. The Iraqis modified Scuds for greater range, but that made the missiles structurally unstable causing them to often break apart in the upper atmosphere. The poor accuracy of this weapon made it difficult to intercept, since its flight path was so unpredictable.[10]

Satan, too, has weapons of mass spiritual destruction. Many are often difficult to detect, but nonetheless dangerous. The Bible warns of Satan's intention in throwing the destruction dart when it says, "The thief comes only to steal and kill and destroy" (John 10:10a). Satan is the destroyer and his weapons prove it. It's not that he has come up with new and improved weapons, these have been around since the "Garden" days. However, he constantly hones his ability to use his ancient weapons with contemporary effectiveness.

One weapon is a flaming dart. When it hits its target, the fire spreads and destroys whatever it touches. These darts are zoned in on marriages and seem to be effective, since recent surveys indicate that among married people, 27 percent of born-again Christians have been divorced, while only 23 percent of non-Christians have been divorced.[11] This dart tends to make people forget their marriage vows and causes them to think that the problem of irreconcilable differences is a good enough reason to walk away from a sacred commitment God intended for life. It deadens people to the consequences—to them personally, to their family, and to their testimony for Christ. I suppose you could call this dart the amnesia dart—that is, until it hits you.

Be careful, for in the line of dart-fire are your family, your testimony, your character, your morals, your body, your mind, your emotions, and your attitude. To hit any one of these affects the rest. That's what makes this dart so dangerous. A satanic victory in any of these areas often means that he wins the trophy, and— to borrow a song line—"another one bites the dust."

## Checking into the Hotel Denial

"I did not have sex with that woman, Ms. Lewinsky." Those words of denial of President Bill Clinton proved to be untrue. Testifying before the grand jury on August 17, 1998, seven months after his Paula Jones deposition, the President acknowledged "inappropriate intimate contact" with Ms. Lewinsky and attempted to explain his earlier denials. As to his denial in the Jones deposition that he and Ms. Lewinsky had had a "sexual relationship," the President maintained that there can be no sexual relationship without sexual intercourse, regardless of what other sexual activities may transpire.

Clinton's denial of his affair with the intern had far-reaching consequences, not least of which were impeachment proceedings. Clinton's family, his integrity, his presidency, his legacy were all damaged by the web of denial he misleadingly wove about his life in office. Only when evidence was presented to contradict all of his denials did Clinton offer—at first an angry, then a tearful—confession: "I misled people, including my wife. I deeply regret that."

Satan's dart of denial hits and results in no one wanting to be responsible. Denial helps to shield a person from dealing with a painful problem or even the plain truth. The denial dart takes many forms:

- Hostility: "I don't have time for such nonsense."
- Nonregistering: "I don't know what you are talking about."
- Noncaring: "Don't blame me. It's not my responsibility."
- Rejection: "If you make that choice, don't come crying back to me."
- Baseless assurance: "Don't worry about it. It'll be okay."

Satan will use fear to produce a target of resentfulness, anger, or defensiveness to allow the denial dart to stick.

Denial is the great cover-up, instead of the great coming-clean. Some years ago, a man was overheard complaining about too much sex and violence on his VCR. In failing to deal with denial, problems continue to progress and become more serious. I have seen denial slowly eat away at marriages where no one wanted to face and deal with the real issues. Couples pretend everything is alright as they smile in public and isolate themselves from each other at home. The only things they share in common are the same address, the same last name, and the children they have brought into the world.

I also commonly see denial in parents who refuse to admit their children have problems and need help. Instead, they throw money and things at their children, set no boundaries for them, and challenge anyone who would dare challenge their children. It's the cover-up syndrome of a mom who told her little boy who stole fruit in the grocery store, "Honey, be sure and chew with your mouth closed."

Perhaps the most dangerous denial to any individual—apart from the denial of the existence of God—is the denial of the existence of Satan himself. Surveys show that nearly two out of three adults (62 percent) agreed that Satan "is not a living being, but is a symbol of evil." Even more surprising is the survey's findings that a majority of born-again Christians deny Satan's existence (52 percent).[12] This is serious because of the nature of Satan's attacks. He works far better undercover and by surprise. To fight him with the weapons God has given to every believer, Christians must know who the enemy is. To deny Satan's reality grants the devil the freedom to attack unsuspecting children of God who won't even know what has hit them until it's too late. Satan's response? He laughs aloud and rejoices over all those who say, "The devil can't be real."

## God's Deflector Shield

In *Star Trek*, the famed TV series-turned-movie sequels, you could count on hearing Captain James T. Kirk command, "Mr. Sulu, raise the deflector shield!" Without the shield's being raised, the Starship Enterprise was vulnerable to attack, and the Klingons would have likely won the battle.

In Scripture, the apostle Paul talks about another kind of deflector shield for Christians—"the shield of faith." Picture it as a large two-foot-by-four-foot shield. When Satan's flaming darts hit it, they will not only be stopped, but they will be extinguished. The shield of faith stops Satan's darts from penetrating your life and your attitude.

> In addition to all, taking up the shield of faith with which you will be able to extinguish all the flaming missiles of the evil one.
>
> —EPHESIANS 6:16 NASB

The King James Version calls the flaming missiles "fiery darts." These missiles, or darts, were flammable in the ancient world and would be lit so that when they hit their target, fire would spread and destroy. You must hold up the shield of faith, trusting in God's presence even when it doesn't look like he's around, believing in God's Word even when it looks like life's circumstances are going to have the last word. You must hold up the shield of faith, standing on the promises of God even when the winds of doubt, floods of discouragement, and the lightning bolts of bad news come violently upon you. Even though your faith is a moving target, God's deflector shield is portable, so you never have to leave home without it.

Jabez put up his shield through believing prayer. If you desire likewise to raise your deflector shield, you must realize that simply repeating the words of a prayer formula will not raise that shield. You must have faith in God to whom you are praying, believing that he not only can protect you from Satan's darts, but that he will do it in response to your staking your trust on his Word. Remember: Believing prayer prepares you for the darts, it does not prevent them; so, be on guard.

Your faith is Satan's diabolic dartboard. Why does he zero in on your faith?

> Your faith pleases God,
> > *And Satan wants you to disappoint God.*
> Your faith overcomes circumstances and brings victory,
> > *And Satan wants to leave you feeling discouraged and defeated.*
> Your faith brings the answer to prayer,
> > *and Satan doesn't want you to pray.*
> Your faith also brings you hope,
> > *and Satan wants you to be discouraged.*
> Your faith provides the shield to protect you,
> > *and Satan does not want you to survive his attacks.*
> Your faith increases as you demonstrate your dependence
> > on God,
> > *and Satan does not want God alone to be the Source of your safety and strength.*

## White Moment

In the game of darts there is a moment in which the victor takes the game from the loser. It is referred to by a Russian term called a "White Moment." It is not necessarily the game-ending throw, but it is that throw of the dart that decides the outcome. A White Moment is that instant in which one competitor's psyche is destroyed and the other's confidence is boosted to the point where the outcome is inevitable. In America, we call it "being in the zone." In Christianity, we call it the cross. Perhaps, it could better be called a "Red Moment," for it is by the shed blood of Christ that the match against the evil one is won. God had the defeat of his opponent in mind when he sent his Son to earth:

> The reason the Son of God appeared was to destroy the devil's works.
>
> —1 JOHN 3:8

**WARNING:** Praying the prayer of Jabez may mean experiencing trials and testing times. When you cooperate with God, however, those become the steps to a greater blessing. When Satan throws his darts, God can use them for our spiritual growth. God is also faithful and offers his shield to deflect those that might destroy you.

Pause now. Pray the prayer of Jabez; however, before you do:

1. What darts is Satan most apt to hurl at you? Seek discernment as you pray about these potentially problematic areas.
2. Ask God to show you any holes in your shield of faith.
3. As you pray this prayer today, think about how God has already given you the ultimate victory over the enemy's darts through Jesus Christ.

> Lord, bless me indeed. . .
> Do something so big in my life that it is obviously from you.
> Increase my influence and opportunities for you,
> And give me a sense of your continual presence and direction.
> Protect me, and keep me from falling into Satan's traps. Amen.

If you really want to bring the supernatural world into your world and more effectively influence people, you may want to continue the experiment.

# Influence: When Two Worlds Connect

*God granted Jabez what he requested.*

**A**s Christians we live in two worlds: this natural visible world and the supernatural invisible world of heaven. To the degree that we allow the spiritual world to influence our earth-bound existence, our world will be positively impacted by our lives. There are no shortcuts, no loopholes, no way around it. If we want to genuinely change our world, we must spend much time in God's world. In order to tap the heavenly Father's limitless resources, we must learn to:

> Abide in his holy presence
> Draw from his inexhaustible strength
> Learn from his infinite wisdom
> Listen to his confident voice
> Lean on his immeasurable mercy
> Trust in his divine guidance
> Follow in his exemplary steps
> Look to his great faithfulness
> Wait for his perfect timing.

The ball rests in our court. We must stop and carefully assess how much we *really* want to impact the world. Do we possess a true passion for pointing this present generation in a God-ward direction? Is it our heart's desire to positively capture the attention of those without Christ and convince them that there is more to life? Are we convinced that we have the potential to persuade the cynical and skeptical about the truthfulness of the things of God? As overwhelming as these questions are, within them lies a challenge—actually, a divine mandate—for us to do something to make a difference in our world. The influence we assert, however, will not come through our God-talk; rather, it will come through our behavior after we have been in God's presence. The impact of which I am speaking can only begin in one place: the place of prayer.

In his book *Don't Just Stand There, Pray Something*, Ron Dunn succinctly shares the influence prayer has on people without God.

> Satan has no defense against this weapon; he does not have an anti-prayer missile. For instance, the unbeliever has many defenses against our evangelistic efforts. He can refuse to attend church, and if he does occasionally show up, he can shift into neutral and count the cracks in the ceiling. You can go to his home, but he doesn't have to let you in. Hand him a tract on the street, and he can throw it away. Get on TV, and he can switch channels. Call him on the phone, and he can hang up. But he cannot prevent the Lord Jesus from knocking at the door of his heart in response to our intercession. People we cannot reach any other way can be reached by way of the throne of grace.[1]

*The Prayer Experiment* can help you to start the journey of influencing your world.

## The "If–Then" Principle

My wife and I have often applied the "if–then" principle to some of our parenting initiatives. When we have wanted our children to accomplish a certain task, we have withheld a privilege until they have completed what they needed to do. For example, when they were younger, we would say, "If you clean your room, then you can go outside and play." As they have gotten older, "If you complete your homework, then you can borrow the car Friday night."

Our heavenly Father utilizes the "if–then" principle—in the form of a covenant—as the primary means to relate to and motivate his children. A covenant is an agreement between God and his people that accentuates the importance of love, obedience, and perseverance. *If* God's people love him and keep his commands, *then* God will bless them. We see God's establishing covenants with Israel throughout the Old Testament (e.g., covenants with Noah, Abraham, Moses, David) and with the church in the New Testament (redemption through Jesus Christ). Both *if* and *then* reflect the conditional terms of a covenant: *If* spells out our part, our responsibility as God's chosen people, and *then* spells out God's faithful response as given in Scripture.

> If we confess our sins, then we will be forgiven.
> If we pray according to his will, then our prayers will be heard.
> If his Word abides in us, then we can ask what we will.
> If we honor God with our money, then we will be blessed.
> If we give, then it will be given to us.
> If we ask, then we will receive.
> If we do his will, then we will be happy.
> If we humble ourselves, then we will be exalted.
> If we are servants, then we will be great.
> If we call on his name, then we will be saved.
> If we are in Christ, then we are new persons.

Whereas a covenant between God and humans is initiated by God, throughout the Bible we also read of God's people initiating another type of agreement called a "vow." A vow is a solemn promise made by a person to God that is binding (Deut. 23:21–23) and should not be made carelessly (Prov. 20:25).

Jabez prayed for God to bless him. As the most honorable of his brothers in his Jewish tribe, he was well acquainted with covenant and vow requirements for God's people. Jabez understood that *if* he desired to be blessed by God, *then* he must love God and keep his commands. Jabez's stating the *if* conditions of the vow ("if thou wilt bless me. . .") without the concluding *then* indicates that this prayer was part of a vow Jabez made to God, and scholars believe it probably had acquired importance sufficient to make it worthy of being handed down only because God had so fulfilled his request.[2]

Paul Harvey, in his broadcast *The Rest of the Story*, told of a most phenomenal coincidence that has been attested by many sworn, legal statements. Swan Quarter, North Carolina, was mostly lowland, but the choicest real estate was on the highest ground. In the 1800s the Methodists of that town had no church building, and the only lot available on which to build one was a far-from-ideal plot of low-lying property on Oyster Creek Road. However, seeking to be obedient to God, the members began constructing their church. The small, white frame building was dedicated on Sunday, September 16, 1876.

Three days later—on Wednesday—a terrible storm lashed Swan Quarter. The wind howled and it rained violently all day long. Devastation and flooding had set in by nightfall. The storm did not let up until Thursday afternoon. As the citizens of Swan Quarter threw back the shutters and peered from what was left of their homes, they saw only a desolate waterscape, a community ravaged by nature. But those within sight of Oyster Creek Road beheld the most incredible sight they had ever seen.

Swan Quarter Methodist Church—the whole building intact—was floating down the street! The floodwaters had gently lifted the entire structure from the brick pilings and had sent it off slowly and silently down Oyster Creek Road. Within minutes, concerned townsfolk were sloshing in waist-deep waters, fighting the rushing current, trying desperately to reach the still moving church so that they could moor it with lengths of rope. But their efforts were in vain. There was no stable structure secure enough to restrain the floating chapel. As the building continued to move on, more attention was attracted and more aid was enlisted—but to no avail. By now the building had made it to the center of town, still traveling down Oyster Creek Road.

Then, as dozens of amazed, helpless citizens watched, the Swan Quarter Methodist Church—still floating—made a sharp, inexplicable right turn and continued down that road, as though it were alive, as though it had a mind of its own. For two more blocks the townspeople fought unsuccessfully with the ropes to hold it back. Finally, in the same decisive manner with which it had moved, the church veered off the road, headed for the center of a vacant lot, and once there . . . stopped. As the floodwaters receded, the church remained there—and is there to this day—on the most desirable property in Swan Quarter.

According to Paul Harvey, it is important to know "the rest of the story." The choice highland lot where the chapel settled was the first choice of the Methodists for their building site, but the prosperous landowner turned them down. However, the next morning after the flood, after discovering the church in the middle of his lot, the landowner went to the Methodist minister and, with trembling hands, presented him with the deed.[3] *If* we obey God, *then* God will do what only he can do—which is often amazing and even unbelievable.

## Just As I Am

Many people today are not familiar with Charlotte Elliott's name, but millions are familiar with one of the hymns she wrote. "Just As I Am" has been used more effectively than any other song as a call to commitment to Christ. We can scarcely think of a Billy Graham evangelistic crusade without thinking about the altar call with the choir's singing Elliott's beloved hymn.

Charlotte Elliott suffered most of her life as an invalid. Her weakened condition was cause for great despair and depression. In 1836, when her brother, H. V. Elliott, was raising funds for St. Mary's Hall of Brighton, England—a college for the daughters of poor clergymen—Charlotte wanted to have a part in helping, but her illness prevented it. As she pondered how she could do something for the cause, she decided to write a poem that would be relevant to others who were physically limited. She remembered the words of a great preacher, Cesar Malon, who had talked to her fourteen years prior. He had told her to come to Jesus "just as you are," words that helped her find Christ.

The resulting poem was published by her sister-in-law without Charlotte's name and without her knowledge. Her doctor handed her the poem, not realizing who the author was. Tears started streaming down her face as she learned that copies of this poem were being sold and the money given to St. Mary's Hall.[4] Although initially feeling like a nobody—as her words in "Just As I Am" reflect—Charlotte's song brought more funds than all the other fund-raising projects combined. Her brother wrote in a letter, "In the course of a long ministry, I hope to have been permitted to see some fruit of my labors; but I feel more has been done by a single hymn of my sister's."[5] Charlotte Elliott simply did what she could, and God used it for significant impact—with eternal influence.

It all begins with surrender. God does not want what we have, he wants us. When he gets us, he gets all that we have, all that we are, all that we face. Jabez had little to offer the Lord, yet he came just as he was to God and gave all he had to God. God has done some extraordinary things through ordinary people, like Jabez, who came just as they were and simply prayed:

| | |
|---|---|
| Just As I Am | I bring my past. |
| Just As I Am | I surrender my future. |
| Just As I Am | I hand over my insecurities. |
| Just As I Am | I lay aside my circumstances. |
| Just As I Am | I abandon all my excuses. |
| Just As I Am | I relinquish my pride. |
| Just As I Am | I let go my failures. |
| Just As I Am | I offer my life. |

I am always moved in profound ways when I hear the singing of "Just As I Am" because I identify with its lyrics. I feel within me a sense of anticipation that God will do something in the hearts and lives of people. When I walked up the steps into the Anaheim, California, stadium where I attended my first Billy Graham crusade, I was immediately taken aback by the sound of this song being rehearsed by the large choir. Hearing that hymn sung in that setting caused me to stop in my tracks and exclaim within my heart and mind, "Yes! This is what it is all about! God is here and is about to make his presence felt in a huge way!" And he did. At the end of Dr. Graham's message, as that moving hymn was sung, thousands responded—just as they were—to what God was doing in their hearts and lives.

Jabez had little to offer the Lord, yet he came just as he was to God and gave all that he had to God.

## Claim It Before You Name It

Not name it and claim it, but claim it before you name it. The "it" to which I refer is answered prayer. Jabez claimed God's promises. Likewise, when we do claim God's promises and meet the conditions of faithful love and obedience, God will answer and bless our prayers. That's what Jabez understood and embraced.

> Delight yourself in the LORD and he will give you the desires of your heart.
>
> —PSALM 37:4

Before we start naming all the things we want, we must first delight in God. When we do that, he will plant his desires within us and put on our hearts the things for which—and about which—we should be praying. When we pray in the manner Paul outlines in Ephesians, we will be in a position to stake our claim on God's promises.

> And pray in the Spirit on all occasions with all kinds of prayers and requests. With this in mind, be alert and always keep on praying for all the saints.
>
> —EPHESIANS 6:18

- Pray... *Lift up our praise and requests to the Lord without fail.*
- Pray in the Spirit... *Pray under the control and direction of the Holy Spirit.*
- Pray on all occasions... *Pray when we feel like it and even when we don't.*
- Pray with all kinds of prayers... *Pray everywhere and in all true ways.*
- Pray always... *Pray persistently and never give up.*
- Pray for all the saints... *Pray continually for other believers.*

Then, what we "name" will be in accord with God's Word and will.

As I began a new pastorate, I immediately sensed an overwhelming personal need to spend much time in intense prayer for the people in my shepherding care. As I did, I became more and more convinced that a stronghold on that congregation was blockading the blessings of God. After weeks of praying and researching the church's "history," God impressed upon me that two things stood in the way of his blessing: rebellion and immorality. I discovered obvious occasions of both. It had damaged the reputation of the church—which the pastor search committee had conveniently kept from me.

Greatly burdened by all I was uncovering, I continued to pray for God's wisdom on how to deal with these strongholds. When I finally felt as though I had thoroughly prayed through the situation, I went before the church and shared my heart. The people responded to the Holy Spirit's convicting urging, and we had a powerfully moving service of repentance and cleansing for the church. Together we—all of us, including new members who were not aware of past problems—confessed to God that our church had failed him. We begged his forgiveness and vowed to start afresh.

A new spirit of freedom, joy, and expectation entered the church. We felt greater liberty for God to work in our midst. We had claimed God's promises and power as we waged spiritual warfare on the oppressive and longstanding work of Satan in this body of Christ. This influenced the entire atmosphere of the church as well as the way that members started influencing others in the community. Everything—conversions, baptisms, giving, attendance, plus a sweet spirit—increased in the aftermath.

Through this difficult but freeing experience, my leadership style began to change. For so long I had felt the need to "help God out" with my making-it-happen, going-for-the-goal, working-it-out attitude. While the class is still in session for me as I continue to grow as a leader, I have learned so much through this and other such life- and ministry-changing experiences. Too often have I attempted to force things and work them out on my own.

> It is far better for me to...
>> seek God
>> wait on God
>> trust God
>> join God
>>> ...and see God do eternally significant things.

## Why You Shouldn't Pray This Prayer

*Late Show* host David Letterman is famous for his "Top Ten" lists. He begins with number ten and works his way up to the number one reason for whatever category he and his writers have chosen for that night. Let me share with you my "Top Ten" list:

---

**Top 10 Reasons Not to Pray the Prayer of Jabez**

Reason #10: I prayed it as the blessing before the meal and the food got cold.

Reason #9: I'm still waiting for God to answer my last prayer.

Reason #8: I want the devil to leave me alone.

Reason #7: I can't kneel to pray because of arthritis in my knees.

Reason #6: I'm using my prayer closet for storage.

Reason #5: I keep getting interrupted.

Reason #4: I have no "No Doze" in the house.

Reason #3: I can't handle the extra blessings right now.

Reason #2: I can't find 1 Chronicles in the Bible.

Reason #1: Jabez who?

---

Now let's consider why you really shouldn't consider praying the prayer of Jabez. Do not pray the prayer of Jabez, if you are looking for a prayer that will:

- put you on Easy Street
- give you an immediate real-good, feel-good feeling
- promise you only happy days
- bring you health, wealth, and prestige
- get God to do it your way

But, by all means pray this prayer if you want to see God:

- bring amazing changes in your life
- give you a heightened awareness of his presence with you
- work through you to influence other people's lives
- do extraordinary things all around you
- use you to impact your world

My assistant, Donna, refused to pray the prayer of Jabez again. She was adamant about it. Because she had observed and experienced the stretching and growing process in so many participants' lives, she had her own top ten reasons why she would not pray it another time. She explains:

> *Because I had seen firsthand the results of praying the prayer of Jabez, I had determined to never pray that prayer again. As good as the results were, people had their faith tested. To be quite honest, I would at times much rather believe God can do something, rather than actually have him do it in my life.*
>
> *Recently, however, as I was sitting at the pastor's desk trying to retrieve an e-mail for him, my eyes caught sight of a paper next to his computer. It was the prayer of Jabez broken down into sections. I started to read the part that says "protect me," and before I had time to think about it, I began to pray for God's divine protection in my life.*
>
> *That night as I was going home after work, I was driving on a one-lane road that is heavily traveled during rush hour.*

*The truck in front of me suddenly came to a stop. Fortunately I had left enough room between us to stop in time to prevent an accident. However, the cars behind me had not. The car directly behind me jammed on his breaks and avoided hitting me, but the car behind him had not seen what was happening so he continued to barrel forward. At the last minute the driver of the third car realized that he would hit us and swerved to the right. He went off the road onto the grass, where his car landed on the passenger's side of my car.*

*Had the driver not swerved when he did, I would have been caught and crushed in the aftermath. It was at that exact moment of seeing the car on the grass next to me that God spoke to my heart and said, "That's my divine protection."*

Donna is now a true believer in the Jabez prayer. She no longer cringes when Jabez's name is mentioned, even though she is still a bit tentative about praying it on a daily basis. She is excited when she hears it and encourages others to pray it as she knows how God can use the in-faith praying of his prayer not only to protect, but also to bless lives in unpredictable ways.

### Need a Professional?

As Jabez touched heaven through prayer, God touched Jabez—and the result was increased influence on his world. Earth reached heaven, heaven responded, and two worlds—the natural and the supernatural—connected. Only then comes true impact. It sounds so simple, yet so many people miss it. When we pray for increased influence and opportunities, we need to be prepared for whatever situation into which he directs us. God may lead us to places we would not normally go and to people we would not normally encounter—or even want to encounter.

A woman received a phone call at work indicating that her daughter was sick with a high fever. So she left work and stopped by the pharmacy to get some medication. Upon returning to her car she found that she had locked her keys inside. She didn't know what to do. She called the babysitter and found out her daughter was getting worse. The sitter suggested that the woman find a coat hanger and try to open the door.

> ▪
> God may lead us to places we would not normally go and to people we would not normally encounter—or even want to encounter.
> ▪

After looking around, she found a rusty hanger that probably had been used by someone else for the same purpose. When she looked at the hanger, she thought, "I don't know how to use this." So she bowed her head and asked God to send some help. Within five minutes, an old car pulled up and out stepped a dirty, bearded man wearing a greasy biker skull-rag on his head. The woman thought, *Lord, this is who you sent to help me?* But she was desperate. The man got out of his car and asked her if he could help. She said, "Yes, my daughter is very sick. I must get home, but I've locked my keys in the car. Please, can you use this hanger to unlock my car?"

The man walked over to the car, and in less than one minute the car was opened. She hugged the man, and through her tears she said, "Thank you so much. You are a very nice man." The man replied, "Lady, I'm not a nice man. I just got out of prison today. I was in prison for car theft and have only been out for about an hour." The woman hugged the man again and while sobbing cried out loud, "Oh, thank you, God. You sent me a professional!"[6]

God will enlarge our borders as we pray the prayer of Jabez. He will guide us to people who have a spiritual vacuum in their lives and who are hungry for God, but don't even know it. We may be the only connection empty, lonely, discouraged, confused, hurting, desperately-seeking-something-more individuals will have with another world—a world of hope. As we seize those opportunities, it is called "increasing our influence."

My wife, Angie, makes frequent trips to the dry cleaners—so much so that we are considering taking out a second mortgage just to pay the cleaning bill each month! We have tried several dry cleaners in town and finally found one close to our home that we like. After going there a few times, Angie befriended Janice, a woman who works there. She began praying for her, took her a cake, listened to her talk about her life, and eventually invited her to church. What a joy it was when Janice showed up for church— and has never stopped coming! She made her profession of faith in Christ and was baptized. This illustrates so well how any Christian can be used to connect two worlds. It doesn't take a professional minister to do God's work. It only takes a yielded and available individual who sincerely professes and proclaims the love of Christ.

## I Don't Wanna Be Here or Stay Here!

As we pray the prayer of Jabez, God may take us to some places we don't want to go and leave us in some surroundings where we don't want to stay until he has used us to accomplish his purpose in those particular settings. The book of Titus provides us an example of a young pastor going somewhere he didn't want to go, the island of Crete, for God to use him to make a big difference. Paul trusted Titus because he had already tackled hard jobs—like delivering the problem-tackling letter of 2 Corinthians to the church at Corinth.

But when Titus accompanied Paul to Crete, it was almost more than he could bear. It was a discouraging place filled with self-centered, hedonistic, hateful people. Titus felt led to ask Paul for a new assignment, but Paul wrote back (the book of Titus) to tell him to stay put. There was much more that needed to be done. The people were off-track with their living for God, and God wanted to use Titus to get them back on course. Likewise, in our lives and ministries God sometimes tells us, "Stay in Crete." He may have much for us to do.

Crete may be the place we live. It may be our job. It may be a position or responsibility that is ours. It may be a person: a relative, coworker, neighbor, friend. It may be some sorrow, suffering, opposition, or temptation we are facing. Paul told Titus, "The reason I left in you Crete was . . ." (Titus 1:5), and went on to tell him why he left him there: to impact the whole place. God may have placed us where we are—even alone and uncertain in Crete—because we are the only ones he wants to use to make a difference there.

This is how we see God operate throughout Scripture:

> Joseph was in the pit and in a prison.
> Moses was on the backside of nowhere.
> David was in a cave.
> Esther was in enemy territory.
> Daniel was in a lion's den.
> Three Hebrews were in a fiery furnace.
> Jesus was in the tomb.
> Paul was in prison.
> John was on Patmos.

Tough surroundings, impossible Cretes, for sure. Yet God worked through these individuals in their settings to change their world.

The book *Jesus Freaks* by dc Talk recounts inspiring stories of Christian martyrs God placed in locations hostile to the Gospel. Yet even in those dangerous-for-Christians settings, these determined-to-remain-faithful-to-God men and women refused to compromise, even to the point of death.

It is said that there are more Christian martyrs today than there were in A.D. 100—in the days of the Roman Empire. According to a study done at Regent University, there were close to 164,000 Christians martyred around the world in 1999. An estimated 165,000 will be martyred in 2000.[7]

Recorded in this incredibly moving book is the martyrdom of Thomas Hauker in England in 1555. "Thomas," his friend lowered his voice so as not to be heard by the guard. "I have to ask you this favor. I need to know if what the others say about the grace of God is true. Tomorrow, when they burn you at the stake, if the pain is tolerable and your mind is still at peace, lift your hands above your head. Do it right before you die. Thomas, I have to know."

Thomas Hauker was bound to the stake and the fire was lit. The fire burned a long time, but Hauker remained motionless. His skin was burnt to a crisp and his fingers were gone. Everyone watching supposed he was dead. Suddenly, miraculously, Hauker lifted his hands, still on fire, over his head. He reached them up to the living God, and then, with great rejoicing, clapped them together three times. The people broke into shouts of praise and applause. Hauker's friend had his answer.[8]

Our faith will cost us our comfort, our convenience, our pride, our time, our money, our reputation—perhaps even our very lives. Wherever we are—wherever our Crete may be—God has placed us there to have an impact for him. Let us lift our hands and applaud the God who knows best where and how to use us.

## Eighteen Inches That Can Change Your World

D. L. Moody made the insightful statement, "Behind every work of God you will always find some kneeling form." His words reflect a timeless God-principle for changing the world. I have heard it said that most people will miss heaven by a mere eighteen inches—the distance between the head and the heart, between intellectual assent and heartfelt belief. I decided to check that out, so I took a tape measure and measured from my head to my heart. Sure enough, it was eighteen inches. I decided to continue my investigation. I measured the distance between my knees and the floor. While this is not the same for everyone, the distance was— you got it—eighteen inches. Therefore, I reason:

- We are only 18 inches away from experiencing God.
- We are only 18 inches away from a life-changing solution.
- We are only 18 inches away from realizing God's dynamic plan.
- We are only 18 inches away from changing our world.

The eighteen-inch difference became important to me as a teenager and as a new Christian. I felt that the best way—possibly the only way—for me to make a difference in the world was for me to kneel and pray. Many nights my mother would come into my room and awaken me as I had fallen asleep on my knees praying. Oh, how I wanted God to use me!

Those eighteen inches made all the difference. God allowed me to begin a prayer fellowship organization called "Partners in Christ," which met before school one day a week. Only God could have packed out that choir room each week and brought so many students to faith in Christ. Only God could have opened the door for the Christian singing group of which I was a part to hold an assembly during the school day in a public school to sing and share the Gospel. Perhaps you are thinking, "That sure couldn't happen today." Oh, don't be too sure. Eighteen inches can always find a way.

> Behind every work of God you will always find some kneeling form.
>
> —D. L. MOODY

The ninety-three students walked in tandem as they processed into the already crowded auditorium. With rich maroon gowns flowing and the traditional tasseled caps, they looked almost as grown-up as they felt. Dads swallowed hard behind broad smiles, and moms freely brushed away tears. This class, however, would not be allowed to pray during the commencement—not by choice, but as the result of a recent court ruling prohibiting it.

The principal and several students were careful to stay within the guidelines dictated by the ruling. They gave inspirational and challenging speeches, but no one mentioned divine guidance and no one asked for blessings on the graduates or their families. The speeches were nice, but they were fairly routine—that is, until the final speech, which received a standing ovation. A solitary student walked proudly to the microphone. He stood still and silent for just a moment, and then he delivered his speech—a resounding sneeze. The rest of the students rose immediately to their feet, and in unison they said, "God bless you." The audience exploded in applause. The graduating class found a unique way to invoke God's blessings on their future—with or without the court's approval.[9]

My passionate desire for wanting God to use me as a teenager cannot compare to my passion for what I want God to do in my life right now. Quite honestly, I have now begun praying the prayer: "Lord, either use me to change the world, or take away my desire to do so." I assure you he has not, and the desire grows in me everyday. I have never been more thrilled about being a Christian. There has never been a more exciting time to exercise and share my faith. I hate to go to bed, and I'm pumped about getting up in the morning. I don't want to miss a minute of what God is doing. Every day I see evidence in my life and ministry that God is at work—and there is nothing I would trade for that! It gives my life purpose and direction.

Not long ago, I received a letter from a business professional who was trying *The Prayer Experiment* and beginning to discover its impact on his life.

> *Dear Pastor,*
>
> *Heretofore, I've always approached things from the intellectual perspective and held the belief that it is the individual's work effort that pretty much controlled his destiny. Because of my admiration for you, I am now making the sincere effort to work my way down the 18" from the head to the heart!*
>
> *Thank you. . .*

I am encouraged—no, I am excited!—each time I learn of individuals who are discovering the difference eighteen inches can make in their lives. Oh, that God would continue to allow me to be used by him to touch lives with the life-transforming Good News. Enough about the great revivals of the past! I want to experience a "now revival" in my generation. Enough of the prophets of doom who declare, "Woe is me!" I choose to believe that this is truly our greatest hour. It's my turn—your turn—to say, "God, I must make a difference in my world."

See!

As I began this book, I shared a personal journal entry about my hesitancy in participating in a civic leadership conference. I "survived" the conference. The following is my journal entry from the evening I returned home.

*Personal Journal*

*Saturday, September 19*

*I believe it was Howard Hendricks who said, "You can impress people from a distance, but you can only influence them up close." God reminded me of that while I was on the retreat this weekend. Despite my telling God why I, as a minister, just didn't fit in that elite gathering, despite my being scared to death about relating to those people, despite my being worried that people wouldn't accept me . . . God went ahead and pushed me into this strange, new environment where he wanted me.*

*Today's experience at the retreat was better than yesterday's. When I awoke early this morning and lay in my bed praying, God impressed upon my heart that he wanted me to experience an opportunity for real impact outside of my safe, religious world. When I went downstairs for breakfast, I noticed a big difference in the way I was able to relate to the others. I think last night's antics made the difference. I finally began to relax—especially after I did my hunka-hunka Elvis impersonation and humor routine for my obligatory introduction of another participant. I may have made a complete fool out of myself, but it sure broke the ice! I began to feel much more at ease. And people began coming up to me wanting to talk. Huh . . . I guess I seemed more approachable to them.*

*Anyway, it was a fun day. I had a blast doing the ropes course with everyone. We had a good time working together, problem solving. Plus, I have had some great conversations today—real God-opportunities to begin forming some wonderful new friendships.*

*God, thank you. . . . Thank you for forcing me out of my comfort zone. Otherwise, I would have missed all that you did*

*in my life today . . . and even yesterday—as painful as that was.
I realize now that you were answering my prayer for greater
impact. As I drove home today, I felt like you were asking me,
"Jay, did you not mean what you prayed?" Oh, God, I am
embarrassed before you. I showed so little faith in the way I
responded to this challenge. While I could offer a lot of excuses,
none would stand up under your scrutiny. I am truly sorry and
beg your forgiveness—particularly for my whining and grum-
bling. I am ashamed that I did not exhibit greater confidence in
your control and in your perfect plan. I just didn't see. . . .*

It turned out to be a weekend I will never forget. Now that I
can look back in life's rearview mirror, I realize that God had set
me up in order to teach me some unforgettable lessons. My prayers
over that weekend were filled with "But, Lord. . ." and "Are you
sure?" as I was trying to legitimize my feelings. However, God
wouldn't buy it—not a bit. While I just wanted the weekend to be
over, the Lord wanted me to experience an opportunity for real
impact outside of my stained-glass-window world, beyond the
King James language. He reminded me Jesus did not die in a
cathedral between two pillars, but in the place where people have
their daily struggles. I couldn't see it then, but in months that have
followed God has chosen to use me in unlikely ways with this
unlikely group of people.

When I returned to Lakeland, I was contacted by one of the
men I met over the weekend. He wanted to get together to talk, so
we met. Quickly a friendship developed between us. We continued
to get together for several months to talk about some of the things
on his heart and mind, and I had the incredible privilege of seeing
this man who is so proud of his Jewish heritage recognize that
Jesus Christ is the promised Messiah and pray to receive him as
his Savior and Lord.

That's not the only relationship that has developed out of that
weekend opportunity. God saw fit to lead another one of the participants to visit the church I pastor. This man and his son ended

up making a profession of faith in Christ at an evangelistic event we held. Now on fire for the Lord, he and his family have become active members of our church, and dear friends as well.

I often cross paths with the other people who were in that group, and each time I do, it serves as a joyful reminder of God's purpose in leading me in new directions. Because of the God-promoted bonding that occurred over that weekend, I now have twenty-nine new friends and increased opportunities to minister to them. Now when I think about this experience, my prayers are ones of thanksgiving—praising God for stretching me beyond whatever I would have attempted on my own. As I try to learn from such growth experiences, I find myself before God, and he again is saying the favorite one-word sentence that usually says to me: "See!"

I know I have pointed out why you may not want to pray this prayer of Jabez. I have warned you that it may be hazardous to spiritual indifference and comfort with status quo Christianity. I have shared honestly that praying this prayer may bring trials into your life. I have attempted to be transparent enough not only to say, but to show you through my experiences, that it may get worse before it gets better.

Now I am asking you—no, actually, I am begging you—to pray it anyway. Go for it. Don't let Satan convince you that God can't use you to change your world. Dare to pray this prayer and watch the amazing things that God can do through it. It may not be easy, and sometimes it won't be fun; but I promise you it will send you on the

> God has great expectations for you and me. He has every right. . . . You yourself can influence more people for God and have a greater role in advancing Christ's cause by prayer than in any other way. It is not the *only* thing you can do, but it is the greatest thing you can do.[10]
>
> —WESLEY L. DUEWEL

most exciting adventure known to the human spirit—that of connecting a lost and hurting world with God's magnificent and life-transforming Word.

As you commit to *The Prayer Experiment* and begin the thirty-day (or even lifetime) experiment, expect in time to hear God speak to your heart and say, "See!"

Pause now. Pray the prayer of Jabez; however, before you do:

1. Say to God, "Just as I am, I offer all that I am to you."
2. Think of all the good reasons you need a more consistent prayer life. Prayerfully consider how undertaking *The Prayer Experiment* might change your life.
3. Commit to praying faithfully the prayer of Jabez for the next thirty days . . . or a lifetime.

> Lord, bless me indeed. . .
> Do something so big in my life that it is obviously from you.
> Increase my influence and opportunities for you,
> And give me a sense of your continual presence and direction.
> Protect me, and keep me from falling into Satan's traps. Amen.

*The Prayer Experiment* has just begun . . .

# Notes

## Chapter 1: Discovering a Prayer That Could Change Your World

1. Christa Ehmann, "The Age Factor in Religious Attitudes and Behavior," *The Gallup Organization Poll Release* (July 14, 1999).

2. Mark I. Pinsky, "The Simpsons: Sinners or Saints," *Tennessean* (August 24, 1999), 2D.

3. Frank Newport, The Gallup Organization, "America Remains Predominantly Christian," *Gallup News Service* (April 21, 2000), 1.

4. David W. Moore, The Gallup Organization, "Two of Three Americans Feel Religion Can Answer Most of Today's Problems," *Gallup News Service* (March 29, 2000), 1.

5. Barna Research Group, "Re-churching the Un-churched," *Barna 2000–2001 Seminar Sessions* online brochure (2000), 1.

6. Barna Research Group, "Americans Identify What They Want Out Of Life," *Barna Research Online* (April 26, 2000), 2.

7. Charles R. Swindoll, *Growing Deep in the Christian Life* (Grand Rapids: Zondervan, 1995), 151.

8. Lisa Miller, *Wall Street Journal* (March 26, 1999).

9. David G. Meyers, *The Great American Paradox* (New Haven, Conn.: Yale University Press, 2000), 262.

10. Massachusetts Medical Society, "Dieting Disorder," *OnHealth Network* (June 2, 1999), 1–2.

11. Brooke Gladstone, "Understanding Eating Disorders," *OnHealth* live broadcast (June 1, 1999).

12. "Conditions A-Z: Anorexia Nervosa," *OnHealth online* (2000), 1.

13. "Conditions A-Z: Bulimia," *OnHealth online* (2000), 1.

14. An Unknown Author, *The Kneeling Christian* (Grand Rapids: Zondervan, 1966), 61.

15. Dan Bornstein, "Gorilla Suits," *Milk.com* (2000).

16. Excerpt from a letter to me written by Pastor Danny Autin, Oak Park Baptist Church, Gainesville, Florida (Sept. 29, 1999).

17. Calvin Miller, *Into the Depths of God* (Minneapolis, Minn.: Bethany House, 2000), 106, 109.

**Chapter 2: If You Think You're the Last Person God Would Use for Big Things . . .**

1. Mark Helprin, "The Russian Reformation," *Wall Street Journal* (April 28, 1998), n.p.

2. Ibid.

3. Denny Mog, ed., "You Look Like a New Woman," *Touched by an E-mail* (North Brunswick, N.J.: Bridge-Logos, 1999), 242–43.

4. Jesse Ventura quote from *Playboy* (Nov. 2, 1999), n.p.

5. Fr. Phil. 3:10–11, TLB. Used by permission of Brad and Misty Bernall.

6. Misty Bernall, *She Said Yes* (Farmington, Pa.: Plough, 1999), 95.

7. Ibid., 12–13.

8. West Bowles Community Church, *Youth Group/Cassie Bernall Tribute*, 1999.

9. "Truck Driver Takes to Skies in Lawn Chair," *The New York Times* (July 3, 1982); "Lawn-Chair Pilot Faces $4,000 in Fines," *The New York Times* (Dec. 19, 1982); Myrna Oliver, "Larry Walters: Soared to Fame in Lawn Chair," *The Los Angeles Times* (Nov. 24, 1993). (Sadly, Larry's story has a tragic ending. He committed suicide at age forty-four.)

10. *The Kneeling Christian*, 22.

11. Ibid., 15.

12. *Christianity Today* (April 6, 1979).

13. Glen Van Ekeren, *Speaker's Sourcebook II* (Englewood Cliffs, N.J.: Prentice Hall, 1994), 351.

**Chapter 3: Motivated to Go Beyond Status Quo**

1. Bernice Kanner, *Are You Normal?* (New York: St. Martin's, 1995), 12–96.

2. Jennifer Lach, "Kids These Days," *American Demographics Magazine online* (April 2000), 1.

3. "Trend Central," *American Demographics Magazine online* (April 2000), 1.

4. John L. Mason, *An Enemy Called Average* (Tulsa, Okla.: Honor Books, 1993), 17.

5. From a fax written by D. James Kennedy, 1999.

6. Daniel Leon, "Ad Slogans Gone Wrong," *Fernstone online* (2000).

7. "Col. Harland Sanders: American Fast Food Pioneer," *Kentucky Fried Chicken online* (2000).

8. Calvin Miller, *The Taste of Joy* (Downers Grove, Ill.: InterVarsity, 1983), 10–11.

9. Roy B. Zuck, *The Speaker's Quote Book* (Grand Rapids: Zondervan, 1997), 215.

10. Raymond McHenry, *McHenry's Quips, Quotes and Other Notes* (Peabody, Mass.: Hendrickson, 1998), 43–44.

11. Thaddeus Wawro, *Radicals & Visionaries* (Irvine, Calif.: Entrepreneur, 2000), 214–16.

12. *Youthworker* (July/August 1999), 10.

## Chapter 4: When Praying Doesn't Remove Your Problems

1. Compiled by Judge William Ray Ingram, *Church Humor Digest* (Memphis, Tenn.: Castle Books, 1991), 35.

2. Michael Busby, "Professional Help from the Enemy," *Civil War online* (1996), 1.

3. Adrian Rogers, *God's Hidden Treasure* (Wheaton, Ill.: Tyndale, 1999), 9.

4. James W. Moore, *Standing on the Promises or Sitting on the Premises* (Nashville: Dimensions for Living, 1995), 62.

5. C. S. Lewis, "Letter I," *The Screwtape Letters* (New York: Macmillan, 1944).

6. Stan Toler and Martha Bolton, *God Has Never Failed Me, But He's Sure Scared Me to Death a Few Times* (Tulsa, Okla.: Honor Books, 1998), 80.

7. "The High Five: Athlete Congratulations," *Knowledge Adventure, Inc. online* (1998), 1.

8. Zig Ziglar, *Something to Smile About* (Nashville: Thomas Nelson, 1997), 63.

## Chapter 5: Risk Dreaming God-Sized Dreams

1. T. E. Lawrence, *Seven Pillars of Wisdom* (New York: Dell, 1935).

2. Edgar Allen Poe, quoted in *Bits and Pieces* (July 21, 1994), 1.

3. Bill Hybels, *Who You Are When No One's Looking* (Downers Grove, Ill.: InterVarsity, 1987), 35.

4. James Hewett, *Illustrations Unlimited* (Wheaton, Ill.: Tyndale, 1988), 408.

5. John L. Mason, *An Enemy Called Average*, 56.

6. Author unknown, "Parasomnias—Arousal Disorders Information," *Stanford University online* (June 16, 1999), 1.

7. Rita Kempley, "Awakenings," *Washington Post* (January 11, 1991).

8. *Time* (September, 1999).

9. Sir Francis Drake, quoted in *OC Missionary Prayer Letter of Jeanie Curryer* (September 1997).

10. Glenn Van Ekeren, *Speaker's Sourcebook*, 2.112–13.

## Chapter 6: God Really Can Do It Through You

1. Michael Hodgin, *1001 More Humorous Illustrations* (Grand Rapids: Zondervan, 1998), 57.

2. Dennis N. T. Perkins, *Leading at the Edge* (New York: AMACOM, 2000), 140.

3. Steven Callahan, *Adrift: Seventy-Six Days Lost at Sea* (New York: Ballantine, 1987), 138–39.

4. Perkins, *Leading at the Edge*, 141–42.

5. Callahan, *Adrift*, 223.

6. Perkins, *Leading at the Edge*, 142–43.

7. Callahan, *Adrift*, 210–11.

8. Perkins, *Leading at the Edge*, 143.

9. Callahan, *Adrift*, 222–23.

10. Lillian Glass, *Toxic People* (New York: Simon and Schuster, 1995), 12.

11. Rick Pitino, *Success Is A Choice* (New York: Broadway, 1997), 81–82.

12. "Chick-fil-A, Inc. Fast Facts," *Chick-fil-A website* (2000).

13. Richard Carlson, re. *Don't Sweat the Small Stuff … And It's All Small Stuff* (New York: Hyperion, 1997), n.p.

14. Donna I. Douglas, *God Stories* (Lancaster, Paq.: Starburst, 1999), 164.

15. Raymond McHenry, *McHenry's Quips, Quotes and Other Notes*, 239.

**Chapter 7: Making a God-Impression**

1. R. G. Lee, *The Bible and Prayer* (Nashville: Broadman, 1950), 41.

2. Peggy and David Newton, "Taste and Smell," *Newton's Apple*, #1101, pbs.org.

3. Author unknown, "Scent of a Market," *American Demographics* (August 1995).

4. Andrea DesJardins, "Sweet Poison: What Your Nose Can't Tell You About the Dangers of Perfume," *Health & Environment Resource Center* (1997), 1–2.

5. Wayne Rice, *More Hot Illustrations for Youth Talks* (Grand Rapids: Youth Specialties/Zondervan, 1985), 82–83.

6. Harold Ellis as quoted by D. A. Benton, *Lions Don't Need to Roar* (New York: Warner, 1992), 15.

7. Canadian Association of Student Activities Advisors, "First Impressions," n.d.

8. R. Michael Franz, as quoted by Benton, *Lions Don't Need to Roar*, 23–24.

9. Ibid., 24.

10. Author unknown, "Smiling Is Important," *Bible Studies Foundation* (1997), n.p.

11. Author unknown, "Why Calvin Klein Has Anne's Nose," *The Express Micro Edition* (Jan. 9, 2000), n.p.

12. Author unknown, "The Fragrance Industry: Perfumes and Fragrances Are a $5 Billion Retail Industry," *American Demographics* (June 1997), 3.

13. Brandy E. Fisher, "Scents and Sensitivity," *Environmental Health Perspectives* 106 (Dec. 12, 1998): 1.

14. Andrea DesJardins, "Sweet Poison," 2.

15. Robert Mann, "Animal Noses," *Nature Bulletin No. 729* (Forest Preserve District of Cook County, Ill.; Oct. 26, 1963), 1.

16. George Barna, *The Second Coming of the Church* (Nashville: Word, 1998).

17. Edited by Dan Bornstein, from "Just Do It," *Forbes*, n.d.

18. George Gallup Jr. and Timothy Jones, *The Next American Spirituality* (Colorado Springs: Cook Communications, 2000), 27.

19. Ibid., 26.

20. Gallup and Jones, *The Next American Spirituality*, 29.

21. Judith Viorst, *Alexander and the Terrible, Horrible, No Good, Very Bad Day* (New York: Simon and Schuster, 1976).

22. Phil Callaway, *Who Put the Skunk in the Trunk?* (Sisters, Ore.: Multnomah, 1999), 150.

23. "The Fragrance Industry: Perfumes and Fragrances," 4–5.

24. Author unknown, "To Think Better, Sniff This," *Self* (April 2000), 116.

25. Glenn Van Ekeren, "Staggering Statistics," *Speaker's Sourcebook II*, 95.

26. "It's 'Moi': Miss Piggy Launches Signature Perfume" and "Fragrance Advice from a Nose—er, Snout—That Knows," *Nando Media* (Dec. 4, 1998).

27. Kathi Keville and Mindy Green, "A History of Fragrance," *Health-World online* (1995), 3.

## Chapter 8: Why Your Opportunities May Be Limited

1. Frank Newport, "Forty Percent of Americans Who Use Glasses Would Consider Laser Eye Surgery," *Gallup News Service* (March 6, 2000), 1.

2. James S. Hewett, *Illustrations Unlimited*, 389–90.

3. Ibid., 2.

4. Barna Research Group, "One Out of Three Adults Is Now Unchurched," *Barna Research online* (Feb. 25, 1999), 2.

5. Luis Palau, *Healthy Habits for Spiritual Growth* (Grand Rapids: Discovery House, 1994), 52.

6. Posted by Julie, "Superstition," *Hourglass2 Outpost online* (Sept. 22, 1999).

7. Matt. 27:5.

8. Luke 10:37.

9. John 13:27b.

10. Rom. 8:28; Wayne Grudem, *Systematic Theology* (Grand Rapids: Zondervan, 1994), 337.

11. WHNT-TV Channel 19, "Radar," *Dan's Wild, Wild Weather Page online* (1999), 1–2.

12. David Watson, *Called and Committed* (Wheaton, Ill.: Harold Shaw, 1982), 83.

13. Wesley L. Duewel, *Ablaze for God* (Grand Rapids: Zondervan, 1989), 71–72.

14. Michael Hodgin, *1001 Humorous Illustrations* (Grand Rapids: Zondervan, 1994), 350.

15. Francis Underhill, "My Time Isn't Always Your Time," *American Diplomacy, University of North Carolina online* (2000), 1–2.

16. James S. Hewitt, *Illustrations Unlimited*, 385.

17. "Internet Time," *Swatch online* (2000).

## Chapter 9: When God Shows Up

1. Bob Meyer, "Compendium of Elvis Sightings," *GeoCities online* (1998), 1.

2. Hillary Rodham Clinton, University of Texas address (1993).

3. Author unknown, "Not Even God Is Spared from Junk Mail," *CNN Interactive* (Feb. 27, 1997), 1.

4. John Naisbitt, *High Tech, High Touch* (New York: Broadway, 1999), 6.

5. Robert Vito, "Madonna Image Still Amazes Florida Visitors," *CNN Interactive* (Dec. 24, 1997), 1–2.

6. Author unknown, "The Healing Water," *MCN online* (2000).

7. Barna Research Group (August 1997).

8. George Barna, *The Index of Leading Spiritual Indicators* (Dallas: Word, 1996), 53.

9. The American Academy of Cosmetic Surgeons, "Cosmetic Surgery: A Comparison Study of Its Growth in the 1990's," *Cosmetic Surgery online* (2000), 1.

10. Author Unknown, "Health: Making Cindy into Barbie?" *BBC Online Network* (Sept. 24, 1998), 1–2.

11. Ted Weatherly, "The Jolt Drinker's Anthem," MIT website, 19 February 2000.

12. Raphael Carter, "Things That Have Been Sold in Vending Machines," *Chaparraltree online* (2000), 1.

13. Richard Cimino and Don Lattin, *Shopping for Faith* (San Francisco: Jossey-Bass, 1998), 23.

14. Barbara Kantrowits, "The Search for the Sacred," *Newsweek* (Nov. 28, 1992), 56.

15. Author unknown, "Dew and Frost," *News and Weather Service online* (National Oceanic and Atmospheric Administration, 2000).

16. Leland Ryken, James C. Wilhoit, Tremper Longman III, *Dictionary of Biblical Imagery* (Downers Grove, Ill.: InterVarsity Press, 1998), 584.

17. Richard Cimino and Don Lattin, *Shopping for Faith*, 63.

18. William D. Hendricks, *Exit Interviews* (Chicago: Moody, 1993), 114.

19. Brother Lawrence, with Harold J. Chadwick, ed., *The Practice of the Presence of God* (Gainesville, Fla.: Bridge-Logos, 1999), n.p.

20. Michael Hodgin, *1001 More Humorous Illustrations*, 21.

21. A. W. Tozer, *The Pursuit of God* (Camp Hill, Pa.: Christian Publications, 1993), 60.

22. Raymond McHenry, *The Best of In Other Words* (Houston: Raymond McHenry, 1996), 233.

23. George Barna, *The Index of Leading Spiritual Indicators*, 55.

24. Barna Research Group, "Christianity Showing No Visible Signs of a Nationwide Revival," *Barna Research online* (March 3, 1998), 2.

25. Ted Kyle and John Todd, *A Treasury of Bible Illustrations* (Chattanooga, Tenn.: AMG, 1995), 28.

26. C. F. Keil and F. Delitzsch, *Commentary on the Old Testament: 1 and 2 Chronicles* (Peabody, Mass.: Hendrickson, 1989), 3:88.

27. The American Institute of Stress, "Stress: America's #1 Health Problem," *Stress online* (2000), 1.

28. Centers for Disease Control and Prevention, "Chronic Fatigue Syndrome Demographics," *CDC online* (2000), 1.

29. Author unknown, "Town's Success with Eating Oatmeal Propels Everyday People into National Ad Campaign," *Quaker Oats online* (2000), 1–2.

## Chapter 10: Posting God's "Keep Out" Sign

1. John Kesler, "How to Keep Your Car From Being Stolen," *Adams Street Shell Auto Theft Prevention Book online* (Shell Services Company, 1997), 1.

2. "Grand Theft Auto," *Stolen Car Recovery online* (2000), 1.

3. "Car Alarms," *Precision Alarm online* (2000), 1.

4. "Uniform Crime Reports: 1998 and 1999," *Federal Bureau of Investigation online* (June, 2000).

5. From *Our Daily Bread*, as published by *Bible Studies Foundation online* (2000).

6. Wayne Grudem, *Systematic Theology*, 337.

7. Dale A. Matthews, *The Faith Factor* (New York: Penguin, 1998), 15–31.

8. Normal Schlenker, "Strategy—Hedging," *The Investment FAQ online* (Dec. 12, 1996), 1.

9. Chand Sooran, "What Is Hedging? Why Do Companies Hedge?" *The Financial Pipeline online* (2000), 1.

10. Heidi Soderstrom, "God's Protection," in "Sermon Illustrations," *Piedmont Baptist Association, North Carolina online* (May 6, 1999).

## Chapter 11: Your Faith—A Moving Target

1. Author unknown, "What Are 'American' Darts and What's an 'American' Dartboard?" *Dartbase online* (2000), 1–2.

2. Author unknown, "Dart Trivia," *Dartbase online* (2000), 3.

3. Bryan Dean, "Magic and Illusion," *About.com Guide* (2000).

4. Author unknown, "Play Your Cards Right," *Ministry online* (January 1999), 1–2.

5. Focus on the Family and Zogby International, in a March 8-10, 2000, survey; see "Zogby Survey Reveals a Growing Percentage of Those Seeking Sexual Fulfillment on the Internet," *Pureintimacy.org.*

6. Ibid.

7. George Barna, *The Second Coming of the Church*, 6.

8. H. B. London, quoted in *Pastor's Weekly Briefing* (Jan. 21, 2000), 1.

9. "Reasons for, and Reporting of, Airline Flight Delays," transcript of a hearing before the U.S. House of Representatives Committee on Transportation and Infrastructure, subcommittee on Aviation, Washington, D.C. (July 27, 1995), 1–2.

10. Thomas A. Keaney and Eliot A. Cohen, "Gulf War Air Power Summary Report" (1993), n.p.

11. George Barna, *The Second Coming of the Church*, 6.

12. Barna Research Group, "Angels Are In—Devil and Holy Spirit Are Out," *Barna Research online* (April 29, 1997), 1.

### Chapter 12: Influence: When Two Worlds Connect

1. Ron Dunn, *Don't Just Stand There, Pray Something* (San Bernardino, Calif.: Here's Life, 1991), 20.

2. C. F. Keil and F. Delitzsch, *1 and 2 Chronicles*, 3:88.

3. Paul Aurandt, *More of Paul Harvey's The Rest of the Story* (New York: Bantam, 1980), 190–92.

4. Lindsay Terry, *Stories Behind Popular Songs and Hymns* (Grand Rapids: Baker, 1990), 171–72.

5. Pamela J. Kennedy, *Hymns of Faith and Inspiration* (Nashville: Ideals, 1990), 85.

6. Denny Mog, *Touched by an E-Mail* (North Brunswick, N.J.: Bridge-Logos, 1999), 170–72.

7. dc Talk, *Jesus Freaks* (Tulsa, Okla.: Albury, 1999), 15.

8. Ibid., 144.

9. Al and Alice Gray, *Stories for a Man's Heart* (Sisters, Ore.: Multnomah, 1999), 133.

10. Wesley L. Duewel, *Touch the World Through Prayer* (Grand Rapids: Zondervan, 1986), 14.

# Appendix A—
# Lab Work:
# Putting the Experiment
# to the Test

*Questions for Further Reflection*

## Chapter 1

1. In your opinion, do you think Christianity is gaining influence or losing positive impact on our culture today? Why or why not?
2. How might "Just Uh" Christianity (according to Homer Simpson) be defined? Do you believe this to be an accurate description of how people of the world view contemporary Christianity?
3. Have there been times in your life when you prayed and you wished you had not? Explain.
4. Diagnose the health of your prayer life. Do you suffer from prayer anorexia or bulimia?
5. Why might prayer be considered an experiment?

## Chapter 2

1. Consider and assess your personal impact for Christ. Is it mostly positive or negative? Why?
2. Name someone you know who, in the eyes of the world, is "highly unlikely," yet who has been used of God in a significant way in your life. In what ways do you admire that person? How and when have you expressed your appreciation to that person?
3. Why might Jabez be considered a "highly unlikely" person for God to use?
4. Compare the public record of Minnesota Governor Jessie "The Body" Ventura's faith stance with that of Littleton, Colorado, student Cassie Bernall.
5. When was the last time you took a difficult stand for God? What was the result or impact of your taking such a stance?

## Chapter 3

1. What ingredients would you include in a recipe for making authentic "Original Recipe" Christian? Identify which ingredients are most often left out.
2. Give your own profile or description of "Average Joe" or "Average Jill" Christian.
3. How does a Christian "get over" the excitement of the Christian life? Would you say this is a common occurrence? Do you think it is a good thing? Why or why not?
4. What damage has been done in the world—and in the church—by Christians who have a holier-than-thou attitude?
5. Describe a time when you were so overwhelmed with meeting responsibilities and needs that you felt like you had to be "Super Christian" in order to handle everything. When did you finally "remove your cape" and allow God to be in charge?

## Chapter 4

1. Have you ever come to that point in your life when you have "raised the white flag" in surrender to God? How did that change how you faced life's challenges?
2. What "blessings in disguise" have you most recently mistaken for unanswered prayer?
3. Is there a "thorn" in your life that you have asked God to remove, but he has not yet answered that prayer and removed it? How has the presence of that thorn changed your life and your relationship to God?
4. What has been some of the toughest "on-the-job training" that you have received in your Christian walk? How has that changed your effectiveness in ministering for Christ?
5. Tell about the most recent episode of your life that should be included in the "T-Files."

## Chapter 5

1. Do your dreams of doing something for God match the size of your God? Discuss possible ways you could dream "bigger."
2. Name some "monsters under your bed" that keep you from pursuing your dreams.
3. What have been people's reactions to your chasing your dreams? Have you recently seen a dream come true? How has that impacted your faith—and your praying?
4. Give an example of a time you felt led by God to do something by faith, but instead you acted by sight. How could this have possibly limited what God could have done through you?
5. What role did his being "honorable" play in Jabez's prayer being answered? What role do you believe honoring God plays in your prayers being answered?

6.  Define "spiritual awakening." Can you point to a time in your life when you experienced one?

## Chapter 6

1.  Give an example of a Christian's being (1) a noun and (2) a verb.
2.  In which zone do you most often reside: the "impossible zone" or the "supernatural zone"? Why is that where you have taken up residence?
3.  Do you think anyone considers you a toxic person? If so, who? Why?
4.  List any "if onlys" or "what ifs" that may be holding you back from doing what you truly believe God wants you to do in your life.
5.  Give an example from your life of your doing something right but doing it at the wrong time because you did not wait on God's perfect timing. What might have been different had you waited on God?
6.  What's packed in your lunch box that God wants given back to him? Do you plan to give it to him? Why or why not?

## Chapter 7

1.  Reality check: Do you most often make a God-impression or a God-turn-off? Why?
2.  When your name comes up in a conversation among people who know you, what do they think—or say—about you?
3.  What is the difference between a "fatal" and a "fantastic" attraction? Give an example of each in your life.
4.  Describe a time when you made a God-impression and a time when you did not.

5. Name the ingredients that go into making a divine scent. Is that the fragrance you most often wear?

6. If we smell like our surroundings, what aroma do you carry with you?

## Chapter 8

1. What things impair a Christian's spiritual vision?

2. Why are the words *luck* and *coincidence* not applicable to a Christian living in the center of God's will?

3. Define "divine appointment." Discuss one you have recently experienced.

4. What prevents you from more often realizing divine appointments?

5. How has a setback in your life turned out to be a divine setup?

## Chapter 9

1. Do you believe most people are searching for God? Explain. Where do those who search look to find him?

2. Why has contemporary culture become addicted to the quick fix in their lives? Is this beneficial or detrimental to developing a relationship with God?

3. How would you define "cafeteria Christianity"? What would be some of the menu offerings?

4. What words or phrase would you have printed on a welcome mat you might put out for God? What art work—if any—would you choose? What colors would you use? What is the significance of your choices?

5. What are the symptoms of "Spiritual Fatigue Syndrome"? Do you have this malady?

## Chapter 10

1. What is God's hedge of protection? When has its presence been most obvious in your life?
2. How did you get God's hedge of protection in your life? How do you activate it in the lives of loved ones?
3. What is Satan's mode of operation (M.O.) in your life? Do you feel you need protection from Satan?
4. What kind of security systems have you installed in your life? Are they operational? Are they effective in deterring or stopping the enemy?
5. Give an example of when your response time to stop temptation was not quick enough. What were the consequences?

## Chapter 11

1. Why do you think Paul described Satan's attack as being like a dart? Describe Satan's attack by using another metaphor or image.
2. Has there ever been a time when you doubted God's goodness or faithfulness in your life? Explain.
3. Which dart of discouragement does Satan most often hurl at you?
4. How does Satan use a deception dart to get you spiritually off-track?
5. What are your greatest physical, emotional, spiritual, and mental struggles?
6. What distractions tend to regularly come up when you are trying to pray? How have they impacted your prayer life? How do you handle these?

## Chapter 12

1.  Do you live with an awareness that there is another world—a supernatural realm—beyond the natural world in which you live? How does that influence your daily living?

2.  What is there about the way you choose to live your life that would indicate to others that you have a passion to impact the world for Christ?

3.  In what ways has God applied the "If–Then" principle to your life?

4.  What is your "Crete"? Why do you think God has put you there?

5.  Describe your eighteen-inch struggle with consistent praying.

6.  Is there anything that would prevent you from performing *The Prayer Experiment* for the next thirty days? If so, what and why?

7.  How has your life changed as a result of reading this book?

# Appendix B— Further Observations

## Suggested reading list

George Barna. *Experience God in Worship*. Loveland, Colo.: Group, 2000.—A compilation of multiple authors' writings on various styles of worship and how each may be utilized in the local church.

George Barna. *The Second Coming of the Church*. Nashville: Word , 1998.—A presentation of statistical information on the condition of the church and Christianity in America.

Henry Blackaby and Claude King. *Experiencing God*. Nashville: Broadman and Holman, 1994.—A practical study on how to join God where he is at work.

Bill Bright and John N. Damoose. *Red Sky In The Morning*. Orlando, Fla.: New Life, 1998.—A glance backwards at the Christian beginnings of America and a forward look at how Christians need to restore morals and values and include God in society through their lives and witness.

Oswald Chambers. *Prayer: A Holy Occupation*. Grand Rapids: Discovery House, 1992.—A collection of quotes related to every aspect of prayer.

Richard Cimino and Don Lattin. *Shopping For Faith*. San Francisco: Jossey-Bass, 1998.—An examination of how people decide which religion or faith to choose.

Jim Cymbala. *Fresh Faith*. Grand Rapids: Zondervan, 1999.—A fresh collection of stories—combined with biblical application—on the power of faith within Christians and the church.

dc Talk and the Voice of The Martyrs. *Jesus Freaks*. Tulsa, Okla.: Albury, 1999.—A new and inspiring look at those who have died for their faith.

Wesley L. Duewel. *Touch the World Through Prayer*. Grand Rapids: Zondervan, 1986.—A testimony of how prayer is the greatest influencer in the world.

Ronald Dunn. *Don't Just Stand There, Pray Something*. San Bernardino, Calif.: Here's Life, 1991.—A revealing work on the power of intercessory prayer in the lives of ordinary people.

George Gallup Jr. *The Next American Spirituality*. Colorado Springs, Colo.: Victor, 2000.—An examination of the spiritual climate of America in the twenty-first century.

Anne Graham Lotz. *Just Give Me Jesus*. Nashville: Word, 2000.—A passionate look at becoming a Christ-centered person through understanding better the revelation of God through his Son.

Josh McDowell and Bob Hostetler. *The New Tolerance*. Wheaton, Ill.: Tyndale, 1998.—An eye-opening account of how Christians are being conditioned to think with less discernment and with greater acceptance of the culture without Christ.

John L. Mason. *An Enemy Called Average*. Tulsa, Okla.: Honor, 1993.—A motivating challenge to move beyond mediocrity in life and faith.

Dale A. Matthews. *The Faith Factor*. New York: Viking/Penguin, 1998.—A presentation of scientific documentation on the connection between health and faith.

David G. Meyers. *The American Paradox*. New Haven, Conn.: Yale University Press, 2000.—A contemporary look at the lessening of purposes in the midst of plenty.

Calvin Miller. *Into the Depths of God*. Minneapolis: Bethany, 2000.—An exploration into the depths of the fullness of God to discover an intimacy with him.

Sally Morgenthaler. *Worship Evangelism*. Grand Rapids: Zondervan, 1995.—A description of the elements of worship when believers worship in spirit and in truth, promoting a powerful atmosphere that calls unbelievers to Christ.

John Naisbitt. *High Tech, High Touch*. New York: Broadway, 1999.—An insightful book about the correlation between living in a high-tech world, yet still searching for meaning to life.

Dennis N. T. Perkins. *Leading at the Edge*. New York: Amacom, 2000.—A fascinating story about how adversity can be the greatest teacher of leadership.

John Piper. *A Hunger for God*. Wheaton, Ill.: Crossway, 1997.—A practical work on how the disciplines of fasting and prayer draw the believer into a more intimate relationship with God.

R. C. Sproul. *The Holiness of God*. Wheaton, Ill.: Tyndale, 1998.—An investigation of the character of God, particularly his holiness, and how it defines who we are and what we do as Christians.

Leonard Sweet. *SoulTsunami*. Grand Rapids,: Zondervan, 1999.—A postmodern wake-up call for the church to rise to the occasion and be the change-agent of society.

Jack Taylor. *Prayer, Life's Limitless Reach*. Nashville: Broadman, 1977.—A classic work on the basics of effective praying.

Elmer Towns and Warren Bird. *Into The Future*. Grand Rapids: Revell, 2000.—A practical guide on the next steps the church should take in reaching this generation and beyond.

A. W. Tozer. *The Pursuit of God*. Camp Hill, Pa.: Christian Publications, 1993.—A classic of the twentieth century that explores the essence of God's nature and inspires readers who thirst for the things of God and desire purer worship of him.

Thaddeus Wawro. *Radicals and Visionaries*. Irvine, Calif.: Entrepreneur, 2000.—A collection of more than seventy stories of how entrepreneurial vision and determination made the difference in America's companies and organizations.

Luder G. Whitlock, Jr.. *The Spiritual Quest*. Grand Rapids: Baker, 2000.—An insightful guide on growing in a deeper understanding of, relationship with, and response to God.

Unknown Author. *The Kneeling Christian*. Grand Rapids: Zondervan, 1966.—A classic work on the power of prayer in the lives of those who are willing to pay the price through time and sacrifice.

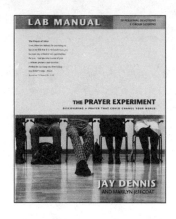

# The Prayer Experiment Lab Manual

### JAY DENNIS AND MARILYN JEFFCOAT

*The Prayer Experiment Lab Manual* provides a thirty-day guide to praying the prayer of Jabez plus six weekly group sessions for mutual encouragement of one's individual prayers to change the way we pray, the desire we have for prayer, and the impact of our praying.

As a companion and supplement to *The Prayer Experiment,* the lab manual not only includes daily devotional guides to encourage individual and/or family praying, but it also includes material to use in small groups: leader lesson material, breakout group discussion questions and activities, closing thoughts for the entire group.

Features:

- Gives thirty days of individual lab sessions, each taking ten to fifteen minutes
- Provides six group sessions with leader helps and group discussion questions
- Companion to *The Prayer Experiment,* based on the popular prayer of Jabez
- Includes the prayer of Jabez and commitment card

Praying the prayer of Jabez has transformed Jay Dennis and his congregation. It can do the same for you. All you need is a willingness to commit thirty days in exchange for a lifetime of possibilities. In God's hands, your life is bigger than you ever imagined. How big? Only God can show you—starting today, if you choose. The biblical guidance is here, along with material to use in small groups. Now can be the time you begin a prayer experiment that will lead you to a God experience.

Softcover 0-310-24235-5

*Pick up a copy today at your favorite bookstore!*

We want to hear from you. Please send your comments about this book to us in care of the address below. Thank you.

GRAND RAPIDS, MICHIGAN 49530

www.zondervan.com